BATTLEFIELDS

—OF THE—

CIVIL WAR

BATTLEFIELDS
OF THE
CIVIL WAR

Roger W Hicks and
Frances E Schultz

Salem House
PUBLISHERS
Topsfield, Massachusetts

Acknowledgements

Our first and greatest thanks must go to Mr. and Mrs. C. Truscott, without whose kind hospitality on the East Coast this book could never have been finished. We would also like to thank Mr. and Mrs. D. Schultz, for hospitality in Kentucky, and Mr. and Mrs. Smith for hospitality in Vicksburg. Also, Prof. B. Collins and his wife Dr. L. Collins gave considerable help and encouragement.

For pictures, we are deeply indebted to Mr. M. Whiney and Mr. R. Hackenbush of the United States Military History Institute at the War College in Carlisle, Pennsylvania; they allowed us access to the photo-archives of the Massachusetts Commandery of the Loyal Legion of the United States. Other pictures came from the National Archives and the Library of Congress in Washington. Many engravings and woodcuts are taken from *Battles and Leaders of the Civil War* and a couple from *Harper's Pictorial History of the Civil War* (see Further Reading).

The National Park Service was often very helpful — many of the Rangers at the park are also very knowledgeable historians — and we cannot recommend the Battlefield Parks too highly. The gentlemen at City Point, at the Jackson Shrine, and at the Surrender House in Dover, Tennessee, were particularly helpful and informative. The Living History crew at Vicksburg, headed by Buzz were also highly impressive. John Kallman of the South Mountain Press, Carlisle, Pennsylvania, also provided us with useful references and introductions; we are indebted to him. Mr. James J. Geary of the New Market Battlefield Park, administered by the Virginia Military Institute, kindly permitted us to use material gathered there. Thanks also to Rand McNally who checked the itineraries on pages 14 and 15.

Finally, the manuscript was read by Prof. Dr. D. Cady, Head of the Department of History at the University of California at Dominguez Hills, although we must emphasize that any errors of fact, or unusual opinions expressed, are our own.

RWH
FES

Guadalupe, California, 1989

For Helen and Chuck

First published in the United States by Salem House Publishers, 1989
462 Boston Street
Topsfield
Massachusetts 01983

Library of Congress Cataloging-in-Publication Data
Hicks, Roger W., 1950 -
    The battlefields of the Civil War
    includes index.
    1. United States -- History--Civil War, 1861-1865 -- Battlefields--Guide-books. 2. United States--Description and travel--1981-   Guide-books. I Schultz, Frances, 1945-   . II. Title.
E641.H53 1989   917 .3'04927
88-26402

Hardback Edition: ISBN 0-88162-401-2
Paperback Edition:ISBN 0-88162-400-4

Phototypesetting in Leamington: Thames Head, a division of BLA Publishing Ltd, East Grinstead, Sussex, England

Origination: Ling Kee, Hong Kong

Printed and bound in Portugal by Resopal

Editorial: Martin Marix Evans
        Jeff Groman
        Elizabeth Harman
        Sheila Mortimer

Design: Maryann Rogers
        Alison Anholt-White

Maps: Sallie Alane Reason

CONTENTS

*Cover photograph:
Statue of Gouverneur
Warren, and cannon,
Little Round Top,
Gettysburg. Half-title: a
crest taken from
Harper's Pictorial
History of the Civil War;
Title page: an Antietam
Cornfield.*

Colonel John S. Mosby.

5

Fort Sumter.

INTRODUCTION

The War between the States did not divide the Union; it reflected a division which already existed long before 1861, and which continues to exist long after 1865. Only in the North is it known as the Civil War; in the South it is still referred to as the War between the States or the War of Northern Aggression.

We did not come to this book as "Civil War buffs," or with any pronounced views in support of either side. Frances is a Yankee, born and brought up in upstate New York; Roger is a Briton. We both suspected that the South was "wrong but wromantic," and that regardless of the rights and wrongs of the situation, a Northern victory was all but inevitable from the start. Both views have since been heavily modified.

Our aim was to report upon the battlefields and to capture some of their mood and reality for readers who might never have visited them, or who might have visited them without having any very clear idea of exactly what happened. Most importantly, we wanted to create what our editor, Martin Marix Evans, so accurately described as the "hair on the back of the neck factor." When you feel the hair on the back of your neck prickle, or a shiver run down your spine, or tears come to your eyes; when you begin to imagine the despair of defeat, the wild exaltation of a victory charge, or just the sheer discomfort of marching in prickly, ill-fitting woolen uniforms in 100° heat; then, we shall have succeeded in our aim.

Confederate sharpshooter.

Likewise, we wanted to convey the terrain of the battle. More than just hills, ravines, streams and forests or woods: the leg-breaking limestone outcrops of Murfreesboro, the tangled underbrush of the Wilderness (and many other battlefields), the rattlesnakes that shared the caves of the besieged inhabitants of Vicksburg, the fire-ants, the poison oak (and ivy, and sumac), and even the goldenrod and ragweed. Hay-fever may seem to be the last thing that a soldier would worry about in battle, but imagine trying to load, aim and fire a musket when your eyes are streaming, you are sneezing constantly, and you can hardly see.

In trying to put ourselves in the position of our 1860s counterparts, the war correspondents, we discovered a number of things. The first was that it is impossible to remain neutral. In the rest of the book, we have tried to suppress our views of the political rights and wrongs and to remain objective. We would be less than honest unless we gave an idea of our bias here.

THE CONSTITUTIONAL QUESTION

First, the United States Constitution does not expressly forbid secession. A strict constitutionalist may therefore argue from the Tenth Amendment: "The powers not delegated to the United States by the Constitution, nor prohibited by it to the States, are reserved to the States respectively, or to the people." The only counter to this is that the several States, by accepting the sovereignty of the United States in various treaties and other national executive decisions, and by acting together in the past, had demonstrated that the United States was indissoluble.

High flown sentiments were the rule on both sides.

While this view may commend itself to many, it is by no means a watertight argument. The "preservation of the Union" was not a God-given law: it was a matter of practical politics and the retention of power in the hands of those who already enjoyed its exercise. Ulysses S. Grant made an excellent argument in his memoirs that those parts of the nation purchased from other sovereigns (Florida, and the Louisiana Purchase) could not secede, because they were bought with the funds of the Union; but President Buchanan, who believed that there was no right of secession, could not find any Constitutional means to coerce the States into remaining within the Union.

SLAVERY - A PRACTICAL ISSUE

Second, slavery was not a moral issue to the politicians on either side: it was a practical issue. Before his election, Lincoln repeatedly stressed that he had no intention of interfering with slavery; the Emancipation Proclamation was (in its own words) "a fit and necessary measure for suppressing said rebellion." It is important to remember that at the time of the War, almost everyone (including the most fervent abolitionist) was "racist," indeed, extremely so seen through modern eyes. Lincoln himself said to Black leaders, "But, even when you cease to be slaves, you are yet far removed from being placed on an equality with the white race... on this broad continent, not a single man of your race is made the equal of a single man of ours." In the same speech (August 14, 1862), he repeated his long-held conviction that freed slaves should be "colonized" or sent somewhere else — perhaps Central America — to get them out of the way of the white people.

In reality, the Emancipation Proclamation was a political ploy to prevent recognition of the Confederate States by Britain and France. Again on the face of the Proclamation, it purported to free only those slaves in Southern-held States; not only Northern States, including the slave-holding state of Delaware, but even Northern-controlled *counties* in Virginia, were permitted to keep their slaves. This led Lord Palmerston to observe that Lincoln undertook to abolish slavery where he was without power to do so, while protecting it where he had power to destroy it.

Third, there were three "media events" in the 1850s which had whipped up North-South antagonism: "Bleeding Kansas," the Dred Scott case, and the Brooks-Sumner affair. The issue was "internal empire," to decide whether Northern or Southern values would prevail in the Territories and the new States.

Dred Scott was a slave who applied for freedom on the grounds that his master had taken him to an area where slavery was prohibited. His master pleaded that Dred Scott was his property, and that he was merely exercizing his constitutional right. The Supreme Court, Constitutionalists to a man, agreed with the master. This effectively nullified any anti-slavery legislation anywhere in the country, but several Northern states then passed unconstitutional laws declaring that slaves would be automatically freed if they entered those states. This wanton disregard of the Constitution was a direct affront to Southern constitutionalists.

Finally, Senator Sumner made an unbelievably offensive speech in the Senate. He called one tall Southern senator "the Don Quixote of slavery," and a shorter one the "Sancho Panza;" and pointing to a Southern senator who had suffered a small stroke which left the side of his mouth paralyzed and was therefore occasionally prone to drool a little, he spoke dramatically of Divine punishment for supporting the sin of slavery. Preston Brooks was the nephew of the third Southern lawgiver: understandably, if intemperately, he later thrashed Sumner. In the South, Preston Brooks societies were formed with a stick as the symbol of thrashing no-good Yankees: in the North, Brooks's action was seen as senseless violence. Certainly, neither side was fully in the right, nor fully in the wrong.

"Bleeding Kansas" was the result of an ill-considered bill by Senator Douglas of *Illinois* to admit slavery in the Territories and the newly-formed states of Kansas and Nebraska in 1854. Constitutionally, Senator Douglas was only upholding the Fourth Amendment, the "right of the people to be secure in their persons, houses, papers and effects," but in practice, he was inviting a free-for-all on the slavery issue. The result was localized civil war as free-soil advocates and pro-slavery advocates fought.

A Louisiana Pelican.

IDEALS AND ANARCHY

This brings us to our fourth consideration. We already know that the people of the 1860s were much like people today. But we must be careful not to attribute to them the specific desires and attitudes of today.

They were far more independently minded. Suffering and death were far more familiar than they are today. With negligible policing, they were far more responsible for their own security and safety. And with a completely different social structure — rural, based on small communities, and with a clear (if often simplistic) moral code — ideas of "right," "wrong" and "kinship" were much stronger than they are today.

In the South, this independence led to something close to anarchy. In the modern world, this is regarded with horror. But stop to consider what "anarchy" means. In a true anarchy, there are no leaders, and all are equal. Surely, this is an ideal impossible to achieve? Individuals therefore give up some of their rights in return for general cooperation. At its most basic, "the freedom of my fist ends where your nose begins." The South wanted to give up as few of their rights as possible; the North wanted to impose the will of the leaders on the people.

WHAT MIGHT HAVE BEEN

And this in turn is our fifth point. The South almost certainly did contain the seeds of its own destruction. But these seeds lay not in the "peculiar institution" of slavery, which was probably dying anyway (though some historians say that the high price of slaves showed how strong the institution was, and that it would have lasted until the 1880s); rather, they lay in its refusal to accept the kind of single-minded dedication which is necessary to win a modern war. Under Lincoln, civil liberties all but vanished: newspapers were suppressed, there were political arrests, and the whole economy was directed towards winning the War. In the South, not a single paper was suppressed; no one was arrested for past views; and the refusal of the States to yield any more control to Richmond than they deemed necessary led to poor coordination of armies and wasted resources. At the end of the War, there were still thousands of good, warm uniforms in the warehouses of some States while soldiers from other States went barefoot and in rags.

The night assault of July 18, 1863, on Battery Wagner; one of the first prior to the re-taking of Fort Sumter by the Union.

Despite all this, the Confederacy *could* have survived. If there had been no war — if the North had simply wished the South good riddance — the Confederacy might well be with us today. And even given the fact that there was a war, there were many, many battles at which the fight, and indeed the whole War, could have gone either way. Two examples will suffice.

In 1862, if the Confederate generals had not squabbled between themselves at Fort Donelson, the Confederate attempt to break out of the encircling Union forces would almost certainly have succeeded. General Grant would not then have received the accolade he did, and his nickname of "Unconditional Surrender" Grant would not have been bestowed. The fickle Northern administration, always desperate for a hero, would probably not have raised him to high command, and General Lee would have continued to run rings around the Northern generals, none of whom ever began to compare with Grant.

"An affair of outposts." This is typical of the confused fighting which characterized the early days of the War.

In 1863, if Early's Confederates had carried Cemetery Hill on the night of July 2, or if Gouverneur Warren had not grasped the importance of Little Round Top, the Confederates would almost certainly have won at Gettysburg. British and French recognition would immediately have followed, and the new nation would have been secure.

ECONOMIC VIEW

One of the best books on the causes of the War is *Civil War in the Making 1815-1860* (Avery O. Craven, Louisiana State University Press, 1959). It contains the thesis that the Union conducted the War along the lines of a Revivalist campaign. A Marxist might delight in further developing Craven's arguments about capitalism. The separation of capital and labor, and the concentration of wealth in a few hands had already led to a discontented society; and when a recession set in at the end of the 1850s, a war was just the thing to stimulate business and take the mind of the ordinary citizen off his deteriorating lot.

VISITING THE SITES

This is a guide to the *battlefields* of the War between the States. Accordingly, it contains only the briefest amount of background necessary to place each battle in context; it is not a history of the War. There is, however, a full chronology on pages 19-21.

This book is meant to be used in one of two ways. If you already know a great deal about the War, but have not visited some of the sites, it provides an excellent chronological guide to the major battlefields and is, we hope, the next best thing to actually being there. If your knowledge of the War is confined to what you learned in school, plus some additional reading since, it bridges the gap between serious study and casual interest.

For most of the battles covered here, the National Park Service maintains a Visitor Information Center and administers at least a part of the battlefield area. The films or slide-shows at these centers are often highly informative, and the park brochures provide an excellent broad guide to the battle or battles covered. There are, however, three potential drawbacks to using these brochures as your sole guide to the battlefields.

One is that they are necessarily brief; even the very best historians would find it extremely difficult to condense all the necessary information into so small a compass. The second is that most of these pamphlets are designed around an automobile tour, with a number of designated stops. Inevitably, these tours cannot follow the course of the battle in strict chronological sequence, and often you will see the battle in quite the wrong order: middle, beginning and end can be hopelessly jumbled. And third, where the same land was fought over more than once (as was often the case), a single brochure covering two battles can be royally confusing.

A living history display, Chickamauga.

GETTING TO THE BATTLEFIELDS

The itinerary shown on the maps on pages 14-15 involves some 3-4,000 miles of driving and visits all the sites described in this book. Few people will have either the time or the stamina to make such a tour in a single trip, but it is quite feasible to divide the journey in two (Eastern Theater and Western Theater) and to make each section the subject of a 2-3 week vacation. If you are able to devote much time to visiting the battlefields, we offer these suggestions based on our experience.

First, consider traveling "out of season." Everywhere will be less crowded; the weather will often be more pleasant; and hotels and motels will be often cheaper. However, you will miss most of the "Living History" shows (see page 196), and you will need to check opening times carefully.

Second, try to get into the parks early. Not only will they be less crowded, but because most battles started at dawn, you will have a better idea both of the terrain and of the mood of the battle.

Third, remember that the season of the year can greatly affect the appearance of the battlefield. In the winter, it is often much easier to see the lie of the land; in summer (when many battles were fought), lines of sight are obscured by foliage.

Fourth, remember also that the appearance of the battlefield during the War was very different from its appearance now. Trenches and earthworks — which are now just gentle, overgrown banks of earth — were then steep, muddy and raw; logs were used to build walls and fortifications; trenches were deeper, walls higher; whole woods were cut down to build fortifications and to clear lines of fire; and paths were blocked by *abatis*. An *abatis* is a line of trees, felled with their interlocking, sharpened tops pointing towards the enemy. These were an effective defense against both infantry and cavalry.

Chevaux-de-frise

Other wooden fortifications included sharpened stakes, set deep in the earth with their points against the enemy, and *chevaux-de-frise*, tree trunks studded with rows of pointed stakes arranged at 90° so that the whole resembled a row of sharpened crosses fastened through their centers. For unfamiliar military or archaic terms, check the Glossary on page 234.

BOOKS, BOOTS AND COMPASSES

You may well find that this book is all you need for visiting the battlefields; it is designed to be fully self-contained, or (at most) to be used with the Park Service brochures.

On the other hand, there are over 100,000 other books on the War between the States, and we cannot pretend to replace all of them. Accordingly, in addition to the Further Reading section (page 235), relevant titles are listed in the "Further Information" panels at the end of each battle section and elsewhere. The bookshops at National Park Service-administered sites are excellent, and stock most books mentioned in these pages.

Virginia Memorial, Gettysburg.

We *heartily* recommend that if you do get out of the car and walk, which is essential for a full appreciation of the battlefields, you dress properly. You may encounter poison ivy and other poisonous plants; fire-ants and other venomous insects are not uncommon; and there are even rattlesnakes, if you venture off the beaten path. High boots, such as cowboy boots, with jeans tucked into them, are best for serious exploration. A lightweight long-sleeved cotton shirt provides better protection against mosquito bites than a T-shirt and bug repellent.

A pair of small, lightweight field-glasses can be useful, but one thing that is essential is a small pocket-compass; many historical markers say "west of here" or "to the north-west," and unless you have a good sense of direction, you can find yourself in difficulties. We have used compass directions in this book.

MAPS

Both for hikers and for serious students, United States Geological Survey (USGS) maps are invaluable. The USGS is on Sunrise Valley Drive, Reston, VA 22092. Obtaining a full range of USGS maps from anywhere else can be expensive, as many bookshops add handsome mark-ups to the official prices.

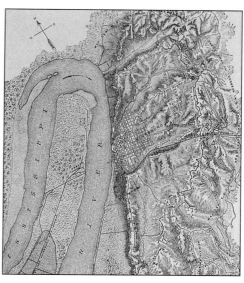

The former course of the Mississippi River.

The references to USGS maps in the "Further Information" sections are all to the 7.5' quadrangle maps, unless otherwise noted. On these, 1″ equals 2,000 feet (1:24,000). At the time of writing, these maps were $2.50 each, but a purchase of $500 qualified for a 50 per cent reduction — a point worth bearing in mind if you are buying many maps.

It is also worth considering the purchase of the *Atlas to Accompany the Official Reports of the Union and Confederate Armies* (abbreviated to *Official Reports Atlas* in the "Further Information" sections), available as a reduced-scale (9/10) reprint at most Park Service bookshops. This handsome volume contains many contemporary maps, including some actually used during the War by both sides, and cost about $40 at the time of writing.

The "Further Information" sections also contain references to the maps in *Battles and Leaders of the Civil War* (abbreviated to *B&L*). For details of this superb book, see Further Reading, page 235.

THE NATIONAL PARK SERVICE

The Visitor Centers already mentioned are far more than just dispensers of brochures. Many of the Park Service staff are extremely knowledgeable, and can provide illuminating answers to all kinds of questions. This is even more true of the staff at the smaller sites — the Surrender House at Fort Donelson, the Jackson Shrine, and the City Point Unit at Richmond immediately spring to mind — who often have a remarkable fund of detailed knowledge. Admittedly, there are some temporary staff who know little or nothing about the site, but you can soon distinguish them from the experts!

The opening hours of the different parts of the various parks vary widely, and they change according to the season. As a general rule, National Parks are open all year except Christmas and New Year, and you can rely on dawn to dusk if there are no gates, or 8 or 9 am to 6 pm (summer) or 5 pm (winter, or in some urban parks all year) for the Visitor Centers. Smaller sites may only be manned during the summer. Many parks provide picnic areas, which are often very attractive, but a surprising number (not all) ban alcohol, so you cannot enjoy a bottle of wine with your picnic. National Park Service information is given in the "Further Information" panel at the end of each battle section.

BATTLEFIELDS AND ITINERARIES

There were over 10,000 engagements, battles and skirmishes in the American Civil War. To reduce this enormous number of widely varying combats to a manageable number of comprehensible battles has not been easy.

What we have tried to do is to give a balanced picture, with all (or almost all) the best-known battles, and a few others which deserve to be better-known either because of the effect they had on the War or simply because they are interesting places to visit. It is a personal choice, but it is a basis on which you can if you wish build a deeper study. There are two "grand tours" in which the battlefields can be visited. Of course, it is possible to visit a single battlefield or a group of battlefields close together, but these two tours allow you to see all the battles covered in this book.

The Eastern itinerary begins at Gettysburg, and then goes on to Antietam (Sharpsburg) and Harper's Ferry; Cedar Creek (Belle Grove) in the Shenandoah Valley; Manassas (Bull Run); Chancellorsville, the Wilderness and Spotsylvania Court House; Fredericksburg; Richmond and the Richmond Peninsula; and finally Petersburg, whose fall marked the beginning of the end for the Confederate States of America. The overall point-to-point distance involved is about 400-500 miles, though you can multiply that by three or more to allow for exploration and battlefield tours. We recommend that you take at least 1-2 weeks.

The Western itinerary is slightly different, consisting of three "legs." The middle leg is the main part; depending on how much you want to see, we recommend that you take a minimum of a week or ten days for this. The full trip could occupy two or three weeks or more. The first leg begins at Vicksburg; from there to Shiloh (Pittsburg Landing), where the second leg begins, is rather over 250 miles. From Shiloh you go up to Forts Henry and Donelson, over to Nashville, down through Murfreesboro (the Battle of Stone's River), on to Chattanooga and Chickamauga (treated together), and then to Atlanta. This is rather over 400 miles. Finally, the third leg follows Sherman's March to the Sea (220-230 miles) and then turns up to Charleston (another 100 miles or so). You can expect at least to double the total mileage to allow for tours and exploration. Astute map-readers will notice that both tours could be run "back to back," as Charleston is only about 50 miles south-east of I-95 (via I-26), maybe 400 miles in all from Petersburg.

The exact routes you take are up to you, and you may well find it more interesting and rewarding to follow minor roads rather than using major highways all the way, but the following itineraries will work: a Rand McNally or AAA road atlas will make life somewhat easier. With the exception of Cedar Creek, most battlefields are well signposted.

A relief monument honoring the Pennsylvania State cavalry on the field at Gettysburg.

WESTERN THEATER

Vicksburg to Shiloh
Take I-20 east to Jackson, about 50 miles. At the junction with I-55, go north for 2-3 miles to the junction with the Natchez Trace Parkway and head north-east towards Kosiusco (55-60 miles) and Tupelo (150 miles or so). From Tupelo take US 45 north through Corinth (about 40 miles) and just after Corinth, take MS 350 for another couple of miles. Then take MS 2 (which becomes TN 22) north for about 10 miles to Shiloh.

Shiloh to Fort Donelson
Follow TN 22 north to Crump (about 5 miles); cross US 64 and join TN 69 for about 10 miles, until it rejoins TN 22; follow the composite road for another mile or so, then again follow TN 69 north (right) beside the Tennessee River via Bath Springs and Parsons to I-40. Cross I-40 and follow US 641 north-west up to US 79 just before Paris. At US 79 junction, turn right (north-east) towards Oak Hill and Clarksville. Fort Donelson National Military Park is about 20 miles from Paris, after you cross the Tennessee River.

Fort Donelson to Nashville
The easy route is US 79 to Clarksville (about 30 miles) followed by TN 112 to Nashville (about 40 miles), but TN 49 via Erin then 47 and 70 is more picturesque.

Nashville to Murfreesboro
Take US 41/US 70S south-east to Stone's River National Battlefield, which is between I-24 to the west and US 41 to the east, about 25 miles.

Murfreesboro to Chickamauga and Chattanooga
Take I24 at Murfreesboro, south to the junction with US 27; Chickamauga and Chattanooga National Military Park is less than 10 miles from this junction.

Chickamauga/Chattanooga to Atlanta
Go back up the 27, 5 miles to GA2. Turn right (east) at Fort Oglethorpe. After 2 miles, join I-75 for Atlanta; turn right (south-east). It is about 100 miles. The main tour ends here.

The "March to the Sea"
Head south-east on I-75 towards Macon; at Pope's Ferry, fork left on I-16; then another 160 miles to Savannah. From Savannah to Charleston, take I-95 north for about 45-50 miles to the junction with US 17. From there, it is about another 45-50 miles north-east.

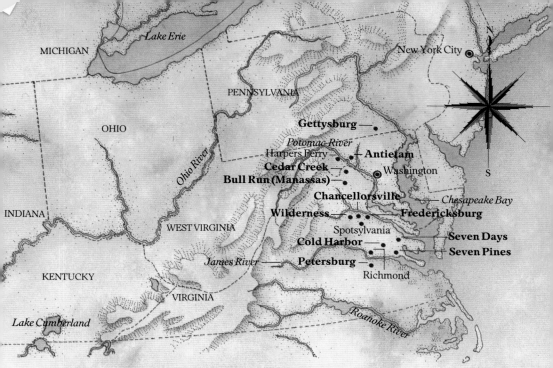

EASTERN THEATER

Gettysburg to Sharpsburg
Go south on US15 (Business) past Fairplay, Emmitsburg (where it rejoins the main US 15). Approximately 8 miles after Emmitsburg, near Catoctin Mountain Park, turn right (west) on MD 77 towards Hagerstown. After approximately 8 more miles, turn left (south) on MD 66 towards Beaver Creek. At Beaver Creek (about 5 miles) cross US 40 and continue on MD 66, heading for Boonsboro. At Boonsboro (5 miles again) take MD 34 for Sharpsburg, and follow signs to the battlefield.

Sharpsburg to Harper's Ferry
Take MD 65 south for Harper's Ferry (about 15 miles). Join US 340 and turn right (west). The National Historical Park is signposted.

Harper's Ferry to Cedar Creek
Go south-west on US 340 through Charles Town (7 miles); cross the VA State line about 10 miles after Charles Town and continue through Berryville and Boyce. Turn right (west) on VA 277 for Stephens City a mile or two after White Post. At Stephens City join I-81/US 11 and turn left (south) for Middletown and the Battle of Cedar Creek (see page 210).

Cedar Creek to Bull Run
From the Strasburg junction follow I-66 east to Gainesville. Manassas (Bull Run) battlefield is signposted after about 45-50 miles.

Manassas to Fredericksburg
From Manassas itself, take the road for Occoquan towards Woodbridge and I-95; after 12-13 miles, join I-95 and turn right (south). About 30 miles later, after the first Fredericksburg exits, the National Military Park is signposted.

Fredericksburg to Richmond
I-95 runs due south to Richmond (50 miles approximately).

Richmond and the Peninsula; Petersburg
I-64 south out of Richmond takes you to Yorktown (about 60 miles). VA 5 will get you back towards Petersburg. Cross the James River after Charles City to Hopewell (formerly City Point); the National Battlefield Park is about 6-7 miles after Hopewell, just before Petersburg. This part of the tour ends here; to continue to Appomattox Court House, it is a surprisingly long way east (about 100 miles) on US 460.

CIVIL WAR LEADERS

UNION LEADERS

Abraham Lincoln. Born Hodgenville, Kentucky, February 12, 1809; 42 when the War began; assassinated April 14, 1865 at age 49. Stood for office (as a Whig) in 1832; first held office (Illinois State legislature) in 1834. Licensed as a lawyer in 1836. Married Mary Todd 1844. US House of Representatives 1847; joined newly formed Republican Party 1856. Elected President 1860. He was so unpopular in the South that his election provided the final spur to Southern secession — the first states left the Union even before he was sworn in.

Abraham Lincoln.

Ambrose Everett Burnside. Born May 23, 1824; West Point 1847; almost 37 when the War started. Burnside correctly doubted his own ability as a leader — he tried to refuse command of the Army of the Potomac — and although he would fight bravely, he seems to have had little grasp of strategy or even tactics. Resigned his commission April 15, 1865; US Senator from 1874 to his death, September 13, 1881, aged 57.

Ulysses S. Grant.

Ulysses Simpson Grant. Born Hiram Ulysses Grant, April 27, 1822; the congressman who engineered his appointment to West Point (Class of 1843) got his name wrong, and Ulysses S. stuck. Almost 39 when the War began. Notorious for heavy drinking, and unlucky in business after his resignation from the army in 1854. Rejoined the army in June 1861. More than anyone else responsible for the Union victory. President 1869-77. Died of throat cancer July 23, 1885, aged 63.

Henry Wager Halleck. Born January 16, 1815; West Point 1839; 46 at the outbreak of war. Nicknamed "Old Brains," a somewhat cold personality masked a great intellect. As a field commander, he was dull and slow but his strategic organization contributed a great deal to the success of Grant. Died January 9, 1872, a week before his 57th birthday.

Joseph Hooker. Born November 13, 1814; West Point 1837; 46 when the War began. Brave but prickly, Hooker made mistakes but would probably have learned from them if he had been given a chance instead of being embroiled in politicking which was mostly of others' making. Died October 31, 1879, aged almost 65.

George Gordon Meade. Born December 31, 1815; West Point 1835; 45 at the outbreak of war. A brave man, luck and Gouverneur Warren (see page 137) were with him at Gettysburg. Died of pneumonia and old war wounds November 6, 1872, aged 56.

George Brinton McClellan. Born December 3, 1826; West Point 1846; 34 when the War began. An able administrator and a brave, intelligent man, McClellan proved a poor, slow general in the Peninsula Campaign (page 58) and at Antietam (page 82). Stood as Democratic candidate against Lincoln 1864. Died October 29, 1885 aged 58.

George G. Meade.

Irvin McDowell. Born October 15, 1818; West Point 1838; 42 at the outbreak of war. A career soldier, McDowell led the ill-prepared Union armies at First Manasses. The loss was more Lincoln's fault than McDowell's, but his reputation suffered; he also had the misfortune to miss his chance during the Peninsula Campaign when Stonewall Jackson's Valley Campaign kept him occupied. He retired from the army in 1882 and died May 4, 1885, aged 66.

John Pope. Born March 16, 1822; West Point 1842; 39 at the outbreak of war. A career soldier with a bombastic personality. Pope was successful in the West in early 1862 but disastrous as a general in the East thereafter. Retired from the army 1866; died September 23, 1892, aged 70.

William Starke Rosecrans. Born September 6, 1819; West Point 1842; 41 at the outbreak of war. Like his opponent Bragg, Rosecrans was a good-to-brilliant strategist who was not too good on the field. He was well liked by the troops (though some accused him of favoring fellow Catholics), and after the War he pursued a political career. Died March 11, 1898, aged 79.

Winfield Scott.

William T. Sherman.

Winfield Scott. Born June 13, 1786; 74 when the War began. Lincoln, obsessed with the idea of a quick, cheap victory, consistently ignored Scott's advice. If the admittedly aging and infirm general had been allowed to develop his strategy at his own pace, Yankee losses would almost certainly have been less and victory could have been achieved more quickly. As it was, he resigned on November 1, 1861. Died May 29, 1866, just short of his 90th birthday.

William Tecumseh Sherman. Born February 8, 1820; West Point 1840; 41 when the War began. A successful soldier and a very fair businessman, he left the army in 1853 and rejoined in 1861. Hated in the South for his conduct of the War (see pp. 208-209), he advocated genocide for Native Americans when serving on the frontier afterwards. Died February 14, 1891, aged 71.

CONFEDERACY LEADERS

Jefferson Finis Davis. Born June 3, 1808 in Christian City, Kentucky; 52 when the War began. West Point 1828, left the army in 1835. Entered Congress 1845. Briefly rejoined the army for the Mexican War, then served as Secretary of War (1853) before returning to the Senate (1857). Disappointed when elected President of the Confederacy rather than being offered high military command. He was a great constitutionalist but a poor politician. Died December 9, 1889, aged 80.

Pierre Gustave Toutant Beauregard. Born May 28, 1818; West Point 1838; almost 43 at the outbreak of war. A thoroughly professional soldier, he was Superintendent of West Point briefly in 1861. He has been criticized as too much of a textbook soldier, but after the War he was offered (and refused) the command of several foreign armies. Died February 20, 1893, aged 74.

Jefferson Finis Davis.

Braxton Bragg. Born March 22, 1817; West Point 1837; almost 44 when the War started. Brilliant organizer and strategist, but apparently completely unable to execute his own plans. Personally unpopular, especially with the troops, but a friend of Jeff Davis. Died September 27, 1876, aged 59.

Jubal Anderson Early. Born November 3, 1816; West Point 1837; 44 at the outbreak of war. Hard drinking, hard fighting, but too impulsive ever to make a great general, Early was a tactician rather than a strategist. He remained an unregenerate secessionist until his death on March 2, 1894, aged 77.

Ambrose Powell Hill. Born November 9, 1825; West Point 1847; 35 at the outbreak of war. He fought well until promoted to Lieutenant-General in May 1863; thereafter, his actions were often ill-judged. He often reported himself sick when action threatened. The sickness was probably psychosomatic in origin. Killed on active service, April 2, 1865, aged 39.

Braxton Bragg.

Thomas Jonathan Jackson.

Thomas Jonathan Jackson. Born January 21, 1824; West Point 1846; 37 when the War began. Resigned from the army in 1851 after becoming a professor at Virginia Military Academy; deeply religious, and known to his students as "Tom Fool" Jackson. Rejoined the army in 1861; acquired the name "Stonewall" at First Manassas (page 22), and served as a brilliant general in his own right in the Shenandoah Valley before forming what was probably the greatest military partnership in history with Robert E. Lee. Died aged 39 on May 10, 1863, after being accidentally shot by his own side.

Joseph Eggleston Johnston. Born February 3, 1807; West Point 1829; 54 when the War started. Conflicting and confusing orders from the President (who disliked Johnston) repeatedly hampered this great Southern general. His skill is attested by the fact that Sherman had the highest respect for him, and was delighted when John Hood replaced him in front of Atlanta in 1864. He had a distinguished political career after the War and died on March 21, 1891, aged 84.

Robert Edward Lee. Born January 19, 1807; West Point 1829; 54 at the outbreak of war. A military genius and a Southern gentleman, Lee is revered almost as a saint in the South to this day. With Stonewall Jackson, he secured a number of military coups. Died October 12, 1870, aged 63.

James Longstreet. Born January 8, 1821; West Point 1842; 40 at the outbreak of war. A good tactical general, if and when he got into battle; he often hesitated in carrying out orders with which he did not agree. Became a Republican after the War, and did his best to soften the blow of Reconstruction. Died January 2, 1904, a few days before his 83rd birthday.

James Ewell Brown ("Jeb") Stuart. Born 1833; West Point 1854; a brilliant cavalry leader, a flamboyant soldier, but a tactician rather than a strategist. Criticized for being more interested in his reputation than in winning the War. Died of wounds May 12, 1864, aged 31.

Robert E. Lee.

CHRONOLOGY OF THE WAR

1784-87	Delegates from South Carolina and Georgia refuse to join the Union if slavery is prohibited by the Constitution
1787	Slavery prohibited on all United States territory north-west of the Ohio River
1820	Missouri Compromise modifies line beyond which slaveholding is illegal
1850	Fugitive Slave Act passed
1859	October: John Brown leads the attack on Harper's Ferry
	December 3: John Brown hanged under Virginia law

1860

Nov 5	Governor William H. Gist of South Carolina recommends Secession from the Union "in the event of Abraham Lincoln's election to the presidency"
Nov 6	Abraham Lincoln elected president
Nov 12	Lawrence M. Keitt, member of the House for South Carolina, says that his state will "shatter the accursed Union"
Dec 20	Ordinance of Secession passed by South Carolina

1861

Feb 18	Jefferson Davis inaugurated as provisional president of the Confederacy
Apr 12	Fort Sumter fired upon
Apr 15	Lincoln calls for 75,000 militia within three months
Apr 17	Ordinance of Secession passed by Virginia
Apr 18	Harper's Ferry arsenal seized by the Confederacy; Portsmouth Navy Yard also occupied
Apr 19	Lincoln declares blockade of Southern ports Factionalist riots in Baltimore
Apr 29	Maryland votes against Secession
May 6	Arkansas and Tennessee secede Confederacy recognizes State of War with United States
May 10	Riots in St. Louis
May 13	Occupation of Baltimore by Union troops
May 20	North Carolina secedes
May 24	Union troops take Alexandria, Virginia
Jul 21	Battle of First Manassas (Bull Run), Virginia
Oct 21	Battle of Ball's Bluff
Oct 24	Transcontinental telegraph completed

Alabama State Capitol

19

1862

Feb 8	Battle of Roanoake Island, North Carolina
Feb 16	Surrender of Fort Donelson, Tennessee
Mar 7/8	Battle of Pea Ridge (or Elkhorn Tavern), Arkansas
Mar 9	Battle of USS *Monitor* and CSS *Virginia (Merrimack)*
Mar 23	First Battle of Kernstown, Virginia
Apr 6/7	Battle of Shiloh or Pittsburg Landing, Tennessee
Apr 11	Fall of Fort Pulaski, Georgia
May	The Peninsula Campaign
May 23	Battle of Front Royal, Virginia
May 25	Battle of Winchester, Virginia
Jun 19	Slavery in Territories prohibited
Jun 25	"Seven Days" Campaign begins
Aug 29/30	Battle of Second Manassas (Bull Run)
Sep 17	Battle of Antietam, Maryland
Oct 3/4	Battle of Corinth, Mississippi
Dec 13	Battle of Fredericksburg, Virginia
Dec 29	Battle of Chickasaw Bayou, Mississippi
Dec 31	Battle of Murfreesboro (Stone's River), Tennessee

Sinking of the USS Monitor, *December 29, 1862.*

1863

Jan 1	Proclamation of Emancipation
May 1-4	Battle of Chancellorsville, Virginia
May 3	Second Battle of Fredericksburg; Salem Church
Jun 14/15	Second Battle of Winchester, Virginia
Jul 1-3	Battle of Gettysburg, Pennsylvania
Jul 4	Surrender of Vicksburg, Mississippi
Jul 13/14	Draft riots and anti-black riots in New York City
Sep 19/20	Battle of Chickamauga, Georgia
Nov 19	Gettysburg Address
Nov 23-25	Battle of Chattanooga, Tennessee
Nov 24	Battle of Lookout Mountain
Nov 25	Battle of Missionary Ridge

Vicksburg Court House, a land-mark during the Siege, from a photograph taken in 1880.

1864

Feb 14	Sherman occupies and destroys Meridian, Mississippi
Feb 20	Battle of Olustee, Florida
Apr 12	Capture of Fort Pillow, Tennessee
May 5-6	Battle of the Wilderness, Virginia

May 7	Sherman begins March on Atlanta
May 8-21	Battle of Spotsylvania Court House
May 15	Battle of New Market, Virginia
May 17	Battle of Drewry's Bluff, Virginia
May 23-26	Battle of the North Anna, Virginia
Jun 1-3	Battle of Cold Harbor, Virginia
Jun 8	Lincoln nominated for second term
Jun 18	Siege of Petersburg begins
Jun 27	Battle of Kennesaw Mountain, Georgia
Jul 11	Confederates invade Washington suburbs.
Jul 14	Battle of Tupelo, Mississippi
Jul 20	Battle of Peachtree Creek, Georgia
Aug 5	Battle of Mobile Bay, Alabama
Aug 18/19	Battle of the Weldon Railroad, Georgia
Aug 25	Battle of Reams's Station, Virginia
Aug 31	McClellan nominated for president
Sep 2	Sherman occupies Atlanta
Sep 7	Sherman orders evacuation of Atlanta
Sep 19	Third Battle of Winchester, Virginia
Sep 22	Battle of Fisher's Hill, Virginia
Sep 29/30	Battles of Fort Harrison and Peebles' Farm, Virginia
Oct 19	Battle of Cedar Creek (Belle Grove), Virginia
Oct 23	Battle of Westport, Missouri
Nov 8	Lincoln re-elected
Nov 16	Sherman's March to the Sea begins
Nov 30	Battle of Franklin, Tennessee
Dec 15/16	Battle of Nashville, Tennessee

Union railroad battery, Petersburg.

1865

Jan 15	Capture of Fort Fisher, North Carolina
Feb 17	Capture and destruction of Columbia, South Carolina
Mar 19-21	Battle of Bentonville, North Carolina
Apr 1	Battle of Five Forks, Virginia
Apr 3	Occupation of Richmond and Petersburg, Virginia
Apr 9	Surrender at Appomattox Court House, Virginia
Apr 12	Surrender of Mobile, Alabama
Apr 14	Lincoln assassinated
May 10	Capture of Jefferson Davis
May 26	Surrender of Army of Trans-Mississippi

Little Bull
Run

Sudley
Springs

Manassas - Sudley Road

Featherbed Lane

Stone Bridge

Stone House

Henry House
Hill

Henry House

Groveton

Warrenton Turnpike

Bull Run

Bald Hill

Chinn Ridge

Vandor Lane

Ball's Ford Road

To Manassas Junction

THE BATTLE OF
FIRST MANASSAS

Bull Run, near Manassas Junction, Virginia
JULY 21 1861

Confederate States	United States
Brig.-Gen. P.G.T. Beauregard	Brig.-Gen. Irvin McDowell
35,000 effectives	37,000 effectives
1,982 casualties	2,896 casualties

To Centreville & Washington

I n Virginia, a small river is commonly called a "run." At Sudley Springs, the Bull Run and the Little Bull Run join; the river meanders south and east past Manassas, ultimately flowing into Occoquan Creek, a tributary of the Potomac.

You can ford both the Bull Run and the Little Bull Run in a number of places, before it grows too swift and deep. The river bottom is mostly stony, though the low banks are surprisingly steep and slippery, so it is more difficult than it looks. Your boots

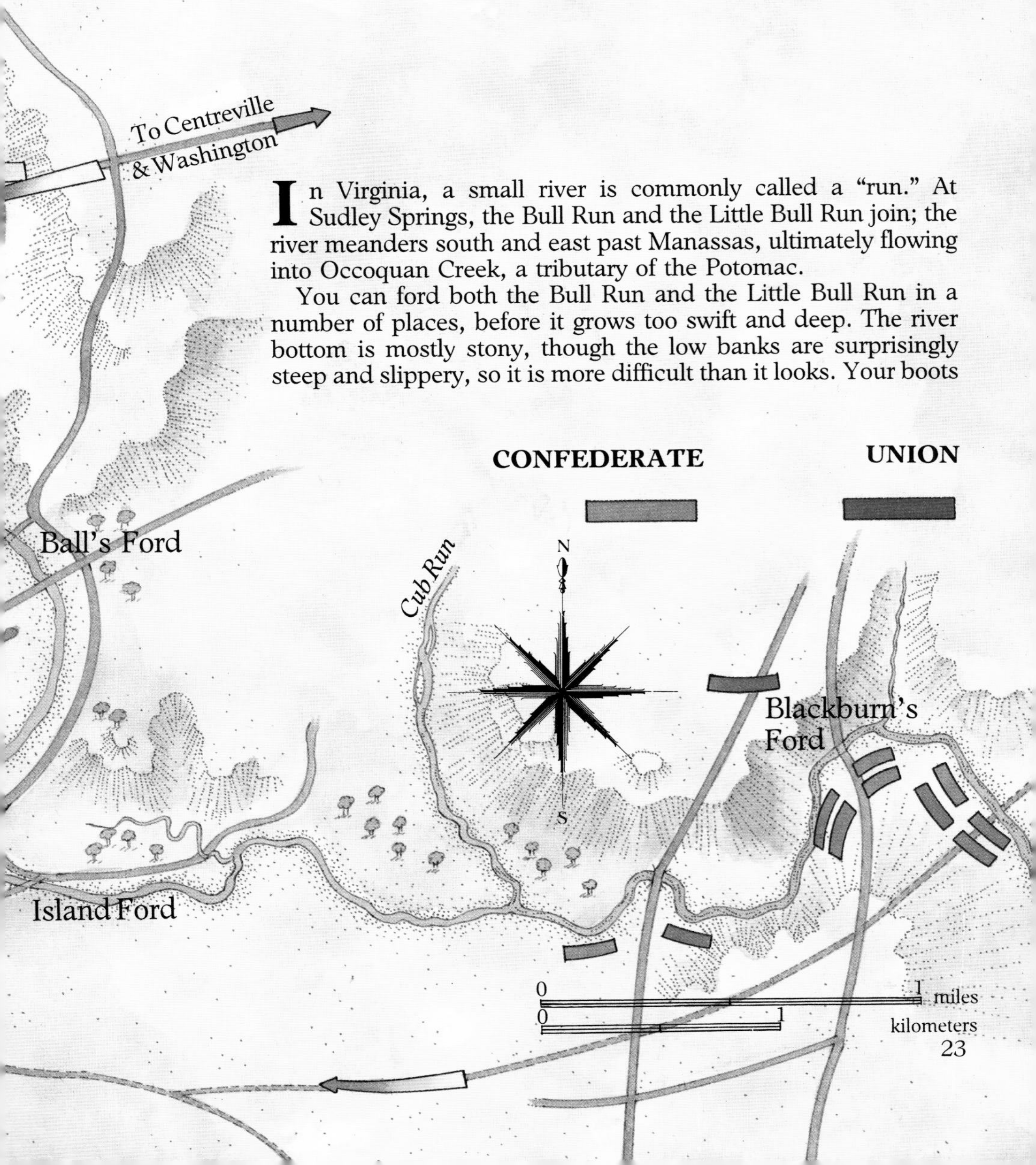

CONFEDERATE   **UNION**

Ball's Ford

Cub Run

N

S

Blackburn's Ford

Island Ford

0   1 miles
0   1 kilometers

fill with water, and squelch afterwards as you walk. This was how many of the Union soldiers fought.

If you would rather see the battle from the Confederate viewpoint, go up to the field around the Henry House, behind the modern Park Visitor Center. There, in a huge field almost completely devoid of cover, you will see how a combination of raw determination and leadership can win a battle in the complete absence of any natural advantages. Look to the north-east; that is where the Yankees came from.

ON TO RICHMOND

The Congress of the Confederate States of America was due to meet in Richmond on July 20, 1861. "BY THAT DATE," screamed the New York *Tribune* in early July, "THE PLACE MUST BE HELD BY THE NATIONAL ARMY." What was more, the initial enlistment of the Yankee 90-day men was nearly over, and their masters in Washington wanted a fight out of them before they went home. "ON TO RICHMOND" was the cry.

Manassas was a major concentration center of Confederate troops for various reasons, but two were decisive. One was the railroad, which ran not only to the south but also to the agriculturally rich Shenandoah Valley in the east (see page 211). The other was the fact that it was as close to Washington (about 30 miles) as the Confederate armies could reasonably be expected to gather. If Richmond was to be occupied by the Yankees, they would first have to fight their way through the Rebels at Manassas.

Winfield Scott, the experienced if elderly and ailing General in Chief of the Union forces, strongly advised against a battle; the men were not ready, he said. He was right. But with the same unerring lack of appreciation of the realities of war which was to dog him for the next four years, Lincoln bowed to public opinion and ordered a battle. In doing so, he very nearly lost the War.

On the way to Manassas — The lighthearted manner in which the War was regarded at its commencement is reflected in the way that both recruits and civilians flocked to Manassas; the former to participate in the potentially brief spell of glory, the latter to witness the action. For this reason, Manassas was also known as "the picnic battle." It was generally thought that the war would be a short-lived affair, a misapprehension to be so harshly disproved at Manassas.

In truth, the battle could very easily have gone either way. The remark attributed to the German soldier General von Moltke was more true here than it would ever be again: the armies *were* just a couple of armed mobs chasing one another around the country-side. It was, however, important for three reasons. To begin with, it was the very first major battle. In the second place, it taught both sides that the War was not going to be over in a few days. Thirdly, and perhaps most importantly of all, it was a Rebel victory. This established a considerable psychological ascendancy on the part of the Rebels; although slightly outnumbered, they put the fear of God into the Yankees and convinced themselves of the truth of all their bravado about how many Yankees a Southern soldier could whip.

THE PICNIC BATTLE

"When the tidings of an impending battle reached Washington, all the idlers in the capital rushed forward to see the sight. Congress-men, newspaper correspondents, and loungers of every grade besieged the livery stables ...

Encouraged by reports of the morning's success, many had ventured beyond Centreville; some had even crossed the Run ..."

(*Harper's Magazine*)

These "idlers and loungers" apparently intended to view the battle from high ground near the field of action. Unfortunately for them, they collided on their way to the battlefield with the fleeing Yankee soldiers who had just left it. *Harper's* likened the result to a whirl-pool, with its vortex on the narrow bridge which crossed Cub Run, the only easy means of retreat to Washington.

This was the last time that either side viewed a battle (literally) as a picnic.

THE OPPOSING ARMIES

Many of the eager soldiers on both sides believed that the War between the States would be over in a few months, or even a few weeks; this was why so many of them rushed to the colors, eager to strike a blow before the war ended. Otherwise, they feared, they would miss the glory.

They were, however, almost completely unprepared for the reality of war. They were hardly armies at all; the concept of military discipline was foreign to most, and their officers had no experience of conducting major battles. The last major American war had been the War of 1812, and although American naval successes had been startling, the armies' showing had been unimpressive. The Mexican War of 1846-48 was a small, professional war (Scott had 13,000 at Tampico, while Santa Ana had 12,000), and was fought in the far West; it did little to prepare anyone for the Civil War.

The Confederate armies had been concentrating at Manassas Junction for some time; Beauregard had about 20,000 men there

Off to War — The railroad, running both south and east, transported the influx of eager Confederate men to Manassas, the first battle in which trains were used to rush troops to the front.

in mid-July, and more were arriving daily. The Union army left Washington on the afternoon of July 16 with 35,000 men, but because they were (in the words of McDowell's adjutant-general J.B. Fry) "not soldiers, but civilians in uniform," it took until July 18 to cover the 20 miles to Centreville. McDowell then spent another two days reconnoitering. Given that security in Washington was non-existent, this delay allowed the Confederacy to build up their armies to a point where resistance would be feasible. As Beauregard himself put it, "arrangements were made which enabled me to receive regularly, from private persons at the Federal capital, most accurate information ..." Sometimes, the Confederates knew the Union battle plans better than their Union counterparts!

At the battle itself, neither side used all of the men available; in fact, only about half the available "effectives" on either side were actually committed. One estimate (Mitchell) pits 18,500 Union troops against 18,000 confederates, but adds that of the Confederates, "the bulk of the fighting was done by only a portion of this number."

TERRAIN

The Bull Run meanders south and east past Sudley, a hamlet to the north-west of Manassas Junction. The junction of the Manassas-Sudley road (roughly north-south) and the Warrenton Turnpike (roughly east-west) was the very center of the battlefield. It is about 29 miles from Washington.

The Warrenton Turnpike crossed the Bull Run at a stone bridge, to the north of Manassas Junction; the Orange and Alexandria Railroad crossed about 6½ miles downstream. The fords are shown on the map; there was a small wooden bridge at Blackburn's Ford.

A rail fence, like this one on the Henry Hill, provides only a little genuine cover but it does make the person behind it much harder to see at a distance. Try it.

The river valley is at an altitude of about 160 feet. The very highest ground, around Sudley Springs and to the north-west of the battlefield, is at no more than 330 feet; most is around the 250-foot mark. The Henry House, to the south-east, is at about 275 feet; the highest part of Chinn Ridge, west of the Henry House, is a few feet higher. Nor are the hills steep; in most places they are very gentle, so that anyone on high ground has a good view as far as the brow of the next hill — a mile or more — unless his line of sight is broken by trees. Nowadays, the Manassas battlefield is rather more open than it was when *Harper's* described it as:

> "Broken and intricate, sparsely dotted with hamlets, plantations, and solitary houses, partly forests of considerable size, and partly of the scrubby growth of pine and oak which springs up spontaneously in the exhausted and abandoned fields of Virginia. It is intersected in every direction by streams ..."

McDowell's plan was to use feints and demonstrations to persuade the Confederates that he was attacking between the

Stone Bridge and the railroad, thereby pinning down the Confederate line, and then to deploy his main force from the north (via Sudley Springs) and attack the Confederates' left flank. The battle was intended to take place around the Bull Run. By pure chance, it actually took place to a large extent on the Henry House hill, which neither side ever anticipated as a battleground.

The ford at Sudley Springs which was the only source of clean, fresh water available during the battle.

During the First Battle of Manassas, the weather was hot — temperatures were probably in the nineties Fahrenheit (over 30°C); the roads were dusty; and the only supply of clean water was from Sudley Springs, though many drank from the Bull Run and the Cub Run.

THE BATTLE

As is so often the case, it is easiest to envisage the battle at dawn, when there are few sightseers about. A clear summer's morning, with the promise of a hot day, re-creates the conditions under which the battle started. If you are a civilian, standing by the Bull Run at Sudley Springs or the Stone Bridge or Blackburn's Ford, you are probably very close in spirit to the recently-enlisted soldiers who fought there. Imagine yourself there, utterly unsure

The Stone Bridge across Bull Run was the site of the second and more significant Union attack. During the retreat, the bridge became a scene of chaos as fleeing Yankee soldiers mingled with panicking civilians who had come to view the battle.

27

of yourself, short of sleep, never having fired a gun in anger, filled with a mixture of pride and terror.

At daybreak, Union troops under Richardson made a feint at Blackburn's Ford. This served as little more than an alarm-clock for the Confederates; it was too transparently a feint. But something was up.

The secondary attack, at the Stone Bridge, was much more convincing; indeed, after the War, Beauregard himself said that it would have been better for the Union to launch their main attack there. It began at 5:15 am, but Colonel Evans (the Confederate commander there) soon realized that this could not be the main attack, or the Union army would have pushed a lot harder. It signalled that the Union had taken a genuine initiative, though, and had the useful effect (for the Confederacy) of mobilizing troops who would otherwise have been resting. They were ordered into a state of readiness at about 7 am.

At precisely that time, the main Union force should have been crossing the fords at Sudley Springs; but the crossing was two hours late. Confederates saw the move at about 9 am and signalled it to all divisions by "wigwag" (semaphore).

Colonel Evans then marched his Confederates smartly towards the main Yankee forces; he was seriously outnumbered, but intended to hold the Union armies until reinforcements arrived. Meanwhile, the Union's Brigadier-General W.T. Sherman had found a ford just north of the Stone Bridge and poured his men across that, in a maneuver apparently unforeseen by the overall Union commander McDowell. Sherman broke the Confederates' lines with his attack on their right flank; the Rebels fled south-west, across Young's Branch and past the Stone House (at the

The contest for the Henry House, which was unexpectedly to dominate the battle, took place on the exposed Henry House Hill which remains substantially unchanged today.

The Henry House and the monument of the First Battle of Manassas, from a photograph taken in 1884.

crossroads) and onto the high ground by the Henry House.

On that high ground, in the words of General Bee, stood General T.J. Jackson, "like a stone wall." "Rally behind the Virginians!" cried Bee; and the Rebels did. Behind Jackson's five regiments, with only the scantiest of cover, the Rebels reformed; the Union armies crashed against them, and the legend of "Stonewall" Jackson was born. It was not yet noon.

This is perhaps the most evocative part of the battlefield of First Manassas. The land around the Henry House is a great open field now, just as it was then, and cover is minimal. There are woods (of second-grown pine) behind you, to the south and east, and they provide a measure of psychological cover as well as potential physical cover; but they are behind you.

"Tom Fool" no more. Of all the equestrian statues on the various battlefields, this one of Professor T.J. Jackson of the Virginia Military Institute is one of the most moving.

Fighting from behind trees, and fences, and shallow depressions in the ground—or most often, standing exposed to the enemy's fire—the Rebels held the Yankees. Colonel "Jeb" Stuart's Confederate cavalry even captured some of the Union guns. But it was close, very close, the armies surging to and fro around the Henry House, like a tide. Then, in the early afternoon, another brigade entered the field.

At Manassas, uniforms were by no means standardized (see page 00), and the Confederate "Stars and Bars" was not the familiar battle flag which most people call by that name. Rather, it resembled a simplified "Stars and Stripes," with seven stars in a circle on a blue ground, and three stripes (red, white, red) instead of the 13 stripes of the Union flag. No one could tell whether these reinforcements were Rebel or Yankee. Then, a gust of wind snapped the flag out. It was the Stars and Bars. Jubal Early's brigade had joined the battle, having marched from near

The Stone House on the Warrenton Turnpike from a photograph taken in March 1862.

Blackburn's Ford where the Union demonstration had proved almost completely ineffectual.

The Rebels took new strength from Early's men; the mere sight of them was enough. With a blood-curdling Rebel yell—the first time it was heard in the thick of battle—they charged down the hill towards the Warrenton Pike, and the Yankee lines broke. As was to become the hallmark of Rebel troops, the Confederates fought like tigers as knives, fists and muskets wielded like clubs terrorized the Union troops.

The Yankee retreat became a rout. Many soldiers did not stop until they reached Washington at daybreak. The Stone Bridge, in particular, became a maelstrom of humanity as Union soldiers joined the panicking spectators who had come to cheer them on. Their carriages jammed inextricably with military transports and guns; fleeing soldiers cut horses from their traces in order to escape faster. This tiny bridge, rebuilt to more or less the same standard of pre-War days, is preserved alongside the modern steel-and-concrete bridge which carries the US 29, as the Warrenton Turnpike is now known. It is a somewhat claustrophobic spot even now; on that hot July afternoon, it must have been hellish.

GENERAL BEE

Trying to rally his own men, Brigadier General Barnard Elliot Bee gave "Tom Fool" Jackson the nickname: "Stonewall." Minutes later, he was mortally wounded. He entered West Point from the then independent Republic of Texas, graduating in 1845, and served in the Mexican War. A career soldier, he left the US Army in 1861, and was appointed Lieutenant-Colonel of the 1st South Carolina Regulars. Confirmation of his rank as Brigadier-General was posthumous. He was 37 years old.

"There stands Jackson." These woods at the Confederates' backs contributed to their rallying and the pine trees you can see now apparently stand much as they did in 1861.

A KEYNOTE BATTLE

It was a spectacular victory for the infant Confederacy. The old boasts about Southern manliness and Northern weakness were reinforced out of all proportion to the truth of the battle, but both sides came to believe the myth. Lincoln's pandering to public opinion and his determination to have a "public-relations" battle almost certainly added years to the war, as it gave the South a long term psychological advantage.

Luckily for Lincoln, he had not made all the mistakes. The Confederates made two disastrous errors. First, they did not appreciate how easily they could have annihilated either half of the Union army which McDowell so obligingly divided for them; and if General Ewell had received his orders on time, he might still have wiped out the Union armies at Centreville. As was to happen so often during the rest of the War, poor staff and communications crippled the Confederates.

Secondly, they were simply too disorganized to follow up their victory with a pursuit; the men were hot, tired, frightened, and insufficiently disciplined to manage a full-scale chase. Arguably, they would not have been able to attack Washington itself: in any case " Lincoln's bodyguard," as the President's detractors called the always-substantial Washington garrison, was there and

35,000 Rebels would probably have been repulsed. Even so, a modest chase might have netted hundreds — or even thousands — of prisoners-of-war, including a few Congressmen and other influential "idlers and loungers."

FURTHER INFORMATION

Maps: USGS 7.5': Manassas, Gainesville
  Official Reports Atlas: 3/1&2; 5/1&7
  B&L: 172, 180, 199, 204, 233

Park: Excellent museum, good "electric map"-type model of battlefield. The Visitor Center is open 8:30 am to 5 pm in winter, 6 pm in summer; the park is open from dawn to dusk. The Stone House is open only during the summer. The picnic area (no alcohol and not very attractive) is on Sudley Road north of the Stone House. Superintendent: Manassas National Battlefield Park, PO Box 130, Manassas, VA 22110; phone (703) 754 7107.

Town: Modern Manassas bears little resemblance to the antebellum town; even the railroad junction is apparently in a different place, probably half a mile from its wartime position. There is a small museum at Manassas itself, but it is not very informative. The majority of the motels are near the I-66 junction.

THE ARMIES

In 1861, there were 16,367 men in the Regular Army of the United States. Close to 300 officers joined the South, leaving just over 800 with the Union.

Given that about 2,000,000 Yankees and 750,000 Rebels bore arms, this meant that there was a severe shortage of trained men on both sides. The army consisted, therefore, of a mish-mash of regular regiments, regiments of militia which do not seem to have been as "well ordered" as the Fourth Amendment envisages (where there was no longer an Indian threat, local militias were often no more than social clubs), and many volunteer regiments.

On numbers alone, the volunteers were most significant; but their abilities as a fighting force varied widely. Some were formed almost as clubs and elected their officers; some were effectively private armies, commanded by the man who brought them together; while others were *ad hoc* organizations whose officers were often political appointees. Later in the War, conscripts would appear; some men joined ahead of conscription, while others (mostly in the North) paid substitutes. Yet others joined on the promise of bounties.

Organization

The standard unit was the regiment, nominally 1,000 men in ten companies of 100 men. Some regiments were over-

strength but others had 500 men or less. Not all would be fit to fight; some would be detailed for other duties, and some would simply have gone home or got lost.

The number of fighting men — "effectives"—might range from one-third to two-thirds of the nominal strength of the regiment. As well as regiments, there were detached batallions (two or more companies or batteries), individual companies and individual batteries. Including regiments, the Union had 3,559 units and the Confederates 1,526.

The question of "effectives" is difficult to judge, as the North counted accountants, sutlers, pork-choppers etc. as "effectives," so their number of *fighting* effectives might be 10% lower than indicated in this book. For the South, all "effectives" were normally fighting men.

Confederate regiments typically maintained an *esprit de corps* by putting new volunteers (and conscripts) into old regiments, while the Union followed the practise of allowing existing regiments to dwindle until they could be amalgamated by a Washington bureaucrat. While this allowed the appointment of politically sound colonels, it hardly promoted morale in the ranks. Also, new bounty regiments

The Awkward Squad — a contemporary cartoon illustrates the fact that the majority of volunteers on both sides were amateurish, inexperienced and ill-equipped for combat.

HARDEE'S
RIFLE AND LIGHT INFANTRY
TACTICS,

FOR THE INSTRUCTION, EXERCISES AND MANŒUVRES OF

RIFLEMEN AND LIGHT INFANTRY.

INCLUDING

SCHOOL OF THE SOLDIER AND SCHOOL OF THE COMPANY.

BY BREVET LIEUT. W. J. HARDEE.

To which is added,
DUTIES OF NON-COMMISSIONED OFFICERS.

MILITARY HONORS TO BE PAID BY TROOPS.

THE ARTICLES OF WAR,

Containing Rules by which the Armies of the United States are governed;
Relating to Courts-Martial; Suppressing Mutiny or Sedition;
Granting Furloughs, Commissary of Musters; Accepting a
Challenge; Chaplains; Sutlers; To whom any Officer
may apply for Redress; Sentinels; False
Alarms; Misbehaviour; Making Known
the Watchword; Engineers; Spies;
How Courts-Martial must be
Authenticated, Etc.,

NEW YORK.
J. O. KANE, PUBLISHER, 126 NASSAU STREET.
1862.

could be used, as at Fredericksburg, "in the front to save the veterans for heavy work" — in other words, as cannon-fodder.

Above regimental level, organization varied. Four regiments would be grouped together on the march to form a brigade, though a battle brigade might be larger or smaller. Brigades in turn were grouped into divisions, typically of two or three brigades, and two or three divisions made up a corps. Finally, the army would consist of a number of corps. The sequence was (in ascending order): Company, Regiment, Brigade, Division, Corps, Army.

Major-General William J. Hardee was a seasoned officer who actively participated in many confrontations throughout the War. His textbook, Rifle and Light Infantry Tactics, *written before the War, became essential reading for both Union and Confederate officers in the early stages when little was known of military procedure and most recruits were raw and untrained.*

For example, at Gettysburg the Army of the Potomac (95,000 infantry) consisted of 51 Brigades organized into 19 Divisions and 7 Corps: the Army of Northern Virginia (73,000 infantry) consisted of 37 Brigades organized into 9 Divisions and 3 Corps.

STRATEGY AND TACTICS

"Strategy" is the art and science of setting goals for long-term ends; thus the repeated attempts at invasion on both sides were strategic. "Tactics" is the art and science of achieving strategic ends on the ground. Thus a *tactical* defeat can be a *strategic* victory if (for example) it delays the enemy and allows you to accomplish something which your opponent would have preferred to prevent.

History often misleads us: because something *did* happen a particular way, we imagine it *had* to happen that way.

But generals often functioned in a "fog of war," and what we call "tactical genius" was normally the result of careful intelligence-gathering and analysis of the options. For an analysis of strategy and tactics in the field, Robert G. Tanner's account of the Shenandoah Valley Campaign of 1862, *Stonewall in the Valley* (Doubleday, New York, 1976) is superb. A more general but equally readable book on tactics is Paddy Griffith's *Rally Once Again* (Crowood Press, Marlborough, Wilts, UK, 1987).

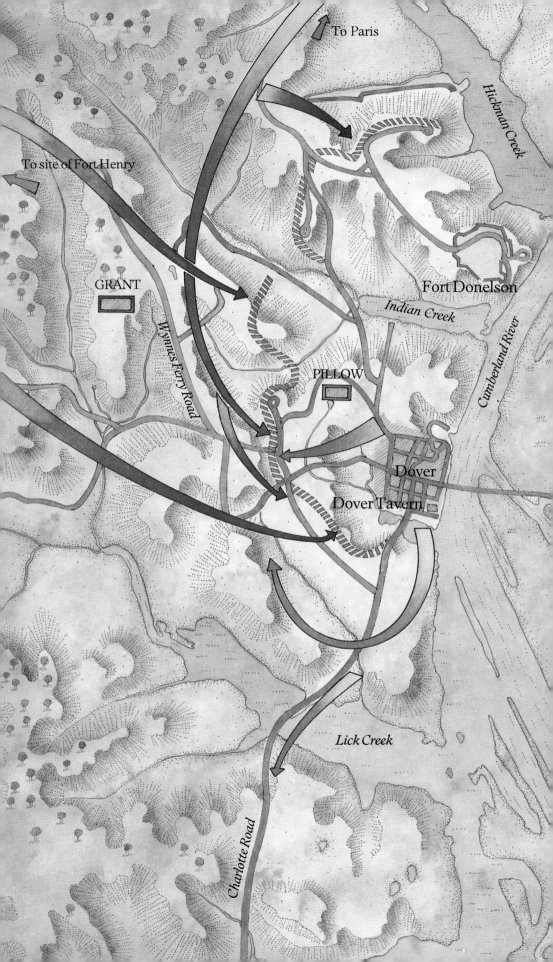

To Paris

Hickman Creek

To site of Fort Henry

GRANT

Fort Donelson

Indian Creek

Cumberland River

Wynne's Ferry Road

PILLOW

Dover

Dover Tavern

Lick Creek

Charlotte Road

THE FALL OF
FORT DONELSON

Also known as Two Rivers
Dover, Tennessee
February 6-16 1862

Union gunboats

Confederate States	United States
Major-General Gideon J. Pillow	Brigadier-General Ulysses S. Grant
12,000 effectives[†]	27,000 effectives[*]
1,500 casualties	2,832 casualties

[*]Plus naval support.

[†]Confederate figures are disputed. Estimates of effectives run from 5,000 to 15,000, but the casualty figure is about right.

To this day, tugs push great rafts of barges along the Tennessee and the Cumberland, the "Two Rivers" which provide the alternative name for the Fort Donelson campaign. On the Cumberland, they pass the long-silent guns of Fort Donelson; on the Tennessee, even the fort which guarded the river (Fort Henry) has been swallowed up by the river itself.

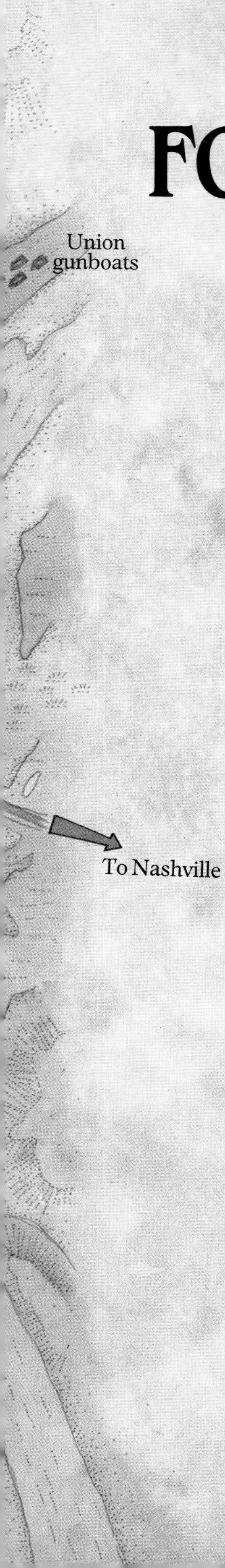

To Nashville

CONFEDERATE   **UNION**

Entrenchments   ////////

S ———— N

0 ——————————————— 1 miles
0 ——————————————— 1 kilometers

The nearest town, Dover, seems little bigger than it was in pre-War days. Although the Park Service maintains an excellent Visitor Center near Fort Donelson, and a superb little exhibit at the Dover Tavern where the Confederates surrendered, the majority of tourists in the area do not come for the history; they come for the fishing, or possibly just for the scenery. Fort Donelson is perhaps a little well-manicured, but it is also nearly deserted. More than in most parks, there is a sense of time hanging still; you know that the huts where they have the "living history" demonstrations are modern replicas, but they do not seem that way.

This picture, from the last century, shows river boats on the Tennessee.

THE TWO RIVERS

The Tennessee and the Cumberland were critical to the survival of the Confederacy — almost as important as the Mississippi. They provided channels for transport and communication (the "internal lines" so beloved of the Swiss military theorist Jomini) and they could *in extremis* act as defensive barriers.

In order to protect them, the Confederates built two earth-and-log forts, Fort Henry and Fort Donelson, rather before the confluence of the rivers.

In late 1861, General Halleck in Washington and General Ulysses S. Grant in the field finally determined to try and break the Confederate lines in northern Tennessee, using combined naval and military force. Grant's position looked extremely dangerous — in hostile territory, surrounded on three sides by the enemy — but his estimate of the situation was that he would prevail; like Lee, he was a superb judge of his opponents. The attack fell first upon Fort Henry.

FORT HENRY

Fort Henry can be dismissed quickly. In the words of the Confederate artillerist Captain Jesse Taylor, "my investigation convinced me that we had a more dangerous force to contend with than the Federals, — namely, the river itself." In fact, if the attack had been delayed for 48 hours, the Confederate powder magazine would have been flooded. The last traces of the fort disappeared in floods during the 1930s, though outlying earthworks remain deep in the woods; they are not marked in any way, or maintained by the Park Service.

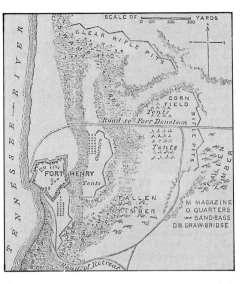

Only a few outworks still remain at the site of Fort Henry, seen here in a map of February 6, 1862.

To make matters worse, the powder was "of very inferior quality" and the Rebels had to resort to "the dangerous expedient of adding to each charge a proportion of quick-burning powder." To cap it all, Captain Taylor did not trust the "pot-metal" 12-pounders which formed a significant part of the fort's defenses. When he tested them, "two of them burst with an ordinary charge," so "the others were set aside as a dangerous encumbrance."

Knowing his position to be indefensible, the Confederate commanding officer of Fort Henry, General Lloyd Tilghman, ordered the majority of his men to march to Fort Donelson some 12 miles to the east; he remained behind with Captain Taylor, a few other officers, and 54 men of Company B, 1st Tennessee Artillery. Their intention was to hold the enemy off for an hour.

In the event, five men were killed, eleven wounded or disabled, and five were missing; but they held out for over two hours. When the Union cutter came ashore to receive the surrender (the army took no part in the action), the river had risen so far that the boat sailed into the infantry sally-port, and "between the fort and the position which had been occupied by the infantry support was a sheet of water a quarter of a mile or more wide, and 'running like a mill-race'." The focus of the action moved to Fort Donelson.

TERRAIN

The Cumberland at Fort Donelson is at 359 feet; the fort itself is on a bluff at about 420-440 feet, some 60-80 feet above the water level. The town of Dover, a mile east of the fort, is at a similar elevation.

The lines outside the fort followed a broad arc with a radius of some 2½ miles, centered on a point mid-way between Fort Donelson and the town of Dover. Wherever possible, they were along the edge of high ground at up to 500 feet. They were anchored at the western end on Hickman Creek, which flows north-east into the Cumberland about 300 yards west of the fort, and at the eastern end on the creek which marks the eastern limits of Dover, Lick Creek. According to one Union map, Hickman Creek was "impassable except by boats and bridges."

FORT DONELSON

After the fall of Fort Henry, Grant's men encircled the Confederate lines at Fort Donelson and sat down to wait for the gunboat support which had already proved so effective at Fort Henry. On February 13, this arrived; the USS *Carondelet* bombarded the fort in the morning, but without any great success. In the afternoon, the weather suddenly changed. It had been mild and fair, but it turned to sleet and freezing rain, with temperatures that night of only 10°F (-12°C).

At this early stage of the War, soldiers were still disposed to throw away blankets and greatcoats during warm weather, because they were too much trouble to carry. Both sides probably suffered equally, with Grant's men having abandoned their kit out of thoughtlessness and the Confederates (or at least, those who had come from Fort Henry) out of necessity.

The Union harassed the Confederates with cannonade and sniper fire; the sharpshooters were equipped with selected Henry 15-shot rifles, remarkably accurate as well as being known as "that damn Yankee rifle they load up on Sunday and fire all week." Fires for cooking were impossible, at least in the outer lines; hardtack and water sustained both sides in the bitter February cold.

On the 14th the bombardment was renewed with a vengeance. Four ironclads and two wooden gunboats pounded the fort mercilessly, but they were answered with well-aimed and heavy Confederate fire. Two ironclads lost their steering gear (the USS *St. Louis* and the USS *Louisville*), and the wooden vessels were simply unable to withstand the Confederate cannonade. Grant's hopes that the gunboats would settle the matter, with the support of sharpshooters and land-based artillery, were dashed. If you stand at the water-batteries, it is easy to understand the gunner in Bidwell's battery who said, "Now, boys, see me take a chimney," and suited deed to word by blowing funnel and mast off a Yankee boat with the next shot. With remarkable bravery, the Union boats fought within 400 yards of the fort.

The Confederates were, however, no better placed in the long run. The Yankees could always outwait them, and with Union gunboats on the river, the chances of Confederate reinforcements being ferried across were poor. The only possibility was to break out, and the Union right (south) flank seemed to be the place to do it.

They prepared for the break-out all through the night of the 14th. Unfortunately, the Park Service now closes the fort before dark, but parts of the battlefield remain open. Get out of your car and sit on a tree-stump, or on the ground; try to imagine the soft clink of harness, muffled footsteps on the snow-covered ground, the whinnying of horses and the occasional buzz of conversation,

Right: The batteries along the riverside at Fort Donelson may look low and ill-protected from above, but if you get down nearer the water line, you see that they are well dug in behind substantial earthworks.

Great rafts of barges carrying coal and other goods still ply the Tennessee and the Cumberland but the guns which guard the river are long silent.

all the while in the bitter cold. You'll feel the uncertainty of war.

They made their grand attempt on the 15th, smashing out from Buckner's positions just south of Dover (a fraction of the original earthworks is preserved here, at Stops 8 and 9 on the Park Tour) and from the town itself, down the Charlotte Road beside Lick Creek and then south-west against Grant's Yankees. A roaring, crashing, yelling attack fell on the Yankees at dawn. By noon, the battle still raged, but the Yankees were running low on ammunition; their only resources were the cartridge boxes of the dead and wounded.

Below: This "Living History" display at Fort Donelson recreates Wartime living quarters for the modern visitor.

Confederate troops under Major-General Pillow broke McLernand's Union line, and laid open an escape route (Wynne's Ferry Road) to Nashville; but General Pillow seems completely to have lost his head. He imagined that Grant's men were in full retreat, and instead of taking care of his own retreat, he decided to pursue them.

The result was a disaster. The Yankees re-formed across the road, and the Confederates running pell-mell in pursuit of what they thought was a fleeing enemy were no match for the almost parade-ground lines. They rebounded, and the fate of the fort was sealed. Heady victory turned to bitter defeat.

Grant now launched a determined counter-attack on the Confederate left (west) flank, near Hickman Creek; he calculated that they must have weakened their defenses in order to attack at all.

The Yankees scrambled up the snow-covered slopes (to the south-west as you stand at Stop 6 on the Park Tour) and succeeded in taking a significant proportion of the outer works. He got no further, but the Rebels were now thoroughly bottled up by a superior force, with no hope of relief.

SIMON BOLIVAR BUCKNER

The general entrusted with the capitulation of Fort Donelson was 38 at the time; he was born in Hart City, Kentucky, on April 1, 1823. He graduated from West Point in 1844, and left the army in 1855. By 1860 he was head of the Kentucky National Guard; he was commissioned Brigadier-General when he joined the Confederate army in September 1861. He owned no slaves, but fought for States' Rights. Much later, at the end of the War, he would also surrender the Army of Trans-Mississippi. After the War, he returned successfully to business, served as Governor of Kentucky 1887-91, and died on January 8, 1914, aged 90.

Captain Edward McAllister's Illinois battery shooting at Rebels on February 13.

NATHAN BEDFORD FORREST

A self-made millionaire who joined the army to become what Sherman called "the most remarkable man our Civil War produced on either side," Forrest was 39 (born July 13, 1821) when he led his troops out of Fort Donelson. He made his fortune in slave dealing, but switched to running a plantation when slaves begged to stay with him. Dashing, brave to the point of foolhardiness, he is known chiefly for his daring cavalry raids into Yankee territory, but he was also a good general in a more conventional battle, as witness Brice's Cross Roads. After the War, he turned back to business and farming, and died on October 29, 1877, aged 66.

THE SURRENDER

The Confederates realized that their position was hopeless, and that surrender was the only answer. Luckily for the South, Nathan Forrest escaped with his cavalry, and a few others also got away; the creeks and hollows to the east of the line around Lick Creek were substantially unguarded by the Yankees, but splashing through the icy water and breaking the ice was slow, hazardous and bitterly cold work. In Lew Wallace's words, "He was next heard of at Nashville."

The Surrender House, Dover, formerly the old Dover Hotel, where Buckner surrendered to Grant.

Generals Floyd and Pillow, afraid that they would not be treated as prisoners of war but rather as traitors, made their escape across the river in small boats. The third in command, General Simon Bolivar Buckner, sent to Grant requesting a meeting to discuss terms; Grant sent back his famous reply, which earned him the name "Unconditional Surrender" Grant and made him a hero in the North: "No terms except unconditional and immediate surrender can be accepted. I propose to move immediately upon your works."

When Buckner was Grant's prisoner, the Union general recognized that Buckner was the only Confederate general to come out of the affair with honor. As they parted, Grant said, "Buckner, you are, I know, separated from your people, and perhaps you need funds; my purse is at your disposal." Buckner declined, but thanked him, and left for prisoner-of-war camp. He was exchanged in the summer of 1862, apparently for a Yankee general expressly captured for the purpose!

THE AFTERMATH

The Two Rivers campaign was to be as much a keynote in the Western Theater as First Manassas in the Eastern Theater. There were two factors at work. One was the thinly-spread forces, with the North always having the advantage in numbers. The other was that it was not so much a question of one side winning a battle; it was more a question of the other losing it. Certainly, the Confederacy had no one of Lee's caliber in the West, while the Union had no one of Grant's caliber in the East. There would still be many Confederate victories in the West; but they would be set against a steady increase in Union power.

As a result of this battle, two important rivers were under Union control, which stifled the Confederate war effort. Kentucky was no longer at issue, and Tennessee was open to Northern invasion. More importantly, the North recognized the genius of the sometimes hard-drinking Ulysses S. Grant. His promotion would hurt the Southern cause more than anything else.

Winter sports in a Confederate camp. Soldiers of both sides experienced severe winter weather for the first time at Fort Donelson and many were ill-prepared; the Yankees had disposed of their cumbersome winter attire to render traveling easier, and the Confederates were simply inadequately equipped. Although the Confederates are seen here making the most of the wintry conditions, their hardship during the grueling defense of Fort Donelson can be imagined.

View of Dover from the Surrender House.
Many modern visitors to Dover care nothing for
the history; it is apparently a fisherman's paradise.

FURTHER INFORMATION

Maps: USGS 7.5': Dover
Official Reports Atlas: 11/1-4; 135/A; 150/F2; 171
B&L: 361; 363; 402

Park: The Visitor Center has an excellent slide presentation and a good little museum. At the Surrender House (open 11 am to 4 pm) there is a superb filmed dramatization of the meeting of Confederate generals as they debated surrender. There are Living History exhibits during the summer. There is a picnic area (lunchtimes only) in the fort itself, though alcohol is banned.

Town: Dover is much as Major-General Lew Wallace described it at the time of the War: "unknown to fame, meager in population, architecturally poor." As a result of fighting over the town during the War, only four pre-War buildings survive. The motels are of a very fair standard, and reasonably priced.

UNIFORMS

The basic function of a uniform is to ensure that in the heat of battle, men can recognize one another as friend or foe. A secondary function is the delineation of rank; and anyone who has ever had to wear uniform will concur that comfort and ease of movement trail a long way behind these two considerations.

By the end of the War — even by 1863 — uniforms served the first purpose reasonably well, with the Union clad usually in dark blue and the Confederacy wearing gray and yellow-brown "butternut." At the beginning of the War, however, there was an outlandish mixture of ancient militia costumes; fanciful "zouave" dress, loosely modeled on the uniforms of the French North African regiments; and pure imagination, such as the all-green uniforms affected by some Irish regiments on both sides, the red and black of the Granville Rifles, or the "Yellow Jackets" from Tennessee. One New York Scottish regiment wore kilts, though not into battle. In some regiments, different *companies* wore different uniforms.

More than once, this cavalier disregard for uniforms meant that men were shot at by their own side, or alternatively, that enemies were ignored because they looked like friends. At Shiloh, the (Confederate) Orleans Guard Battalion wore blue while Grant's men did not want to wear Union issue uniforms; they preferred the well-made, comfortable gray in which they had gone to war. Other examples could be furnished on both sides. The Second Wisconsins and the Thirteenth Indiana (both Union) wore gray and sustained casualties from their own side as a result. Particularly striking uniforms rendered the wearer highly conspicuous, and had the additional disadvantage of being impractical for the wear and tear of rigorous combat. At Fredericksburg the ragged Confederates stripped dead Yankees in order to get some warm

Confederate uniforms. Although the South officially adopted gray uniform, each regiment equipped itself, and there were many interpretations of the standard issue.

CONFEDERATE UNIFORMS

NORTH CAROLINA MILITIA.　REG. INFANTRY PRIVATE.　WASHINGTON ARTILLERY.　MONTGOMERY TRUE BLUE.　FIELD OFFICER OF INFANTRY.　GEN. LEE'S UNIFORM.　REG. CAVALRY PRIVATE.　LOUISIANA TIGER.　LOUISIANA ZOUAVE.　REG. ARTILLERY PRIVATE.

clothing against the bitter cold, giving further scope for confusion in battle. One Yankee commentator, writing after the War, made especial comment that this did *not* happen at Shiloh.

Later in the War, when the blockade began to bite, many Confederate uniforms were yellowish-brown home-dyed "butternut." Even early in the War, some uniforms were issued undyed; the Second Texas Regiment received grayish-white uniforms just before Shiloh, which apparently led one Union prisoner to ask, "Who were them hell-cats that went into battle dressed in their grave-clothes?"

The supply of uniforms to the troops provided textile manufacturers with the opportunity to make quick fortunes and there were many accusations of sharp practice. A new material was produced consisting of yarn woven from the shredded fiber of previously used material

Yankee uniforms. After the confusion at the beginning of the War, the Quartermaster Bureau streamlined the issue of uniforms to the North, which resulted in the Union having the best supplied army of the time.

giving rise to the word "shoddy." Uniforms made from this cloth fell apart very quickly.

As the War wore on, uniforms became more standardized. The "Boys in Blue" wore a dark blue fatigue blouse with paler blue trousers, both of which tended to fade in actual service; dress jackets resembled those of the higher ranks, reaching below the hips. Sergeants and officers wore epaulettes; very senior ranks wore darker trousers. Many items of uniform, such as the stiff leather stock or "dog collar," were very unpopular and were never worn; and in the summer, greatcoats (and even blankets) were often thrown away in order to lighten the load upon the march.

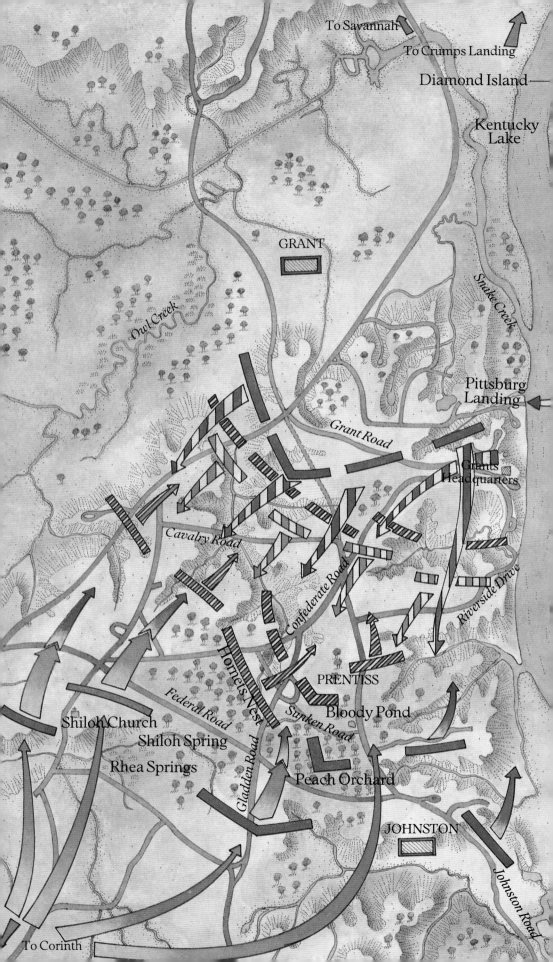

To Savannah

To Crumps Landing

Diamond Island

Kentucky Lake

GRANT

Owl Creek

Snake Creek

Grant Road

Pittsburg Landing

Grants Headquarters

Cavalry Road

Confederate Road

Riverside Drive

PRENTISS

Hornet's Nest

Federal Road

Sunken Road

Bloody Pond

Shiloh Church

Shiloh Spring

Rhea Springs

Gladden Road

Peach Orchard

JOHNSTON

Johnston Road

To Corinth

THE BATTLE OF SHILOH

Also known as Pittsburg Landing, Tennessee
APRIL 6 AND 7 1862

Confederate States
General Albert Sidney Johnston
40,000 effectives
10,700 casualties

United States
General Ulysses S. Grant
42,000 effectives*
13,000 casualties

*At the start of battle on April 6; 20,000 reinforcements arrived late in the afternoon and during the night.

By its very name, Shiloh now conveys a sense of dread. Once, the "Place of Peace" had a different connotation, but now it is the peace of the graveyard, the peace of death.

There is no major town nearby. Pittsburg Landing was a useful landing for the steam-boats which plied the Tennessee River; Shiloh Church, a small Methodist chapel about 2¼ miles south-west of the landing, provided another focus for the people of the

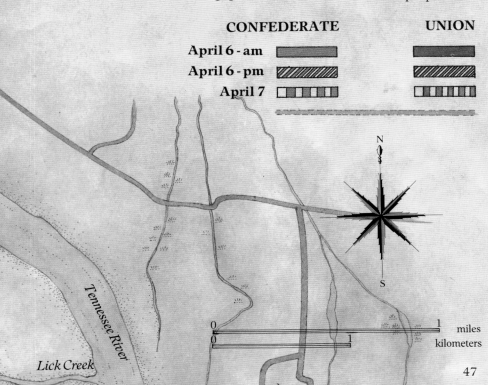

	CONFEDERATE	UNION
April 6 - am		
April 6 - pm		
April 7		

scattered farms who lived in the area. The modern Shiloh Church is a recent structure which is spiritually, rather than materially, related to the building which stood there in 1862.

There is no longer a "landing" of any kind at Pittsburg Landing, but here the steam-ships are seen in the heyday of the place.

Perhaps it is imagination, but across those fields and woods the sun does not seem to shine so brightly, even from a cloudless sky; the birds do not seem to sing, nor the flowers to be as colorful. The peaches which grow in the peach orchard beside the Hornets' Nest are sweet enough — they reach the senses clearly — and the river flows timelessly on; but the overall impression of the place is as if it were seen through a glass, darkly.

THE SHILOH CAMPAIGN

The fall of Fort Donelson in mid-February had broken the Confederates' northern line of defense; worse, it had led to the destruction of the east-west rail link between Nashville and Memphis. The Confederate commander, A. S. Johnston, knew that unless he could attack Grant's Union forces before they were reinforced by Buell's 50,000 men, he would be fighting not against slightly superior numbers, but against odds of more than two to one.

In order to fight on his own terms, Johnston would have to attack as fast as possible. The original plan called for an attack on April 5; this meant that the Confederate army would have to march the 20 or 30 miles north-east from Corinth in two days. Untried and untrained as they were, they were simply unable to meet this relatively modest requirement, which led to the attack being postponed for a full day — with disastrous consequences for the South.

On the Union side, Halleck (who was in supreme command of the Union armies) apparently had a major personality conflict with Grant. At its height, according to Grant, Halleck effectively had him under arrest. The allegation was that the subordinate general had failed to react to telegrams sent by Halleck, though a less charitable interpretation is that Halleck was simply jealous of the fame that Grant had won at Fort Donelson. This "war by telegraph" was to be a recurring flaw in Union strategy, and at Shiloh it may have cost the Union a true victory, as Grant was unwilling to exceed his authority by one iota.

TERRAIN

At Pittsburg Landing on the west bank of the Tennessee River, the water itself is at an elevation of about 360-365 feet. The shore rises precipitately for the first 10 or 20 feet (less at the Landing), then rises still steeply to an altitude of about 460-470 feet at what is now the National Cemetery but was in 1862 Grant's headquarters.

South of the Landing there are deep ravines with steep sides, trails zigzag rather than meeting such slopes head-on. Some of these ravines were full of water at the time of Shiloh, because the river was unusually high. Most of the rest of the battlefield, half a mile or so west of the river, is between 450 and 500 feet.

The elevation was, however, less important in most cases than the ground cover. Although there was more woodland in the 1860s, and less open land, the overall terrain today is still fairly similar: open fields (then under cultivation), the Peach Orchard (where peaches still grow), and thick, tangled woods. Some of these woods are in the hollows and ravines; others, notably the Hornets' Nest, occupy higher ground. In the woods, poison ivy, poison oak and a little poison sumac combine to make a very unattractive undergrowth. There were also numerous creeks and streams, most of them readily fordable.

The result was that the whole area was intersected with roads, though many of them were little more than trails by modern standards. Trying to walk "off the beaten path" was hard work, and maneuvring large bodies of men in precise formation was substantially impossible once you left the fields and clearings. Some of these roads are now park roads, some remain as trails, and others have all but vanished. Access to a number of these roads is restricted; motor vehicles are banned from many. Shiloh Church is about 2¼ miles from the Landing.

The battleground was limited at its northern extreme by Snake Creek and Owl Creek. The two creeks come together about 2½ miles west of the Tennessee; the Snake at this point has been flowing south-east, the Owl north-west. Although they flow into the Tennessee almost due west, the combined creek (still called Snake Creek) loops northwards in an arc 1½ miles wide before joining the main river.

At the southern extreme, about 3½ miles south of Snake Creek, Lick Creek flows north-east into the northward-flowing Tennessee River. As the map shows, at least five of the other creeks are big enough to warrant names, and the

This pen and ink sketch, made two days before the battle, shows the original Shiloh Church which has subsequently been rebuilt and enlarged twice.

network of streams is considerable. The ground is damp, but only around the south of Owl Creek was it marshy.

Between Owl Creek and Lick Creek, a distance of some 6 miles, there is an area of high ground which runs roughly east-west. This marks the remaining boundary of the battlefield, which may be thought of as a triangle with its base here and its apex in the loop of Snake Creek. The left side is formed by Owl Creek and Snake Creek; the right side is formed by Lick Creek and the Tennessee River.

THE BATTLE

Grant's forces were camped along the high ground (up to 500 feet) between Owl Creek and Lick Creek, in the southern part of the modern Military Park, and although (as later reported by Grant) "The water in these streams was very high at the time, and contributed to protect our flanks," they cannot really be said to have formed lines or to have protected their position at all well. Grant himself had established his headquarters on board the steamer USS *Tigress* some 9 miles north at Savannah, Tennessee, waiting to meet Buell when he arrived, and neither he nor his men were expecting a battle.

The Union troops had camped wherever they could find clearings, but they seem simply to have thrown down their bedrolls, pitched their tents, and left it at that. There were no earthworks to speak of — indeed, many Union commanders at that stage of the War believed that defensive earthworks were counter-productive, as they discouraged men from advancing. Also, pickets, sentries and videttes (outlying mounted sentries) seem hardly to have existed; the general lack of security was incredible. They appear to have been completely unaware that the Confederates were even in the neighborhood.

On the first night at Shiloh, the Union troops were (for once) even more uncomfortable than their Confederate counterparts.

Despite the advantage of almost complete surprise, the Confederates' dawn attack (it began at six o'clock) was something of a shambles. Instead of being organized into three clearly defined wings (left, center, right), the three Confederate corps attacked instead in three waves, throwing the command structure and the men themselves into confusion. If Johnston had used a three-wing approach, he would have stood an excellent chance of realising his intention of forcing the Union's left flank back from Pittsburg Landing and bottling them up against Owl Creek and Snake Creek.

The confusion was greater still in the Union camp, however. Breakfast was simmering in pots and frying pans — the smell of cooking must have been a torment to Confederate noses — and many men were still relaxing in their sleeping-rolls, just thinking about getting up. The more fortunate were taken prisoner, while the less fortunate were shot or bayonetted where they lay. When the Confederate attack burst upon them to the accompaniment of a full-throated cannonade, they were taken utterly by surprise.

They broke and ran. With the exception of Prentiss's division (see below), they were completely routed. There seemed to be every sign that this was going to be an utter Confederate victory — and, had Grant not been in charge, so it might have been.

Pittsburg Landing as it is today.

When Grant heard the cannon's roar, he immediately cast off and sailed to Pittsburg Landing. What he found then was not encouraging. Sullen crowds of Union soldiers, many of whom had abandoned their weapons, had come to the Landing in the hope of escape. Grant rode against the tide of men — perhaps as many as 5,000 — whom Buell was trying to rally, still moving towards the sound of the guns.

Because of the incoherent Confederate attack, and the widely dispersed nature of the Union camp, the battle was actually proceeding as a series of private fights. Union regiments and divisions had all fallen back, with a variety of responses which ran from outright flight to a desperate rearguard struggle. The most prominent salient in the fast-retreating Union lines was formed by the remains of Prentiss's division; because of the fury of their defense, this became known as "The Hornets' Nest."

The Sunken Road inside the Hornets' Nest was little mentioned in the original battle reports - the wood was regarded as much more significant - but it has grown in importance with the re-telling.

Their position was a thick wood, with open fields on either side, and a (very slightly) sunken road running through it. To the west, the Union right, there was open land; to the east, the Union left flank, there was a peach orchard. Walking along those portions of the Sunken Road which still exist is perhaps the best place to imagine that terrible defense, men huddled together and fighting against

charge after charge. In the gloom of the wood, it is even easier to imagine the claustrophobia of the position, though when you walk into that blighted sunlight behind the rail fences to your right or the peach trees to your left, you also understand the terrible vulnerability of the Yankees. After six hours of fighting, the Hornets' Nest finally fell under a last Confederate assault which was supported by no fewer than 62 guns gathered from all over the field by the Confederate general Daniel Ruggles.

General Johnston pointed out that once the Yankees were bottled up, there was a limit to how wide a battle-line they could form. This is a part of the "final line."

The time they bought was, however, invaluable for the Union cause as it gave Grant time to arrive, to appraise the battle, and to re-order his troops. The armchair warrior's diagnosis is easy: the Confederates should have isolated it and then bypassed it, using artillery fire to contain it instead of trying to take it by frontal assault. Indeed, had any of the Confederate command been more experienced, they might have tried this, but as it was, they simply sent more and more men against the Hornet's Nest. Not until the afternoon did they surround it, finally forcing its surrender at about 5:30.

Another major factor which prevented a Rebel victory was the death of the Confederate leader. General Albert Sidney Johnston died after a bullet severed an artery in his leg in the afternoon; his command devolved upon General Beauregard. Johnston's death was a serious blow to the morale of the Confederacy since many people had expected him to mature into a great leader. It was loss of blood that killed him, but he was unwilling to get off his horse and relinquish control of the battle; a simple tourniquet would almost certainly have saved his life.

Yet a third factor was that the Confederates needed a swift victory — a matter of hours — if they were to win at all. They were running out of ammunition by the late afternoon, and they were also physically exhausted. They had marched for two days in order to get to the battle, on short rations, and they had not the stamina to fight on. Later in the War, when they had become battle-hardened and used to privation, they would have found it easy: but now, they were hungry, tired, scared farm-boys. In fact, many stragglers had taken time off from the War to eat the food that the Yankees had so obligingly abandoned in the now-overrun camps. The strength of the Union commissary was a great change from what they were used to.

The net result was that at the end of the first day's fighting, the Union had been forced back at least 3 miles from the positions they had occupied that morning, but they had a good line anchored on Snake Creek on the left (northern) flank and on Pittsburg Landing on the Tennessee on the right (southern or eastern) flank. What was more, their flank on Snake Creek was just by the road to Crump's Landing and Savannah, along which they expected Buell's men to arrive shortly. Their artillery was set up along the edge of the ravine just south of the Landing, and this tiny, compact position was much easier to hold than their original straggling lines. The ground they commanded was as high as almost any on the field, and the thick woods made a Confederate flank attack impracticable. Only frontal attacks were feasible.

General Beauregard called off the Confederate attack at six o'clock — 12 hours after the initial attack — but because of delays in receiving the orders, Braxton Bragg did launch one more (unsuccessful) Confederate attack. A whole brigade advanced against Union positions, armed only with the bayonet; they had no ammunition left. Pause to imagine that, as you drive your automobile along Riverside Drive: running towards shot and shell, armed only with a bayonet.

That night, Union and Confederate wounded alike dragged their shattered bodies to one spot near where the fighting had been heaviest: the Bloody Pond, just to the east of the Hornets' Nest. Broken wagons and artillery limbers lay in the water, which had been churned by wheels and hooves; the already red-muddied waters were stained a true red by the blood of dead and wounded men and horses. But still, they drank there. It was the only water they had.

ALBERT SIDNEY JOHNSTON

The "Lost Hope" of the Confederacy was born on February 2, 1803; he was 58 when the War began, 59 when he died. He graduated from West Point in 1826, served as the Secretary of War for the then-independent Republic of Texas, and when the War came he made the long, dangerous trek from the West to join the Confederate army. It is not clear why he was so highly regarded. Grant, normally very fair in such matters, wrote that "after studying the orders and dispatches of Johnston ... my judgement is now that he was vacillating and undecided in his actions." He also wrote that "the Confederates fought with courage at Shiloh, but the particular skill claimed I could not, and still cannot, see; though there is nothing to criticize except the claims put forward for it since."

THE SECOND DAY

Although "Old Brains" Halleck was theoretically in command of the Union forces, he was not on the scene; and Grant, although the senior general present, was unwilling to assume command of Buell's forces, which had begun to arrive the previous afternoon and who had arrived in force during the night. As a result, although the Union army was now greatly superior in numbers, the two generals launched essentially separate, uncoordinated attacks which began at 5:00 am on the 7th. As Grant pointed out, "a great moral advantage would be gained by becoming the attacking party."

The Confederates, exhausted and often without any ammunition, were forced back by the enormously larger Union armies; but it was slow, bloody work for Buell and Grant. The roads had been turned into muddy tracks by endless rain. By noon, Beauregard realized that he had failed to achieve his aim of breaking Grant's army, and ordered a retreat; a rearguard covered his passage to Corinth, whence he had started on the third of April. In Grant's words again, "I knew the enemy were ready to break, and only wanted a little encouragement from us to go quicky and join their friends who had started earlier..." Retreat always comes hard, but retreat after apparent victory is still harder.

DON CARLOS BUELL

The "other" Union general at Shiloh was born on March 23, 1818, graduated from West Point in 1841, and was 44 at Shiloh. Sometimes derided as overly cautious, it is not impossible that if he had been allowed to develop as a general, he would have achieved greatness; he was responsible for Bragg's defeat at Perryville (October 8, 1862), but he was never quite successful enough for Lincoln or the American public. He never commanded an army again after October 24, 1862; after the War he returned to business and public service, and died in Paradise, Kentucky, on November 19, 1898, aged 80.

Carp now live in the Bloody Pond where some of the fiercest fighting of the battle took place, but in the right light, algae stain the water an eerie red.

Fortunately for the Confederates, neither Union general ordered a pursuit. Grant said "I wanted to pursue, but had not the heart to order the men who had fought desperately for two days, lying in the mud and rain whenever not fighting, and I did not feel disposed positively to order Buell..."

The Confederates were however beaten; despite their brave show on the battlefield, the army which retreated was a rag-tag rabble, men and officers separated from their regiments, with no provisions and precious little ammunition. The road across which they passed was a mire; all were utterly dispirited. As Braxton Bragg put it, "If we are pursued with a vigorous force, we will lose all in our rear. The whole road presents the scene of a rout, and no mortal power could restrain it."

THE AFTERMATH

Although the battle was in one sense indecisive — neither side "won" in any straightforward sense — it was (like Fort Donelson) a harbinger of things to come. The Confederates had failed to achieve their objective, and had lost large numbers of men, including a general of whom they had high hopes. The Union had made a fair show of ineptitude, but Grant at least was a man who would learn from his mistakes. This was the real beginning of Grant's rise to fame in the War.

The dead, it may well be, do not care where they sleep, but the soldiers in this Confederate mass grave were never exhumed and re-interred like the men they fought.

FURTHER INFORMATION

Maps: USGS 7.5': Pittsburg Landing, TN and Counce, TN
 Official Reports Atlas: 10/10; 12/4; 13/1; 14/2; 98/4
 B&L: 466; 470; 497; 502/3; 508; 545; 551; 560; 566; 608

Book: James Lee McDonough, *SHILOH - In Hell Before Night* (University of Tennessee Press, 1977). A first-class book.

Park: The National Park Service has organized the park superbly; everything is easy to see and to understand, and even the markers are coded to tell you whether they refer to the first day's fighting or the second. In addition to the regular museum, there is a "please touch" museum of replica equipment (clothes, canteens, muskets, etc). The slide/tape presentation is, however, unimpressive and relatively uninformative; it consists mainly of modern artwork. You can picnic at a number of places, but alcohol is banned. Superintendent: Shiloh, TN 38376.

Town: There are no towns near the battlefield, and no attempts to exploit it commercially. The nearest major town is Corinth, an unattractive (and dry) city with a number of hotels and motels ranging from quite good to downright sleazy. There are not many restaurants, and it is a dry county. The nearest villages, Crump and Adamsville, are tiny.

WEAPONS

The Confederates were at a severe disadvantage at the start of the War because they had no experience of manufacturing rifles, cannon or ammunition. In 1860, 97 per cent of the country's firearms were produced in the North. Some Confederate volunteers enlisted with their own weapons ranging from bowie knives and Colt revolvers to shotguns and hunting rifles.

Josiah Gorgas, appointed as chief of ordnance in April 1861, organized the purchase of enough arms and ammunition from Europe to equip the South for the first year of the War, until he could set up the local manufacture of small arms and artillery.

Muskets

The rifled musket was the weapon *par excellence* of the Civil War. By modern standards, bores were very large (.54, .58 and even .69 inch, or 13.7mm, 14.7mm and 17.5mm) and although projectiles were referred to as "balls" they were usually elongated "Minie balls." An almost complete lack of bore standardization made the quartermaster's task a nightmare.

The rifled musket was very much more accurate than the muzzle-loader, had a longer range (accurate up to 500-700 yards, still deadly at 1,000 yards, though few soldiers could hit a man even at 200 yards) and more tolerant of sloppy loading, but it was still extremely slow (three shots a minute was fast) and the musketeer normally had to stand up to reload. All black powder guns foul badly, and for real accuracy the bore really needed to be swabbed every two or three shots.

Like the smooth-bore it superseded, the rifled musket was usually a muzzle-loader: a "cartridge" was a paper cylinder containing a pre-measured quantity of powder and a ball. With the gun at half cock, the top had to be torn off the cartridge (usually with the teeth), the powder tipped down the barrel, the bullet started with the thumb and then rammed home with the ramrod. A percussion cap on the nipple then made the gun ready to cock and fire.

The Enfield rifle, pictured here, was the British equivalent of the Springfield rifled musket (standard US Army issue after 1855) and took the same bullets. In 1861, James D.Bulloch reached the Confederate army at Savannah with a steamer loaded with 11,000 Enfield rifles.

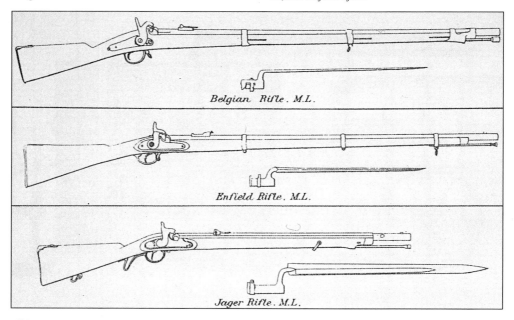

Belgian Rifle. M.L.

Enfield Rifle. M.L.

Jager Rifle. M.L.

This pistol was buried by Corporal Bull of the 23rd Ohio infantry after he was mortally wounded at Antietam. His comrade James Hayes dug it up almost 17 years afterwards in May 1879.

Breech-loaders with metallic cartridges were just coming in, but many military men opposed them because they used up ammunition too fast. The single-shot .52 caliber (13.2mm) Sharps with its linen cartridge was one of the most highly regarded breech-loaders; the Spencer, made in several calibers, was magazine-loaded with metallic cartridges as was the .44 (11.2 mm) caliber Henry. A breech-loader can of course be loaded lying down.

Swords, Knives and Bayonets

Swords were more symbolic than functional in most cases — officers used them to urge their troops on — and the bayonet was used far more rarely than you might expect: in the Wilderness, only six out of 7,302 wounded were reported as having been injured by sword or bayonet.

The knife was another matter, and was sometimes used in hand-to-hand combat. The Rebels, in particular, were keen on knives; often, they were big, heavy "Bowie" type knives. A particularly unusual knife was the heavy *caisson* knife, which was more like a cleaver. It was used to break the legs of horses when cavalry stormed a gun emplacement; when the horse went down, the rider was normally incapacitated or killed.

Pistols

The range of pistols in use in the Civil War was even greater than the range of rifles; everything from old single-shot percussion guns or flintlocks (up to .58) to cap-and-ball or metallic-cartridge revolvers in a wild proliferation of bores, though .44 (11.2mm) was popular.

Most revolvers were cap-and-ball types, which meant the same rigmarole as for loading a musket, but five, six or seven times, once for each cylinder; it was also a good idea to grease the neck of each chamber to guard against chain-fires, which were a bit like holding a hand-grenade. Most were single-action, and had to be cocked (with the thumb) before firing.

Accuracy was negligible — hitting a man at 15 yards was regarded as pretty good — and because reloading took several minutes and was impracticable in the heat of battle, many cavalrymen (the most enthusiastic users of revolvers) often carried two, three, four or even five revolvers "acquired" during their campaigning.

57

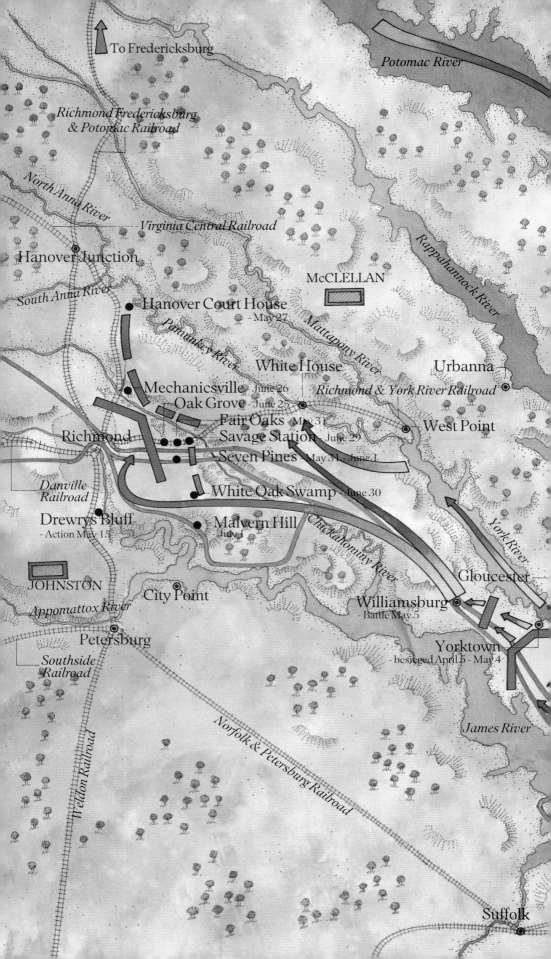

To Fredericksburg

Potomac River

Richmond Fredericksburg
& Potomac Railroad

North Anna River

Virginia Central Railroad

Rappahannock River

Hanover Junction

McCLELLAN

South Anna River

Hanover Court House
- May 27

Pamunkey River

Mattapony River

Urbanna

White House

Richmond & York River Railroad

Mechanicsville — June 26
Oak Grove — June 25

Fair Oaks — May 31

West Point

Richmond

Savage Station — June 29

Seven Pines — May 31 - June 1

Danville
Railroad

White Oak Swamp — June 30

Chickahominy River

York River

Drewrys Bluff
- Action May 15

Malvern Hill
- July 1

Gloucester

JOHNSTON

Williamsburg
- Battle May 5

Appomattox River

City Point

Yorktown
- besieged April 5 - May 4

Petersburg

Southside
Railroad

James River

Weldon Railroad

Norfolk & Petersburg Railroad

Suffolk

THE PENINSULA CAMPAIGN AND THE SEVEN DAYS

Richmond Peninsula, Virginia
March - July 1862

Confederate States
General J.E. Johnston
General Robert E. Lee
80-90,000 engaged*
20,000 losses*

United States
Major-General George B. McClellan
80-100,000 effectives*
16,000 losses*

*For the whole Seven Days campaign

The Richmond Peninsula is rather a magical place. Low, soft hills rise from a tangle of intersecting rivers, creeks and inlets. At dawn and dusk, the sun reflects in still water; ducks are everywhere. It was one of the first parts of North America to be settled by Europeans. If you avoid the more self-consciously touristy parts, the overall effect is a curious blend of mellow history and surprisingly untamed wilderness.

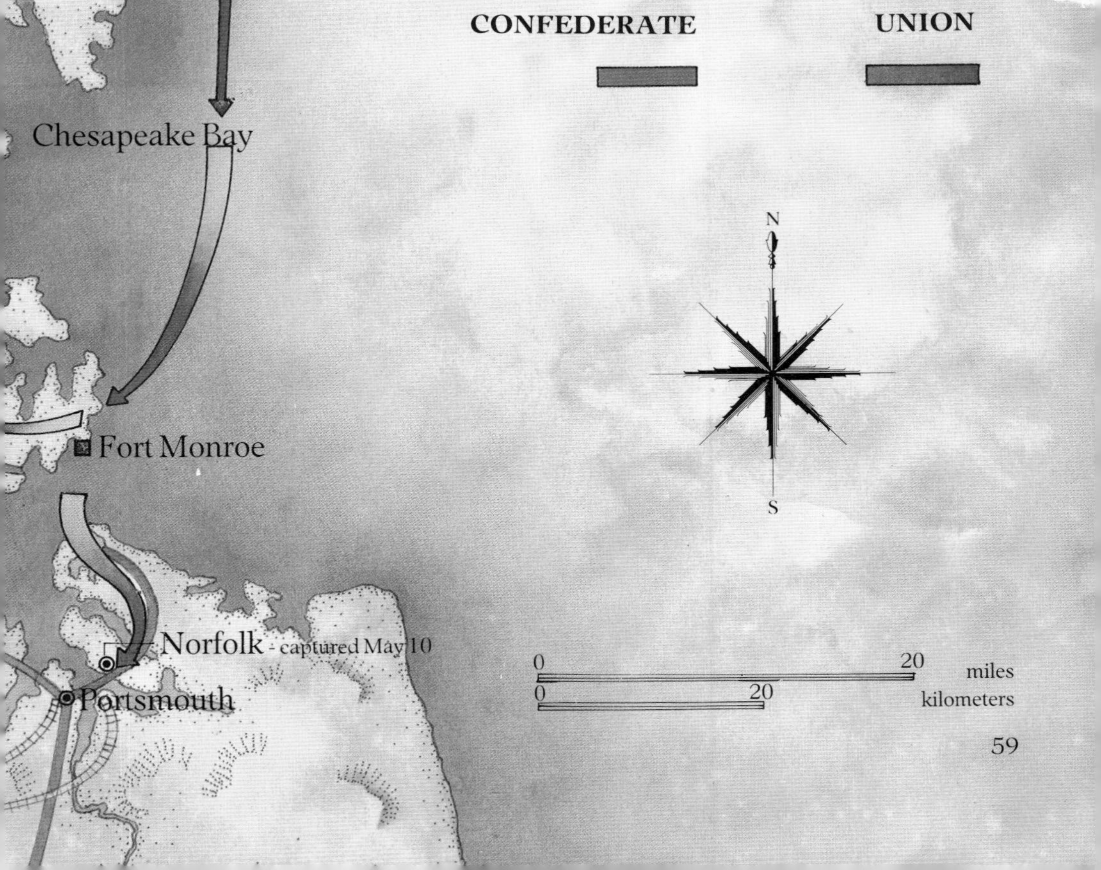

CONFEDERATE

UNION

N

S

Chesapeake Bay

Fort Monroe

Norfolk - captured May 10

Portsmouth

| 0 | | | 20 | miles |
| 0 | | 20 | | kilometers |

THE LANDING ON THE PENINSULA AND THE SIEGE OF YORKTOWN

Since November 1861, McClellan had been nursing a plan to move the Army of the Potomac by sea and by river to the end of the Richmond Peninsula, and to fight his way up to Richmond from there. The plan was finally approved in Washington on March 13, 1862, two days after Lincoln had relieved McClellan as Commander-in-Chief of the Federal Armies while leaving him in charge of the Department and of the Army of the Potomac.

The landing site finally chosen was the Union-held Fortress Monroe, at the very end of the Peninsula, and the transshipment began at the end of March. By the first week in April, McClellan had 100,000 men on the Peninsula. His first opposition was a mere 15,000 Confederates at Yorktown.

Drewry's Bluff, scene of the river action, and the Confederate stronghold on the James River, from which Union gunboat attacks were repulsed. The fort served as a Confederate naval and marine training center.

Astonishingly, using adaptations of the old Revolutionary earthworks, they held him up for almost a month, from April 5 to May 3. Knowing the reasons for his sloth does, however, make it more understandable. One was the way Lincoln had treated him on March 11. A second was that his intelligence staff (headed by Pinkerton, the founder of the detective agency) received good raw data, but then inflated it so that McClellan thought he was facing up to 200,000 Confederates. Thirdly, after agreeing to let McClellan have reinforcements, Lincoln insisted on a good part of the projected force being left to protect Washington, so McClellan never had as many men as he had hoped. Also, in the words of Colonel T.J. Cram, the Chief Topographical Engineer of the Department of Virginia:

> As a general rule in advancing beyond Southwest Br[anch] of Back River and Watts' Creek, the roads will be found blocked with felled trees wherever there is a wood, and there are many such places. Again on the Northwest Br[anch] of the Back River where fordable, trees have been felled to obstruct the fords, wherever there is wood to answer.

Subsequent battles were to demonstrate three things. First, both armies had a lot to learn — the Yankees were chronically over-cautious, while the Rebels were impetuous and ill-cordinated. Second, a "drive to Richmond" was a rash undertaking, because the soldiers of the South would be defending their country while the Union men were operating in unfamiliar and unfriendly terrain. And third, there was no lack of bravery on either side.

As they retreated, the Confederates left land mines or "torpedos" behind them. Debate raged about when their use was proper; they were apparently acceptable to reinforce fortifications, but leaving them in the road was regarded as cowardly. This was one of the first debates about "total war" (see pages 208-209), even though the "infernal machines" were left to delay the advancing army so were used only against soldiers.

SEVEN PINES AND THE SEVEN DAYS

The Battle of Seven Pines (or Fair Oaks) took place when McClellan finally got within striking distance of Richmond, at the end of May. He had fought the Battle of Williamsburg on May 5 and occupied the colonial town on the 6th, then trundled slowly up the Peninsula. The Battle of Drewry's Bluff (May 15) was mainly a river action, in which Confederate shore batteries prevented a passage of the James River by Union vessels, and on May 24 Lincoln gave McClellan more excuses for failure by ordering him to set aside the movement on Richmond and send 20,000 men toward the Shenandoah in an attempt "to capture the forces of Jackson and Ewell."

The so-called "Seven Days" battles took place from June 25 to July 1, though there was not actually a battle on the 28th. They represented the failure of McClellan's Peninsula Campaign and the end of the second attempted strike against Richmond. They were Oak Grove (also known as King's School House, French's Field or The Orchard) on June 25; Mechanicsville (or Beaver Dam Creek or Ellerson's Mill), June 26; Gaines's Mill (First Cold Harbor, The Chickahominy), June 27; Savage's Station, June 29; White Oak Swamp (or Charles City Cross Roads or Frayser's Farm or Glendale or Nelson's Cross Roads or New Market Road or Turkey Bridge or Willis's Church), June 30; and Malvern Hill, July 1.

The bridge across the Chickahominy to Mechanicsville Road.

TERRAIN

Colonel Cram's assessment, quoted above, gives a fair idea of the terrain. Over such a large area it is impossible to be too specific, but the following information is useful.

From Richmond to the tip of the Peninsula is no more than 70 miles to the south-east as the crow flies; but by road, it is at least 80 and could be as much as 100, depending on the route. To this day, the back-roads of the Richmond Peninsula are dirt tracks through the woods, and in 1862 this was the general standard of highways. Numerous creeks and rivers cut all through the Peninsula, which is mostly below 100 feet in elevation, and there are many areas of swamp.

Visibility in the heavily-broken and thickly-wooded countryside is usually limited. This is especially true in the summer; the view from Chickahominy Bluff, for example, is clear in March but completely obscured by foliage by June or July.

As you travel inland, the hills become slightly higher and often steeper — and they can be quite steep on the Peninsula! — so that by Richmond itself they frequently top 160 feet. The valleys between the hills are often swampy and filled with all kinds of undergrowth. In 100 yards you could splash through swamp, wade through standing water 3-4 feet deep, and then have to push your way through scrub oaks. There are patches of cultivated land, sometimes quite large.

Beaver Dam Swamp gives a very fair impression of the kind of country in which much of the Seven Days' fighting was done.

SEVEN PINES
May 31 - June 1

Maps: USGS 7.5': Seven Pines

Official Reports Atlas: 20/1
B&L: 227; 240

McClellan's Union forces were divided by the Chickahominy, very much swollen as a result of heavy rains, and the Confederate General Joseph E. Johnston thought he saw the position of the two corps south of the river as very vulnerable.

These two corps were oriented north-south, crossing the railroad and the roads which lead east from Richmond. The National Cemetery at the junction of the US 60 and the VA 33 is close to the right flank of the Union position.

The attack was to come from Nine Mile Road (the modern VA 33), the Williamsburg Road (US 60) and the Charles City road (still shown on USGS maps under its old name), running south-east. The Union right was at Seven Pines. The terrain is relatively flat, at an elevation of 150-160 feet, and was mostly wooded with farms and clearings at the time of the War.

Fort Brady is one of the many forts on the Richmond Peninsula.

Unfortunately for the Confederates, the various parts of their armies displayed the same lack of coordination which was to dog them throughout the rest of this campaign. Orders were confused; General James Longstreet took the roads intended for other brigades, and entangled the whole business; and instead of a full-spirited, concerted attack there was an indecisive, piecemeal but bloody engagement spearheaded by General Daniel H. Hill's Confederates.

The Confederates managed to divide the Yankee lines, pushing some of the army northwards to Fair Oaks, but there the Union men were reinforced by Major-General Sumner's troops whom he had managed to get across the Chickahominy — no mean feat. At their southern (left) extreme, the Union men withdrew twice but finally managed to hold their third position. Losses were 5,031 on the Union side, 6,134 for the Confederates.

The result was a tactical stalemate, but it had two strategic repercussions of immense importance. The first was that Lee replaced Johnston, with results which do not need to be explained, and the other was that McClellan was so unnerved by the sight of the "mangled corpses" of his men that he lost what little resolve he had. The Confederates would have an invaluable psychological advantage for the remainder of the battles of the Peninsula Campaign.

OAK GROVE
(or King's School House)
June 25

Maps: USGS 7.5': Seven Pines
Official Reports Atlas: 20/1

Oak Grove is usually described as an "engagement" rather than a "battle;" even General Lee's map (*Official Reports Atlas*: 21/1) does not show it as a battle.

The Union General McClellan wanted control of an area of bog just south of the Williamsburg Road (modern US 60) to secure his front before a general advance, but although his troops succeeded in clearing it partially, they could not dislodge the Confederates from their main earthworks before nightfall, when the action fizzled out. Federal losses were 516, Confederate 316.

The engagement took place just to the west of the modern Seven Pines; there is next to nothing to see there now.

MECHANICSVILLE
(or Beaver Dam Creek)
June 26

Maps: USGS 7.5': Seven Pines
Official Reports Atlas: 21/7; 63/8; 90/9
B&L: 328

The right flank of the Union forces were concentrated (and dug in) along the east bank of Beaver Dam Creek, which runs roughly north-south past the east side of Mechanicsville.

Lee planned to attack the end of the line, while Jackson came up behind them.

The charge of the Confederates under Ripley and Pender at Beaver Dam Creek, just above Ellerson's Mill.

For no known reason, Jackson never actually reached the battle — indeed, he made camp a few miles from Mechanicsville — and Lee found his opponents better dug in than he expected. A costly frontal attack gained no ground, though it reinforced the Union conviction that there was no likelihood that they would carry Richmond during that campaign.

You can get an excellent idea of the extraordinary terrain over which both sides were fighting if you turn off the VA 156 to see the Beaver Dam Creek stop on the Park map. The banks were (and still are) "so steep as to be impassable without bridges" (Confederate General James Longstreet); the water is supposedly up to waist-deep (no-one would try it unless they had to), with a muddy bottom and plenty of snags, tree-stumps and insects.

The Rebels did attack, and were repulsed; again in Longstreet's words, "We attacked at Beaver Dam, and had failed to make an impression at that point, losing several thousand men and officers. This demonstrated that the position was safe." It also threw away an awful lot of lives.

Incredibly, the Federals then evacuated their position (Longstreet called it "very unwise"), and "in withdrawing not only abandoned a strong position, but gave up the *morale* of their success, and transferred it to our somewhat disheartened forces; for, next to Malvern Hill [see below], the sacrifice at Beaver Dam was unequalled in demoralization during the entire summer."

GAINES'S MILL
June 27

Maps: USGS 7.5': Seven Pines VA
      Official Reports Atlas: 42/3; 63/8
      B&L: 334

This battle saw Union troops, covering the Union retreat, in a strong position behind Boatswain Swamp (Boatswain Creek) about ¾ mile north of the Chickahominy.

After a long and indecisive battle, the final Confederate charge came at seven in the evening. The terrain for the charge is incredible: tangled undergrowth, a swampy bottom, and a long steep slope down from the Confederate position and up to the Union — the swamp is at about 90 feet, the armies' positions were both at 140-150 feet, and the total distance of the charge was no more than 500 yards from front to front. Looking at it, the immediate reaction is disbelief that anyone would even attempt such an onslaught, let alone succeed. But they did, capturing "many thousand stand of arms, fifty-two pieces of artillery, and many prisoners" (Longstreet). Admittedly, the cost was serious — 8,750 Confederates killed and wounded against 6,837 Union losses — but from the Union viewpoint, the delay it gained at least permitted the orderly retreat to continue.

The swamps around Richmond have not changed much in a hundred years or more. Compare this picture of the Chickahominy Swamp from Battles and Leaders *with the modern photograph of Beaver Dam Swamp on page 62.*

SAVAGE'S STATION
June 29

Maps: USGS 7.5': Seven Pines

Official Reports Atlas: 20/1
B&L: 374

The Battle of Savage's (or Savage) Station was an attempt by Lee to pursue and destroy the retreating Union armies.

The station was on the Richmond and York River railroad, about 10 or 11 miles east of Richmond. Lee was once again frustrated by the tardiness of his lieutenants, and there was hardly a battle at all.

WHITE OAK SWAMP
June 30

Maps: USGS 7.5': Seven Pines and Dutch Gap

Official Reports Atlas: 21/8
B&L: 397

White Oak Swamp was a fight to secure an orderly retreat for the Union armies; but the Yankee line held as the fighting bogged down in the swamp. Hand-to-hand fighting, ambushes by small groups of men, and sudden fire from the murk continued well into the night, the result of another failure of Lee's armies to coordinate their attacks.

MALVERN HILL
July 1

Maps: USGS 7.5': Dutch Gap and Roxbury

Official Reports Atlas: 21/10
B&L 392; 412

Sharp-shooters in the cornfield, Malvern Hill.

Malvern Hill was the last of the "Seven Days" battles. It was a tactical Confederate defeat at the end of their strategic victory. The site is about 5 miles south of White Oak Swamp, or 15 miles south-east of Richmond. The highest point of the hill itself is at about 140-150 feet. The retreating Yankees were on the crest of the hill, facing north and west, their backs to their supply base at Harrison's Landing, 10 miles to the south-east.

On the Union left (west and south) were the steep slopes of Malvern Hill, while on their right were the swampy and well-wooded bottoms of Turkey Island Creek and Western Run, at about 50-60 feet. This left the approach from the north, up a gently-shelving field, as the only possible route for a Confederate charge. The Yankees did not even dig in.

Reinforced with artillery, they stood in parade-ground order and raked the field in front with fire.

THE AFTERMATH

A view from the south side of the Richmond Peninsula.

On July 14, the Union General John Pope brought the newly-created Army of Virginia between the Confederates and Washington to relieve the pressure on McClellan, and to calm Northern fears. Pope proved no match for Lee, though, who pushed him back across the Rappahannock and soon it was time for McClellan to come to Pope's aid. Between McClellan's excess of caution, and Pope's excess of self-confidence (both of which were equally misplaced), the Peninsula Campaign had come to a halt. The next big battle in the East would once again be fought at Manassas.

FURTHER INFORMATION

Maps: USGS 1:250,000 (*not* 7.5'): Richmond
Official Reports Atlas: 17/1; 18/1&2; 19/1-3; 20/1
B&L (see also individual battles above): 164; 167; 188; 204; 272; 320; 384

Park: The main Park Service establishment is on the site of the old Chimborazo Hospital, inside the city. The orientation presentation is good but not outstanding. Many sites are unmanned and accessible at all times. The Park Service brochure is essential.

Town: Richmond is a busy, modern town comparable with any. Accommodation of all kinds is widely available. The most expensive is near Richmond itself or at the Colonial sites on the Peninsula; there are also many places for cheaper accommodation, including Newport News at the end of the Peninsula and Hopewell (formerly City Point). There are many good museums in the area, but one of the very best is the Confederate Museum in Richmond, next to the White House of the Confederacy (the official residence of the President). It is open from 9:00 am to 5:00 pm throughout the majority of the year (some holidays excluded).

ARTILLERY

Field-guns

Designed to be portable, typically they were pulled by six horses behind a *limber*, which carried an ammunition chest. Another team of six horses pulled the *caisson*, with three more ammunition chests. The three drivers rode the left-side horses, with the *guidon-bearer* (flag-bearer) on the right lead horse. All three pairs of horses (called *lead, swing* and *wheel* pairs) were yoked with quickly-detachable traces so that they could be unhitched and interchanged if necessary. The cannoneers rode on the jolting, unsprung limber and caisson — literally sitting on a powder-keg.

The workhorse field-gun on both sides was the muzzle-loading smooth bore 12-pdr Napoleon, strictly a "gun-howitzer" with a more curved trajectory than a true gun, but smaller and lighter. It had a range of up to 2,000 yards.

There were various rifled field-guns too, some breech-loading and some muzzle-loading; the 10-pdr cast-iron muzzle-loading Parrott was common. Although rifles such as the British Whitworth had a longer range (up to 3,000 yards) and packed more punch than smooth bores, much of their advantage was lost at short range, when the big bore of the cannon made it far more dangerous.

Siege and Coastal Guns

Monsters like the 30-pdr Parrott were moved only when a siege was likely; even bigger guns like the 300-pdr Parrott were used only as permanently-mounted coastal guns. Maximum range came from the 80-pdr Whitworth rifle, with a 4-ton barrel and a range of over 13,500 yards.

Mountain Guns

Lightweight field pieces which could be carried in the conventional way, on a carriage, on pack-mules, or *in extremis* manhandled. A 12-pdr mountain howitzer had a range of under 1,000 yards.

Mortars

Designed to hurl a shell high into the air, to fall inside fortifications or a besieged city. Some mortars of truly spectacular

A 30 pdr Parrott rifle positioned near Lee's command post on the Confederate lines during the Battle of Fredericksburg.

dimensions were made. The 13 in mortar used a 20 lb firing charge to lob a shell or "bomb" which weighed nearly 90 lb (including an 11 lb bursting charge) for a mile and a half. At the other extreme, the 24 pdr (5.82 inch) Coehorn could be lifted by four strong men.

Columbiads

Enormous smooth bores, capable of functioning as guns, howitzers or mortars with a remarkable range. Although versatile, they were cumbersome; the rise of the rifle spelled their doom, and the War saw their demise.

Projectiles

Included solid shot (both round and elongated), explosive shells of various kinds, and "canister" and "grape." Solid shot, round or rifled, had the best range and accuracy and was good for battering at fortifications, or for use against troops at ranges where explosive shells might endanger the artillerist. Explosive shells and "spherical case" (shrapnel) were used at greater ranges against troops; explosive charges were typically too small to be useful against substantial fortifications. Fuses for explosive shells often failed to go off at all, while others went off prematurely, sometimes at the cannon's mouth. Percussion fuses were not yet in widespread use. "Canister" was a thin metal canister of cast-iron balls designed to be used against troops at close ranges (350 yards or less). This was where the large diameter of the smooth bore was so valuable, turning the gun into a giant sawed-off shotgun. In grapeshot, used mostly at sea, the shot were held between plates secured by a central through-bolt parallel with the bore.

Gunlaying

This was far from accurate, for a number of reasons. Powder was unreliable, ranging techniques were not well developed, and with smooth bores the ball fitted poorly in the barrel. High trajectories meant that there were large "safe zones" where shell would pass over the heads of troops in the middle distance, while remaining deadly at close range or at maximum range. This was why relatively flat trajectories (typically 5° elevation) were the rule in land battles, even at the expense of range.

This photograph of captured munitions in the arsenal at Charleston, South Carolina, gives some idea of the lack of standardization which plagued both sides.

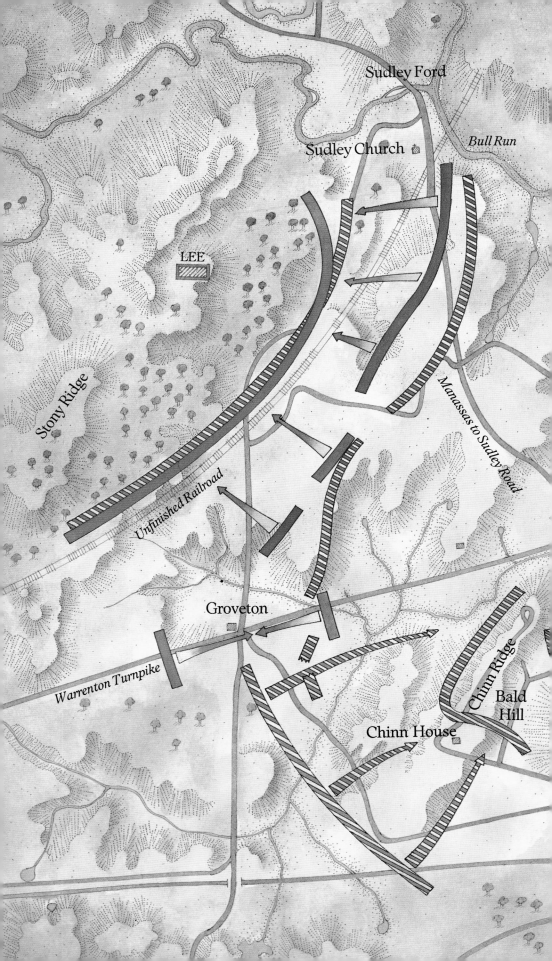

Sudley Ford

Sudley Church

Bull Run

LEE

Stony Ridge

Manassas to Sudley Road

Unfinished Railroad

Groveton

Warrenton Turnpike

Chinn House

Chinn Ridge

Bald Hill

THE BATTLE OF SECOND MANASSAS

Also known as Second Bull Run, or the Battle of Groveton
Bull Run, near Manassas Junction, Virginia
August 29-30 1862

Confederate States	United States
General Robert E. Lee	Major-General John Pope
48,500 effectives*	75,000 effectives*
9,197 casualties*	16,054 casualties*

*Figures are for campaign August 27-September 2.

POPE

Stone House

Henry House Hill

Henry House

In 1862, the rail-bed of the Independent Manassas Gap Railroad had been surveyed and partially graded; it was never to be completed. The rail-bed was, as the history books put it, "an excellent line of defense." It was on the north-western side of that

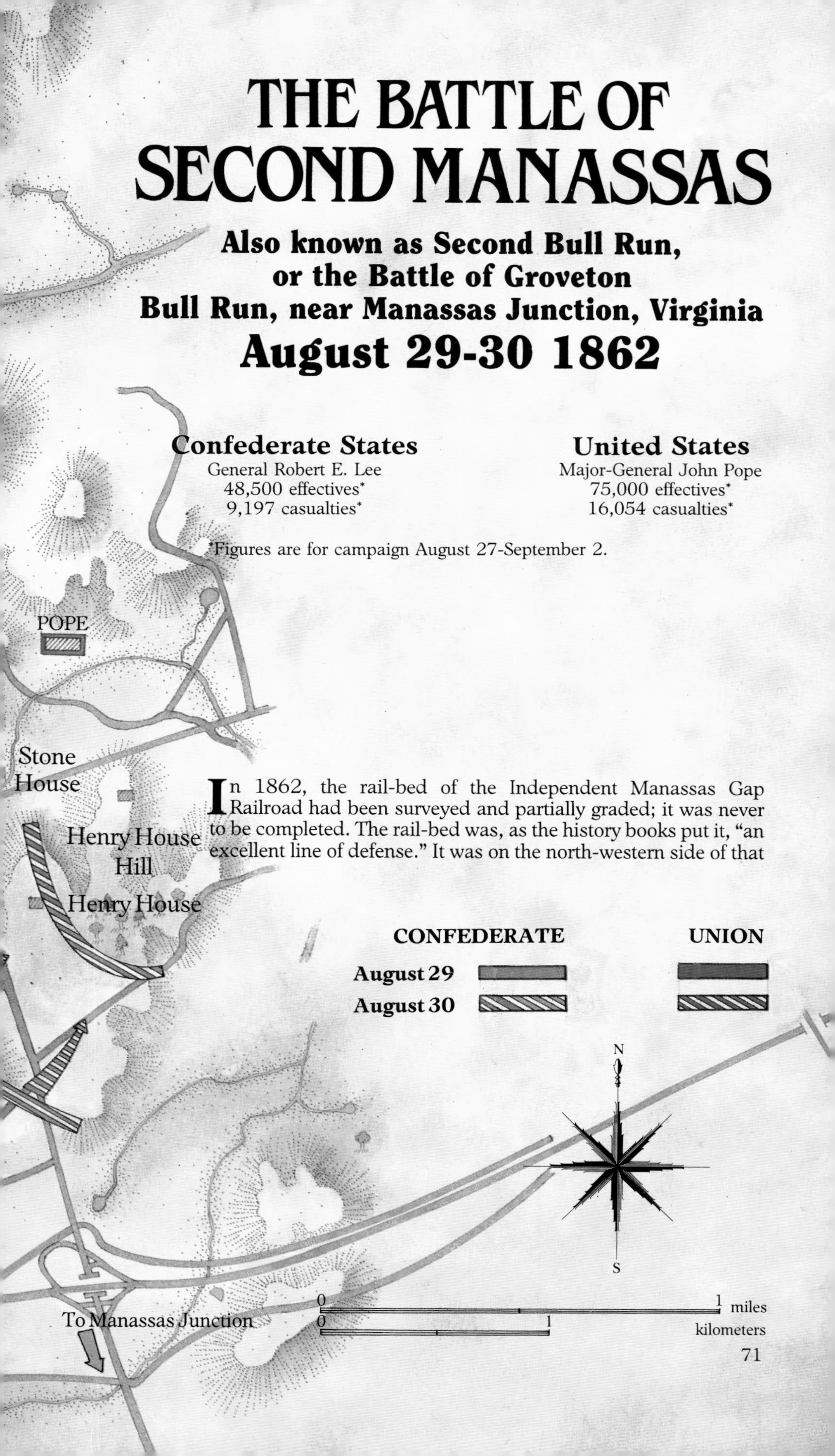

	CONFEDERATE	UNION
August 29		
August 30		

N

S

To Manassas Junction

0   1 miles

0   1 kilometers

rail-bed that Jackson's Confederates repulsed repeated Union attacks, sometimes running out of ammunition and throwing rocks or swinging their empty muskets like clubs.

That rail-bed still stands. If you walk along it, two things strike you. The first is that it does not provide such good cover as the history books say; as on any railroad, there are transitions between banks and cuttings, and there are parts which are more or less level with the rest of the wood through which it passes. The second thing is that the rocks which were used to grade the bed would have made excellent weapons.

Most country boys can throw a fair-sized rock with devastating accuracy; Jackson's Rebels were probably accustomed to knocking over squirrels for the pot, if they were lucky, with a flung rock. There are enough of these rocks around today that you can heft them in your hand; at 10 or 20 yards, a hard-thrown rock could put a man's eye out, or even crack his skull. In that close, crowded forest, a good deal of musket fire was exchanged at distances no greater than this.

The rocks in the railroad cut are well-suited to throwing.

LEE'S ATTEMPT TO DESTROY POPE

During the Seven Days, the main concern in the South had been to protect Richmond. With that goal accomplished, Lee and Jackson could afford to turn their attention to the other Union forces, greatly superior in numbers, which were scattered all over northern Virginia.

Major-General John Pope had been appointed in June to command these forces. He was a bombastic and unpopular man who upon his appointment in June pompously announced that his headquarters were in the saddle; this prompted Confederate wits to point out that the hindquarters usually occupied that position. He seems to have had very little idea of where the Confederates were, and as the Union had not yet learned how to use cavalry for reconnaissance, he marched and countermarched his men around the general area of Manassas, Groveton and Centreville in a desperate attempt to find them.

What is more, Lincoln had made not just one bad appointment, but two: Pope was in the field, and General Henry Wager Halleck came to Washington as General in Chief with effect from July 11. "Old Brains" Halleck (he had written several books) had done well at Corinth, but he tended to think in terms of cities rather than armies, and he was no match for the sheer speed and brilliance of the Lee/Jackson combination.

In the words of General Longstreet, describing "Our March Against Pope:" "For centuries there has been among soldiers a maxim: 'Don't despise your enemy'." Pope was to be rudely disabused of his apparent contempt for the Confederacy.

Lee, on the other hand, rarely if ever underestimated his opposing generals; but in the light of Pope's remarks, he formed the opinion described by Longstreet; Pope was "quite ambitious to accomplish great results, but unwilling to study closely and properly the means necessary to gratify his desires in that direction."

Lee was right, but by sheer bad luck the Yankees captured Lee's attack orders; the intended battle of Gordonsville never took place, as Pope rapidly withdrew his outnumbered army to the far shore of the Rappahannock. If those orders had not been found, Lee's 54,000 men (30,000 under Lee and 24,000 under Jackson) could well have annihilated Pope's 45,000.

On August 22, a stroke of equally bad luck befell the Union: Jeb Stuart captured Pope's personal baggage train, complete with Pope's attack orders. From this, Lee learned that Pope would have 70,000 men by the 24th, and perhaps 100,000 a few days later. Speedy attack was essential.

LEE DIVIDES HIS ARMY

Lee's response was characteristically original. He divided his already outnumbered army, and sent Jackson's Foot Cavalry right around behind Pope. Jackson's army covered almost 60 miles between Monday morning (the 25th) and Tuesday sunset; they took Manassas Junction, where they burned what they could not carry.

The capture of Manassas Junction provided a rich catch for the Confederates - 50,000 lbs of bacon, 1,000 barrels of beef, 2,000 of pork and 2,000 of flour, according to Lee's report. After a day of eating their fill, Jackson's troops set fire to what remained and Manassas Junction was left in ruins.

MANASSAS JUNCTION

Jackson's Foot Cavalry had been fighting for months when they made their extraordinary march to Manassas Junction, captured on August 26 by Fitzhugh Lee's Confederate cavalry. Their clothes were in rags, their boots were worn out, and many of them were barefoot when they made the long, gruelling march over dirt roads in the hot summer sun.

At Manassas, there was the most tremendous range of food, clothing, and *matériel*; even the Union generals had commented on the sheer quantities of material goods accumulated for the armies. Now, it went to men who had almost forgotten what such things were like. They gorged themselves on potted meat, lobster and champagne; they took whatever clothes they wanted, including the luxury of perfectly-fitting boots; after all, they could just keep trying them on until they found a pair they liked. In the words of one participant, "Streams of spirits ran like water through the sands of Manassas, and the soldiers on hands and knees drank it greedily from the ground as it ran."

After their brief hours of luxury, they burned the rest. Manassas Junction was so thoroughly destroyed that the modern railroad does not even follow the precise course of the old; the modern town of Manassas is almost entirely post-bellum.

From Manassas Junction, Jackson's men went on via the Sudley Springs road, and via a more circuitous route through Centreville, to take up positions on August 28 behind the soon-to-be-famous unfinished railroad. Lee, meanwhile, was bringing Longstreet's Confederates from the Shenandoah Valley to join Jackson; they would arrive at noon on the 29th, after the Second Battle of Manassas had already started.

The men at the front are throwing rocks, not hand grenades: this is the Deep Cut.

The Deep Cut is now just a shallow depression. In 1862 it would have been deeper and with steeper sides; in some places it was a cut, as here, while in others it was an embankment.

TERRAIN

The general terrain of the Manassas/Centreville/Groveton area has already been described on page 26. The most important thing to add is a description of the woods in which Jackson had dug in; this was effectively where the battle was decided, as the Union troops wore themselves out against the Confederates.

The ground is undulating and deceptive, interspersed (as usual) with many streams and rivulets, and with a certain amount of boggy ground to the south-east of the woods. The wood itself is dry, but covered underfoot with a treacherous duff of leaves, branches and undergrowth. There is some poison ivy.

The woods themselves were more extensive in 1862, though there were a number of cleared or open patches; the trees were particularly dense along Stony Ridge and on the Manassas side of the Groveton-Centreville road. The maximum height of Stony Ridge is about 330 feet, though it is mostly around 300 feet; the course of the Bull Run is at about 180 feet, and the surrounding countryside at 200-250 feet. The railroad bed runs along the foot of Stony Ridge, near the edge of the woods, at about 250-270 feet.

A relic of Pope's retreat along the Manassas railroad.

THE BATTLE

The campaign effectively lasted from August 26 or 27 to September 2. On the 28th, Jackson deliberately drew attention to himself with a demonstration against King's Union troops which turned into a fierce fight.

By the morning of the 29th, Pope had decided where Jackson was, but instead of concentrating his forces and making a serious attack, he threw in brigades and regiments as they arrived, piecemeal. The result was a slaughter of brave Yankees, who attacked Jackson's strong position frontally. The Union troops were tired out by the marches and countermarches of the previous days; although Jackson's men were also tired, they had much more trust in their generals. To give an example of the scale of Yankee losses, one of Hooker's brigades (under Cuvier Grover) lost 484 men out of 2,000 in 20 minutes.

PHILIP KEARNY

Major-General Philip Kearny was one of the romantic figures of the War. Born on June 2, 1815, as a young man he was left a million dollars by his grandfather but preferred a military life. He studied at the French Cavalry School at Saumur and saw service in Algeria before fighting in the Mexican War where he lost his left arm. In 1859, he won the Legion of Honor at Solferino, fighting with Napoleon's Imperial Guard. At Second Manassas, he commanded one of the Union divisions that pressed Jackson so hard, but on the evening of September 1 he rode by mistake into Confederate lines and was shot as he wheeled his horse and tried to escape. He was 47. His opponent, General A.P. Hill, said "Poor Kearny! He deserved a better death than this."

It might have been possible to roll up Jackson's line either from the left flank or the right. The left (north) flank originally followed the railroad to the Bull Run, but there was nothing to "tie" the flank and an attack would have been feasible. As it was, the attack was quite insufficient and Jackson's men fell back to the north and west to take advantage of a small stream and wooded and higher ground. The right (south) flank was also less protected than the center, but the ground was boggy and Lee arrived to reinforce Jackson at about noon. Fierce fighting continued all day, with the Confederate reinforcements arriving in the nick of time. This was when General A.P. Hill described the Confederate position as follows:

> Soon my reserves were all in, and up to six o'clock my division, assisted by the Louisiana brigade of General Hayes, with a heroic courage and obstinacy almost beyond parallel, had met and repulsed six distinct and separate assaults, a portion of the time the majority of the men being without a cartridge.

The retreat over the Stone Bridge on Saturday evening, August 30th.

By the end of the day, the battle was indecisive; the Rebels had neither advanced nor retreated, though they had repeatedly and bloodily repulsed the Yankees. Indeed, "indecisive" was a key word for the Union; Halleck was furiously telegraphing McClellan in an attempt to get him to join Pope, but McClellan displayed less than zeal in carrying out the orders, possibly because of his personal antipathy towards Pope. And all the while, Lincoln in Washington was wringing his hands. He telegraphed Pope three times to ask "What news?", telegrams such as these not being calculated to help a general who is concentrating on fighting a major battle.

During the night, for some extraordinary reason, Pope conceived the notion that the Rebels were retreating. Given that he often did not know where his own men were (and they were in no hurry to tell him, so many enemies had he made), this is less surprising than it might be in the case of another general.

The Chinn House is now reduced to a low wall, a few feet high, showing the general outline of the original house.

The small railroad halt still proclaims the name "Manassas."

Accordingly, Pope launched a full-scale attack on the Confederate left. This was a tremendous strain on Jackson's men, but they were able to take it, and it allowed Longstreet (on the right or southern flank) to launch an attack of his own.

From his original position along Chinn Ridge, Longstreet was able to advance to Bald Hill (where his artillery had a fine commanding position at an elevation of 270 feet) and then to drive the rest of Pope's army back to the Henry House Hill, scene of the main action at First Manassas. The Union successfully defended this last position, but they had lost, and there was nothing they could do to improve their position. With their left (southern) flank threatened, Pope's men had to call off the attack on the Confederate flank. Pope's only hope was to slink back to Washington to lick his wounds. On September 2, Lincoln restored McClellan to full command; Pope was left out in the cold.

This monument to Union dead beside the Deep Cut was built just after the battle, but within a very short time it had been stripped of shells etc. by souvenir-hunters.

FURTHER INFORMATION

Maps: USGS 7.5': Gainesville quadrangle. Manassas quadrangle is useful for information, but the battlefield proper is in the Gainesville Quadrangle. Infuriatingly, the railroad bed is not shown; it does *not* follow the "pipeline" shown on the map.
Official Reports Atlas: 22/4; 111/1
B&L: 450; 459; 464; 467; 469; 472; 473; 482; 503; 505 (two); 509; 525

Park/Town: See page 31.

SIGNALLING

Communication is obviously central to conducting a war. Commanders need to coordinate their movements and to pass orders along to their subordinates, and subordinates need to inform their superiors of what is going on. During the 1860s, the many traditional methods of military communication had been supplemented by a new one: the telegraph.

Signal corps near the Rapidan River. The tripod-mounted telescope is a typical piece of signalling apparatus, found in many museums; field glasses were just beginning to gain popularity. The difficulties of visual signalling, and of relaying signals, are not immediately apparent to a modern soldier brought up on radios and field-telephones.

Messengers

The traditional approach, using foot-messengers or horsemen ("gallopers") to carry messages was still one of the most reliable. Normally, an important message would be sent by two or more messengers, often with a verbal message to supplement the written instructions. The dangers of such orders were, of course, that they were slow and prone to capture, and that unless the messenger understood his business the order might not be understood by the recipient.

Visual Signalling

Flags and even uniforms constitute a form of "signalling": they say "I am on your side" or "So-and-so's division is over here." For sending messages, though, you need something capable of sending the letters of the alphabet; signal flags, widely used in the navy, were never widespread in the army.

One of the oldest systems is semaphore, where a man holds two flags and the relative positions of the two flags represent different letters (both straight out, inverted Vee, Vee, one up/one down and so forth). Semaphore can be surprisingly quick, but the flag-man is a good target for a sniper and unless the message is sent in code it is normally as accessible to the enemy as to the intended recipient. To increase range and reduce the risk of snipers, both sides used mechanical semaphores or "wigwags" which resembled demented railroad signals. High towers and telescopes increased the effective distance of line-of-sight signalling.

Heliography (using mirrors to flash messages in Morse code) seems to have been relatively little used in the Civil War, as does the use of signal lanterns. Both of these methods are (or can be) surprisingly secure, even for messages "in clear."

Signal towers were usually rickety-looking structures often incorporating living trees. They were also very attractive targets for enemy sharp-shooters and cannoneers. Some, like this, were made from felled lumber.

Telegraphy

This locomotive, the General, (now in the General Museum, Kennesaw, Georgia), was stolen by Union spies intending to escape to the North and cut telegraph wires, burn bridges etc. en route. Luck and judgement were against the Yankees; the bridges were too wet to burn, and the General ran out of fuel.

The electric telegraph was the cutting edge of communications technology in the 1860s. It was, however, slow, because messages could only be transmitted in Morse code; there was no possibility of voice (telephone) communication. Obviously, translating a message into dots and dashes, tapping them out letter by letter, and then reassembling them at the other end is time-consuming, but it allowed "real-time" communication across hundreds and even thousands of miles. "Real-time" communication means that (for example) a commanding general in Washington could receive a report from the battlefield and send a reply fast enough to influence the field commander's actions. A letter, by contrast, would be "yesterday's newspaper."

The telegraph was dependent on wires, and these wires could be cut, intercepted, or even used to send false messages — a favorite Confederate trick. An experienced telegraphist could recognise the "fist" or rhythm of other telegraphists he had worked with before; and some telegraphists could cut a wire in the field, touch the ends to their tongue, and read the message from the tingling sensations they received.

Drums and Bugles

Drums and bugles are so associated with the pageantry of soldiering that it is easy to forget why they are used. Both produce a clear, distinctive sound which can be heard even over gunfire. Only a limited range of "codes" can be used, and they cannot easily be changed, but for controlling bodies of men in battle they are surprisingly useful.

Upper Bridge

Mondell Road

North Woods

Monument Road

Pry Ford

East Woods

West Woods

Dunker
Church

Sunken Road
Bloody
Lane

Observation Tower

Hagerstown Pike

Middle Bridge

LEE

Antietam Creek

Boonsboro Road

Sharpsburg

Burnside Bridge

Millers Sawmill Road

Harpers Ferry Road

Ford

Potomac River

To Harpers Ferry

THE BATTLE OF ANTIETAM

Also known as the Battle of Sharpsburg
Antietam Creek, near Sharpsburg, Maryland
September 17 1862

Confederate States
General Robert E. Lee
40,000 effectives
10,000 casualties

United States
Major-General George B. McClellan
80,000 effectives (58,000 engaged)
12,000 casualties

McCLELLAN

The so-called Burnside Bridge across Antietam Creek is one of the most rustically beautiful sites of the Civil War. For the benefit of non-American readers, "Antietam" is pronounced "Ann-tee-t'm." If you stare at it, you can mentally switch between its gentle beauty now, and that day in 1862 when men struggled and fell atop the bodies of their comrades, as they were cut down by the deadly Confederate fire of the few who had been left to hold the position. With your eyes open, you see the green trees

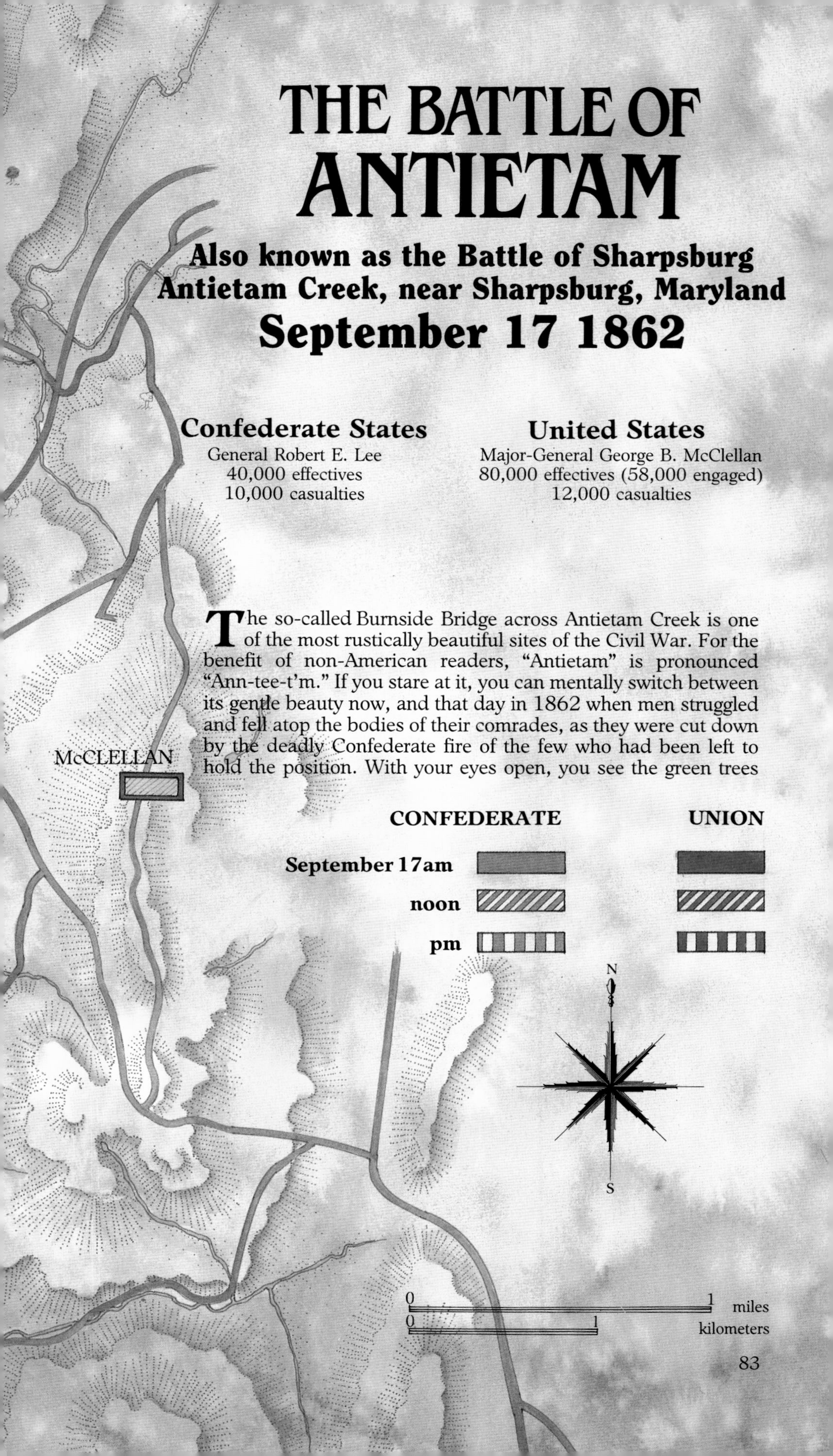

	CONFEDERATE	UNION
September 17 am		
noon		
pm		

N
O
S

0   1   miles
0   1   kilometers

Jackson's men wading the Potomac at White's Ford, Antietam.

and feel the gentle breeze; close them, and you hear the crackle and crash of musketry, and smell the blue powder-smoke on the air.

The other place which really brings home the battle of Antietam Creek — in which more Americans died in battle than on any other day of the Civil War — is the Bloody Lane, a small sunken road. When the Yankees overran it, you could walk from one end to the other on the bodies of Confederate dead.

In one sense, the battle of Antietam Creek was indecisive; at best, the North won a modest tactical victory. But strategically, it represented another blow in a war of attrition which could only harm the South more as it dragged on, and it represented a Northern repulse of the first Southern attempt to invade.

FIRST INVASION OF THE NORTH

Second Manassas had shown that the Yankees could not take anything for granted; but equally, it showed that the South could not take Washington even when they were pursuing a defeated

---

IN LEE'S FOOTSTEPS

Rather confusingly for those who do not know the geography of the area, the South Mountains are a *northward* extension of the Blue Ridge Mountains, and indeed are marked as the Blue Ridge Mountains on some maps.

It is not easy to relate to modern roads the precise routes taken by any of the four columns, but if you want to follow (very roughly) the route via the South Mountains, try taking the modern US 15 from Manassas to Leesburg and on up to Point of Rocks; US 340 up to Frederick; and I-70 over the mountains. Turner's Gap is about 12 miles north and 7 or 8 miles east of Harper's Ferry, or 2 miles north and 7 miles west of Sharpsburg.

army. The North simply had too many men and too much *matériel* for this to be possible. The Confederate army was, however, well placed on an axis between Centreville and Alexandria.

What Richmond now needed was a Confederate invasion of the North. It would show that the Confederates were not merely fighting a defensive war; it would provide more ammunition for the strong peace movement in the North. And it might even achieve the long-dreamed-of Southern goal of recognition from major European countries such as France and Britain. There was also considerable hope that the populace of Maryland might spontaneously rise up and aid the Southern cause once they had a Southern army in their state. The South was to be disappointed in all of these hopes, most cruelly in the last, but they did not know that at the time.

Accordingly, the Confederacy hatched yet another daring plan. As Colonel Henry Kyd Douglas, CSA, put it, "On the 3rd of September, 1862, the Federal army under General Pope having been confounded, General Lee turned his columns toward the Potomac..." On September 9, 1862 — little more than a week after Second Manassas — Lee issued Special Orders No 191. The plan was to split the army in four, with three columns taking different routes to Harper's Ferry and the fourth marching up between the Catoctin Mountains and the South Mountains, looping around to the east of the other three columns. Harper's Ferry was about 45 miles north-west of the Confederate armies' position around Centreville.

LAFAYETTE McLAWS

Major-General Lafayette McLaws was born in Georgia on January 15, 1821, and served under James Longstreet from Williamsburg to the Wilderness; his name appears often in histories as a supporting general. Reliable rather than brilliant, he was briefly under a cloud as a result of the unsuccessful attack on Fort Sanders in November 1863, but he was found guiltless and served until the end of the War. Subsequently he worked for the IRS as well as being a postmaster. He died, aged 76, on July 24, 1897.

Special Orders No. 191 was the famous "Lost Order," which came into McClellan's hands just after noon on September 13 when a couple of Union soldiers found it wrapped around three cigars. Such utter lack of security has never been explained, the more so as one recipient (Major-General John G. Walker) "pinned it securely in an inside pocket" and another "memorized the order and then 'chewed it up'."

McClellan now had a golden opportunity to destroy Lee's armies. The only practicable route through the mountains was via Turner's Gap (see panel *In Lee's Footsteps*). If McClellan had set out on the evening of the 13th, he would have had a good chance not only of reinforcing Harper's Ferry but also of destroying Lee's modest force of 13,000 men by using his greatly superior numbers. Fortunately for Lee, McClellan did not set out until the morning of the 14th; and as Lee had learned of the Yankee's luck (via a sympathetic aide who overheard careless talk in the Union camp) on the 13th, he tried to salvage the Confederate position.

Accordingly, Lee started every available man for Turner's Gap and Crampton's Gap. When the two sides met, the fighting was fierce. In the resulting battles on September 14, the Federals lost 2,325 men out of about 28,000 and the Confederates lost between 2½-3,000 out of 18,000. The Union Major-General William B. Franklin promptly dug in at Crampton's Gap, believing he was outnumbered, and while the Confederates suffered a tactical defeat at both passes, they won a strategic victory. By their defeat, they delayed and distracted the Yankees while Lee gathered his forces. At this time, of course, Lee did not know whether Harper's Ferry had been taken.

Harper's Ferry, captured by Jackson on September 15, 1862, seen here as it is today.

Lee's position was desperate, and he decided to retreat towards the Potomac as fast as possible. On the evening of the 15th, he learned that Harper's Ferry had fallen that very day, and decided to take a stand by Antietam Creek. Overnight, Jackson was able to join him from Harper's Ferry, and Lafayette McLaws set out from Crampton's Gap. A.P. Hill's men would not arrive until the battle was under way, on Wednesday 17.

TERRAIN

The battle of Antietam was fought over quite a large area, and a confusing one at that. The Battlefield Park (which reflects the battle quite well) is about 4 miles from north to south, and an average of a couple of miles wide, though it is wider at the top than at the bottom. Sharpsburg is about two-thirds of the way down, and on the western edge of the park, about a mile east of the Potomac. Antietam Creek flows roughly from north to south (via a good number of curves and meanders) along the eastern side of the park; it empties into the Potomac about 3 miles south of Sharpsburg.

The bed of the creek is at an elevation of about 320 feet, while the old town is at about 480 feet. Occasional hills top 500 feet, with the highest ground above 520 feet.

The northern part of the battlefield is mostly rolling farmland, as steep as can conveniently be worked. At the time of the battle, much of it was under corn; some was under grass; and at least

one field was recently plowed. The undulations of the ground are sufficiently steep that it is difficult to see what is going on in the next field if you are in a dip; and even if you are on high ground (and a good target for a sniper) there is a good deal of "dead" ground which could easily conceal troops lying down or crawling.

This photograph of the rebuilt Mumma's farm reflects the nature of the terrain around Antietam; mostly steep, hilly farmland, planted in places with various crops.

The southern part of the battlefield is much more rugged, and there are many areas where the ground drops away at 45° — a very steep slope, hard to scramble up. There are a few places where sheer drops of 10 or 20 feet are encountered, especially on the east side of the creek; the creek generally is in a very noticeable valley. This ground is mostly covered with grass.

In various places, there are open woodlands with a relatively clear floor; the trees are widely spaced. In 1862, these woods were much more extensive than they are now, but they were still not widespread. Around the river, however, the woods are somewhat thicker.

THE OBSERVATION TOWER

At the north end of the "Bloody Lane" there is a massive stone observation tower. It is a long climb, but it gives you an excellent view of the northern part of the battlefield. It also shows you how the "dead ground" could make troop movements hard to spot. Visit it early in the morning or late in the day, when the shadows are long, as this emphasizes the undulations of the ground. A pair of binoculars or field glasses will also be useful for picking out features such as the various farms.

The "Bloody Lane" - a sunken farm road in which fierce fighting took place at midday on September 17, 1862.

THE BATTLE

The Union threw away a large number of chances in this battle. If they had attacked on September 16 instead of September 17, they would have been up against a Confederate army of half the size. Lee gambled — successfully — on Jackson's proven speed and McClellan's proven sloth.

He also gambled successfully on McClellan's inability to handle his men for the best. In the event, the Battle of Antietam

87

turned out to be a series of five assaults by the Union forces, beginning on the Confederates' northern (left) flank at dawn and winding towards their southern (right) flank in the middle of the afternoon. And his third gamble — also successful — was that McClellan would not renew his attack on the 18th. By keeping his men in Maryland for 36 hours after the battle, he could honestly praise them for never having been driven from a field of battle.

Union Charge of Irwin's brigade (Smith's Division), at the Dunker Church, from a sketch made at the time.

McClellan's original plan, which would almost certainly have succeeded, was for a simultaneous attack against the whole Confederate front. It was not until the morning of the 17th that he changed it; the revised plan was to attack the Confederates' left (north) flank, then "as soon as matters looked favorably there" to attack their right flank. It all went hopelessly wrong.

The first attack, from the north at 6:00 am, came from General Hooker's Union corps; it was resisted by Major-General John

JOHN BELL HOOD

Hood was one of the bravest and most aggressive of all Confederate generals — he was to lose the use of his left arm at Gettysburg and his right leg at Chickamauga — and in a situation like Antietam he was at his best. Born on June 1, 1831, he graduated from West Point in 1853 and was 31 at Antietam. As a strategist, however, he was to prove less than successful at Atlanta (see pages 203-204). He died in poverty on August 30, 1879, of yellow fever, aged 48; his wife and eldest child had died a few days before. Friends arranged for the publication of his memoirs (*Advance and Retreat*, 1880) to afford some support to his remaining children.

Hood's men and Brigadier-General Jubal Early's men. Fierce fighting lasted rather over an hour, mostly on John Poffenberger's cornfields. The Confederates yielded a little ground at first, but then recovered it. Eventually, Hooker's men fell back; they would not be called upon to fight again that day.

At about 7:30, General Mansfield's corps took the place of Hooker's men. The Union general himself was killed in the first few minutes of fighting, but his men fought bravely on against the increasingly weary Confederates, who were driven back about a mile to the Dunker Church, around which fighting raged. By ten, a Union victory seemed assured; Confederate losses were heavy, both from infantry attack and from Union shelling from high (500 feet) ground to the east.

Some time after nine, the Union General Sumner also joined the fight for the Dunker Church, even though he only had one of the three divisions of his corps to hand. At almost the same moment, two Confederate divisions joined the fray; they had arrived an hour earlier after a forced march, and after a rest, they were sent into the lines. It was the appearance of McLaws' division, from South Mountain, which stopped Sumner's division and indeed turned the tide; within half an hour, the Union had lost 2,000 men. With the aid of their reinforcements, the Confederates fought the Union advance to a standstill around the Dunker Church, by about ten thirty or eleven.

The regiments of the 51st New York and the 51st Pennsylvania charged the Burnside Bridge to secure it for the Union forces, but Burnside's failure to consolidate is regarded as one of the great lost opportunities of the War.

Sumner's Union forces had sustained severe casualties in the fight for the Dunker Church. In moving to assist Sumner, General French's division came into combat with Confederates positioned along the sunken road now known as the Bloody Lane. At first, the Union took terrific casualties, but by sheer blood-and-guts fighting, they reached a position from which they could take the sunken lane. The Confederate defenders were slaughtered, and the 61st and 64th New York took the ground. A union victory must again have seemed certain, as it did at ten in the morning — it was now about two in the afternoon.

Once again, McClellan snatched defeat from the jaws of victory. He had a corps of 12,000 men under Franklin, who had arrived a couple of hours earlier from Pleasant Valley, and for some inexplicable reason he failed to commit them. The Dunker Church was still no-man's-land, and a strong drive with this corps could have broken right through the Rebel army.

The reason may be partly due to the incredible bravery of General A.P. Hill. He had led 5,000 men at South Mountain, and had lost 2,000. Of the 3,000 survivors he had brought to Antietam, almost half had been lost. But now, like some hero from a Greek or Roman legend, he seized an infantryman's musket and rallied a tiny force of about 150 men against the Yankees, who were (in Hill's own words) "completely deceived by their boldness, and ... made no farther attempt to pierce our centre, except on a small scale." It is not unreasonable to suggest that he reversed the tide of battle almost single-handed.

The last attack of the day was on the Confederate right, or

southern flank, and came from Major-General Burnside. This was the attack which should have taken place "as soon as matters looked favorably" on the other flank — in other words, at about ten. The bridge itself was barely defended; about 500 riflemen were all that the Rebels could spare. The fords (which Burnside apparently never attempted to find) were not protected at all, and the river is about hip- or waist-deep.

Burnside initially dashed two regiments against the bridge, and according to legend, it was finally stormed at 1 pm when Burnside promised personally to overrule the teetotallers in Washington who were blocking the men's liquor allowance. His whole corps, some 14,000 strong, soon crossed the river without opposition. But then, for reasons which no one alive today knows, Burnside decided to concentrate his forces for a couple of hours. It was only after he had received repeated orders to advance that he moved forward to engage the Rebel troops.

Initially, his attack was successful; if he had attacked earlier, he might well have carried the day. But the remnant of Hill's corps from Harper's Ferry — about 2,000 men — had recently arrived. Once again, it was Hill's men who turned the tide; together with fewer than 1,000 from Toombs's brigade, Hill's Confederates (who were outnumbered five to one on this part of the field) simply drove Burnside back. Union casualties killed and wounded were more than double Confederate losses. The fighting here was across the toughest of all the terrain in the battle, and it may be that the Rebel boys were simply more at home on such marginal land.

Antietam seen from the artillery position on the ridge, from which Confederate troops repulsed Burnside's brave but ill-fated attacks in the afternoon of September 17, 1862. The arrival of General A.P. Hill's Confederates turned the tide just when it looked as though Burnside's men might break through.

Whatever the reason, the final effort by Hill's men meant that a tired, ragged, under-equipped Confederate army had fought to a standstill a Union army which outnumbered them three to two in the field, or two to one in total strength; and they could honestly boast that they had never been driven from the field of battle. Nor would they ever be.

The end of the campaign is bathos. McClellan had almost as many fresh troops as the Confederates had total troops; and as *Harper's* put it, "those who were worst off were in better plight than the best of the enemy." Even so, he decided to postpone a continuation of the battle. Had he attacked on the 18th, he could hardly have failed to win; but by the morning of the 19th, when he planned to attack, the Confederates were all safely back across the Potomac. The First Invasion was over.

The infamous Burnside Bridge at Antietam: now one of the most photogenic relics of the entire Civil War, but at the time a scene of carnage. Burnside apparently did not know of (or disdained to use) a ford a few yards downstream, where his men could have crossed without wetting their belts.

FURTHER INFORMATION

Maps: USGS 7.5': Keedysville Quadrangle (contains the vast majority of the battlefield) and Sheperdstown Quadrangle (necessary only for completeness; not particularly informative)
Official Reports Atlas: 28/1&2&6; 29/1&2
B&L Vol. II: 553; 568; 593; 606; 636

Book: Jay Luvas and Harold W. Nelson, *The Army War College Guide to the Battle of Antietam* (South Mountain Press, Carlisle, PA 1987). Supremely detailed; a self-guided tour. Sometimes difficult to follow the directions, but the military information is superbly considered.

Park: The Park Visitor Center is up to the usual high standards of the Park Service. The orientation program is a good reenactment movie. Burnside Bridge is a fine place for a picnic and a discreet drink with your meal is allowed.

Town: Sharpsburg is surprisingly (and mercifully) undeveloped, though the visitor will find more than adequate accommodation and some very fair restaurants.

SLAVERY

It is extremely difficult to discuss slavery in a modern context; it is so awful, so terrible, that the freeing of the slaves as a result of the War is seen as an unmitigated blessing. Even so, we cannot deny that there were people of goodwill in the South; and we cannot deny that although there were only about 385,000 slaveowners in total, something like 600,000 Southerners fought for the Confederacy. Was war the best way to free the slaves?

The Northern View

The Northern view was simplistic in the extreme. Slaveholding was sinful; the slaveholders should therefore repent and give up their sin. The abolitionists had absolutely no plans for compensating slaveowners; for providing a transition to a wage economy for the slaves; or for minimizing the disruption of the Southern economy.

"Get that team out of the mud!"
An invective to get the slaves to work harder.

The Southern View

Increasing numbers of Southerners were manumitting (freeing) their slaves as the War approached: "Free Black" populations doubled between 1850 and 1860, while slave populations rose by about 10 per cent. Admittedly, there were diehards who wanted to keep the institution of slavery alive; but public opinion was slowly turning against them.

Over half of Southern slaveholders owned fewer than five slaves; almost 90 per cent owned fewer than 20. Most slaveholders would have said, with a clear conscience, that they treated their slaves well. Of course, they were operating on a very different standard from the ones we apply nowadays, but slaveholders normally provided at least basic food and shelter to the aged, young or infirm. Subsistence for slaves may have been horrifyingly low by modern criteria, but so were the living standards of free people in many states, or in England, Ireland or Scotland for that matter.

Left: Slaves at Drayton Point, South Carolina.

Those who had not freed their slaves were mostly looking for some sort of compensation. After all, they argued, they had paid an average of a thousand dollars for an able-bodied slave, and the money had normally gone to a Northerner (most slave-running was done by Yankee-owned ships, with a few from Britain and other nations). Even if they wanted to free the slaves, they simply could not see how they were going to afford to do it.

Below: Slaves laboring at night on the Confederate earthworks at Corinth.

Root, Hog or Die

One of Lincoln's own stories concerns a farmer who decided to raise pigs and let them dig up their own potatoes. When another farmer asked him what would happen when the winter arrived and when the ground froze, the farmer's reply was "It'll be hard on their snouts, but I reckon it'll be root, hog or die." This tended to be the Northern attitude to the South; and when Sherman and the Carpetbaggers had finished, very many Southerners (including blacks) had died.

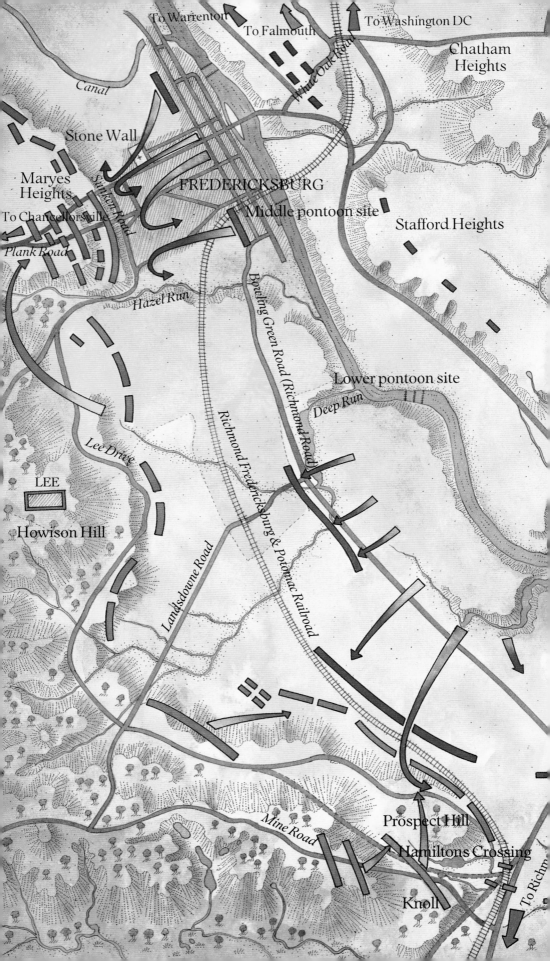

To Warrenton

To Falmouth

To Washington DC

Chatham Heights

Canal

Stone Wall

White Oak Road

Maryes Heights

FREDERICKSBURG

Stafford Heights

Sunken Road

Middle pontoon site

To Chancellorsville

Plank Road

Hazel Run

Bowling Green Road (Richmond Road)

Lower pontoon site

Deep Run

Lee Drive

LEE

Howison Hill

Richmond Fredericksburg & Potomac Railroad

Landsdowne Road

Mine Road

Prospect Hill

Hamiltons Crossing

Knoll

To Richm...

THE BATTLE OF
FREDERICKSBURG

Fredericksburg, Virginia
December 13 1862

Confederate States
General Robert E. Lee
78,000 effectives
5,300 casualties

United States
Major-General Ambrose E. Burnside
120,000 effectives
12,600 casualties

O ne of the most moving memorials of the Battle of Fredericksburg — and to the tragedy of war and the greatness of bravery — is the statue of Sergeant Richard Kirkland of the 2nd South Carolina Volunteers. The night after the Battle of Fredericksburg, the 19-year-old sergeant climbed out of the Sunken Road from which the Confederates had done such deadly execution, and walked among the Union wounded who lay

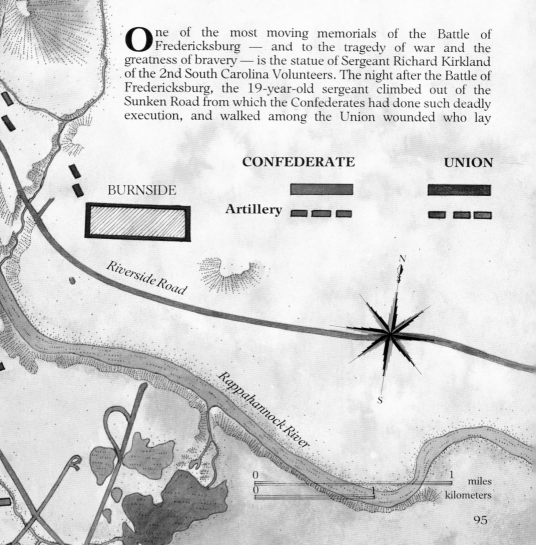

CONFEDERATE   UNION

Artillery

BURNSIDE

Riverside Road

Rappahannock River

N

S

0   1   miles
0   1   kilometers

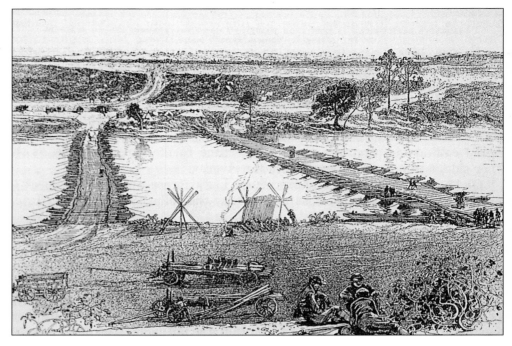

thickly on the frozen ground. He carried no flag of truce, just water for the dying men; his was the last face many Union soldiers saw. Both sides held their fire. When he went back over the stone wall to his regiment, over an hour later, the watching Union soldiers saluted him with a great cheer. He was killed at Chickamauga, ten months later.

Pontoon bridges at Franklin's Crossing.

A LOYAL SOUTHERN TOWN

Fredericksburg, which lies less than 50 miles south of Washington and a little to the west, was doubly important as a military objective. Strategically, it commanded road and rail links with Richmond, and it was just across the water from Falmouth, little more than a 10 mile train ride south from Aquia Landing on the Potomac. It was a loyal Southern town to which many Southern families (including Lee's) traced their ancestry. The South would be unlikely to let it fall without a struggle.

If the Union could take Fredericksburg, therefore, they could demonstrate to their own people that something was happening in the Eastern theater of war — so far, they had little to show for 20 months of war — and they would clear the way to Richmond.

The man to whom the plan is normally credited was the new general of the Army of the Potomac, Major General Ambrose E. Burnside: the same man whose sloth had proved so calamitous at Antietam Creek. Lincoln had made yet another disastrous choice of generals when he appointed Burnside in McClellan's place.

Burnside was unquestionably a man who was personally brave and honorable, and to his eternal credit he had tried his best to refuse the command on the grounds that he was not fit for it — a much more accurate assessment than his president made. But then, the politician and orator in Lincoln was always more able than the statesman or leader. He also told an old friend on the other side, whom (incredibly to modern eyes) he invited over for dinner under a flag of truce after the battle, that he was not responsible for the attack on Fredericksburg, as he was himself under orders and was not much more than a figure-head.

McClellan was personally popular, and there was talk of a political future for him in the Democratic Party; Lincoln feared for his own position. On November 4, the Democrats made significant gains in the Federal elections; Lincoln appointed Burnside on the 5th. Lee regretted parting with McClellan, "for we always understood each other so well. I fear they may continue to make these changes till they find someone I don't understand."

In fairness to Lincoln, McClellan had not been diligent in pursuing the Rebels; under the right man, Antietam might have decided the War in the Union's favor. As events would transpire, Fredericksburg could have done the same for the Confederacy, but it didn't.

BACKGROUND TO THE BATTLE

Burnside hoped to deceive Lee by appearing to concentrate his forces near Warrenton, half-way between Manassas and the Rappahannock on the Orange and Alexandria Railroad, when in reality he was planning an attack from Falmouth (opposite Fredericksburg) almost 30 miles to the south-west. Lincoln approved the plan on November 14. By November 17, the first Union troops were in Falmouth; Major-General Sumner (who had distinguished himself at Antietam — see page 89) wanted to ford the river and attack that day, knowing that Fredericksburg was very lightly defended; the force there was about the size of an infantry regiment.

He was overruled by Burnside, who expected his pontoons to arrive the next day; then, reasoned Burnside, the whole army could cross in relative safety and take the town easily. Unfortunately for him, someone in Washington had screwed up; the pontoons did not begin to arrive until the 25th, and it was not until the very end of the month that pontoons for all three crossings were available.

This gave Lee all the time he needed. By now, it was clear that Fredericksburg was the Union objective, so Lee brought in both corps of his reorganized army. Longstreet arrived on the 21st, Jackson on the 30th. They dug in and cut down trees to clear lines of fire and make *abatis*. Their only weaknesses were first, that their line was perforce very long and thin (if the men had been evenly spaced, they would have been 5-10 feet apart) and second, that the southern or right flank was more exposed than the northern or left flank. The majority of the men were concentrated on the left and right flanks, though reinforcements were behind the center.

The Union used both canvas and wooden pontoons to build bridges like those across this river.

97

TERRAIN

Just above Fredericksburg, the Rappahannock is at about 40 feet above sea level; it runs between bluffs which are up to 200 feet high. At Fredericksburg, the ground is flatter; Chatham Heights, on the Falmouth side of the river, are at less than 100 feet while the old town of Fredericksburg is about 10 or 20 feet above the river at 50-60 feet.

South of Fredericksburg, the river runs through an alluvial plain some 2 or 3 miles wide, but a chain of hills runs from north to south just west of the town. Marye's Heights (pronounced "Marie's") are an oasis in modern Fredericksburg, but they were well outside the western boundary of the town in 1862. They begin to rise steeply (from 70 feet to 140 feet in only 100 feet) about three-quarters of a mile from the river. A sunken road runs along the foot of Marye's Heights, and this was where Lee anchored his left (northern) flank. To make this position still more impregnable, a drainage canal paralleled the Confederate lines about 200 yards east of the sunken road.

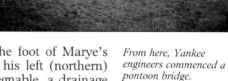

From here, Yankee engineers commenced a pontoon bridge.

The rest of Lee's lines were distributed along what is now Lee Drive, broadly following the 100 foot contour as it sweeps south along the edge of the hills. In places, the line dipped as low as 80 feet; in others, it was as high as 120-130 feet. What it had throughout its length, though, was a commanding view of the plain 30-50 feet lower; and, of course, the artillery and command posts were positioned higher still, with Lee's command post at a height of about 200 feet. The right flank was by the railroad at Hamilton's Crossing, again at about the 100 foot mark.

In order to reach Lee's lines, the Union soldiers would have to advance across almost dead-flat land, raked by artillery and small-arms fire. Cover was negligible: a handful of scattered houses, a few stream-beds (especially Deep Run, about half a mile downstream from the town), and a few trees — but the Confederate lines were just in front of the main bodies of woods all along the ridge.

The Sunken Road in Fredericksburg, from which the Confederates put up a courageous and successful defense.

THE BATTLE

The battle can be divided into two parts. The first was the crossing of the Rappahannock by pontoon and the storming of the town. The second was the assault on the Confederate lines proper.

The logical places to throw pontoons across were at the town itself and to the south, just by Deep Run; this was as clear to Lee as to Burnside. Fording the river was not feasible; the ice was half an inch to an inch thick, and more men would have been lost to exposure than to shot and shell. Some Union soldiers later tried to ford the drainage canal in front of Marye's Heights — it was about 4 feet deep — and many perished from the cold.

The southern crossing was achieved almost without trouble; the pontoons were laid on the 11th, and the Union armies crossed easily. In Fredericksburg itself, the Confederates simply

On the other side, in Fredericksburg, a few houses commanded a formidable glacis. Initially, Union engineers were simply blown off their pontoons by Southern fire.

shot the engineers off the pontoons. Despite very heavy Union shelling, which reduced much of the attractive old colonial town to rubble, the snipers in the basements of the houses proved almost impossible to eradicate. It was not until troops were ferried across, sustaining substantial losses in the process, that a bridgehead could be established on the western shore and the pontoons could be completed. The Confederates immediately withdrew behind their main lines. The Union crossing was complete by the evening of the 12th; they occupied the town, and in the words of one of their own major-generals, "There was considerable looting."

The main battle took place on the 13th. The Union plan was to turn the Confederates' right (south) flank, attacking under cover of fog, but for some reason, Burnside changed his mind about committing the whole of his left Grand Division; part was kept back.

As the fog began to clear, the Confederates realized where the attack was coming from — and young Major John Pelham of Jeb Stuart's Horse Artillery decided to head it off. With one Blakely rifled cannon and one smooth-bore Napoleon, he charged in front of his own lines and began to shell the Union. The Blakely was destroyed after one shot, but the old Napoleon poured solid shot into the blue lines. His single gun was the target for four batteries of Union cannon, but he and his men did not withdraw (with the Napoleon) until they were almost out of ammunition, having held up the Union advance for half an hour. Seeing his young major in action, Lee said to his aides, "It is glorious to see such courage in one so young." "The Gallant Pelham," as he is known to history, was killed on March 17, 1863, aged 25.

Barksdale's Mississippians opposing the laying of the pontoon bridges.

The Union batteries now commenced their pounding of the Confederate positions; but the Rebels were so well dug in that casualties were surprisingly light. Jackson had instructed his artillery not to fire until the Union infantry advanced; he did not

want them to give away their positions. After an hour's bombardment, by which time Union commanders assumed the Confederate batteries had been silenced, the Union infantry were ordered forwards.

A contemporary pen and ink sketch of the bombardment of Fredericksburg.

Then the Confederates fired. Union bravery was no match for strong entrenchments and solid shot. Before noon, the soldiers in blue began to fall back. Incredibly, they did so in good order; this was not the army that had broken and run at First Manassas.

Just after noon, Meade's Yankees charged up the swampy bed of a nameless stream a couple of miles south of Deep Run; its mouth is now lost in the gravel pits three or more miles downstream from Fredericksburg, but the Meade Pyramid beside the Richmond, Fredericksburg and Potomac Railroad (on the other side of the tracks from Lee Drive) shows where the Union nearly broke through. The weather was so cold that they could advance over the lightly-defended swamps, which were frozen

Stop 3 on the park tour, by the Meade Pyramid, shows where the Federal troops nearly broke the Confederate lines.

almost solid. The Confederate lines were weak here at the meeting-point of Lane's and Archer's brigades of Hill's division. Meade took 3,000 prisoners; if the whole of Burnside's left Grand Division had been there, the battle might have ended shortly.

As it was, Early's Confederate reserves rushed forward to plug the gap, and indeed counterattacked; they did this to such good effect that the Yankees were driven back from the small amount of land they had captured, and this time the retreat did become a rout as the jubilant Rebels chased them across the plain. It was only a counter-counterattack from Brigadier-General David Birney's division (formed along the Old Richmond Road parallel with the river) that stopped another First Manassas, bringing forth from Jackson the sour comment, "I did not think that a little red earth would frighten them. I am sorry that they are gone. I am sorry I fortified."

THE SUNKEN ROAD

On the other flank, the battle was taking a very different course. The Sunken Road at the foot of Marye's Heights was the perfect defensive position, and a soldier resting his musket on the wall which bounded it could aim with deadly effect at the massed ranks of Union men advancing towards him.

Today, the Sunken Road is a pleasantly rustic little spot; the wall which bounds it is actually a reconstruction, built in 1939; the land across which the Union advanced is now covered with houses. It is hard to visualize the slaughter on that bitterly cold day in 1862. But in the words of Colonel Alexander, Longstreet's acting chief of artillery, "General, we cover that ground now so well that we will comb it as with a fine-tooth comb. A chicken could not live in that field when we open on it." And in James Longstreet's words, when Lee expressed doubt about the position, "General, if you put every man now on the other side of the Potomac on that field to approach me over the same line, and give me plenty of ammunition, I will kill them all before they reach my line."

Behind the wall at Marye's Heights.

It is not difficult to imagine the terror of trying to attack the Sunken Road. Fourteen separate assaults were launched, and they all failed; almost 6,000 Union men fell there. Charging across that field, you would be dodging around not just the dead, but also the dying — men who might reach out, or try to stand up, at the most inopportune moment. If you tripped, you would find that dead and dying men were your only parapet; you would know that if you attempted to stand up and continue the charge, you would stand a very good chance of joining them. But if you stayed where you were, you might not only think yourself a coward; immobile on the frozen ground, praying not to be hit, you might well die of exposure.

Confederate picket with blanket-capote and rawhide moccasins.

It is perhaps more difficult to imagine how the Rebels felt. On the one hand, there must have been the fierce exaltation of battle, the almost mechanical sequence of load-and-fire, load-and-fire, load-and-fire underlying a godlike sense of power. On the other, there was the terrible sight of those falling, squirming, twitching bodies — though according to one Yankee, the Rebels amused themselves by shooting chickens "when the higher game in blue uniform was not in sight." It was during the awful night which followed that carnage that Sergeant Kirkland made his mission of mercy.

SERGEANT PLUNKETT

Union losses at Fredericksburg were considerable. The troops fought with exemplary courage, withstanding the onslaught of almost uninterrupted fire from the Confederates in the Sunken Road.

Sergeant Plunkett's courage was typical; he was a Union colorbearer who lost both forearms to cannon fire, but continued to clasp the colors in his bleeding stumps.

THE AFTERMATH

Action on the southern flank had effectively finished when Birney halted the pursuing Confederates; Jackson wanted to counterattack, but Union artillery was too strong.

Burnside was all for renewing the attack on the Sunken Road in the morning; he wanted to lead the first charge himself. He even wrote orders for such an attack. No-one questioned his bravery, but all his subordinates questioned his wisdom. Mercifully for his troops, he was dissuaded, but not before the Rebels had captured the original orders. When the Yankees did not attack, Lee suspected a ruse, but no surprises were forthcoming. In the afternoon, a truce was arranged; the Union buried their dead, many of whom had been stripped during the night by Confederate soldiers desperate for warm clothing. That night, Burnside's withdrawal across the Rappahannock was as

masterful as Lee's had been across the Potomac after Antietam.

In front of the Sunken Road.

One major question remains for historians: why did Lee not counterattack on the 14th? And why did he let Burnside slip away? There is no easy answer. As we have already seen, Lee expected Burnside to renew the attack. When he did not, Lee said, "Had I divined that was to have been his only effort he would have had more of it." Perhaps, knowing that the Union artillery had stopped Jackson, he feared that the same might happen again. Or perhaps, little knowing how much longer the War was to last, and having just won a victory against an army which outnumbered his by three to two, he was simply tired. Longstreet said, after the War, that "attempts to break up an army by following on its line of retreat are hazardous and rarely successful," though he added that "movements against the flanks and rear increase the demoralization and offer better opportunities for great results." There were no "great results" here; Lee's failure to smash the retreating Union armies led to another two and a half years of war.

FURTHER INFORMATION

Maps: USGS 7.5': Fredericksburg Quadrangle (which contains most of the battlefield) and Guinea Quadrangle (the southern tip of the battlefield)
Official Reports Atlas: 25/4; 30/3-4; 31/4; 32/2; 33/1; 63/7
B&L:74

Park: The main Visitor Center, with a good orientation show, is near the Sunken Road. Most of the remainder of the battlefield is open all the time.

Town: Fredericksburg relies heavily on tourism (it stresses its pre-Revolutionary origins as well as the War), but is a pleasant town withal.

PHOTOGRAPHY

Most Civil War photographs (with the exception of some portraits) were taken using "wet-plate" cameras, so called because the photographer had to prepare and sensitize his own glass plates, then expose them while they were still wet; the "dry plate" (the forerunner of modern films) was not invented until 1871, and George Eastman would not introduce his roll-film Kodak until 1888. Plates were loaded individually into single or double plate-holders or darkslides.

Because enlarging was extremely rare, almost all photographers used cameras which produced a negative the same size as the final print — sometimes as big as 10×12 inches, or even bigger. Cameras were always tripod-mounted; plates were very slow (the equivalent of a modern ISO $1/2$ to ISO 2) and most exposures were made at f/16 or less (the f/8 "Rapid Rectilinear" was not patented until 1866). The result was that exposures were several seconds long; even in bright sunlight, $1/4$ second was unusual. Many photographers used their hat as a "shutter," holding it over the lens as they opened the plate-holder, removing it for the exposure, and then replacing it again.

Types of Photographs

Portrait photographers sometimes used wet plates, but others still used the old Daguerreotype process (published 1839) and many used tintypes or ambrotypes. Daguerreotypes are made by sensitizing a silver-coated copper plate with mercury; the image (the "mirror with a memory") is very fragile, and can only be seen at certain angles. Exposures were enormously long, often several minutes.

Tintypes (ferrotypes) consist of a wet collodion emulsion on a black japanned metal plate; they are more robust than Daguerrotypes, and because of their relatively low cost they were popular

Bergstresser's Photographic Studio.

among soldiers who wanted a "likeness" to send home. A tintype is actually a direct negative, which looks positive because of the black backing. An Ambrotype is another direct negative, this time on glass, backed with black varnish, paper or velvet; the principle is the same as the tintype. Both processes were introduced in 1851 and were still novelties during the Civil War. Because the emulsion could be under-exposed in these processes, "instantaneous" pictures could be made between 1 second and $\frac{1}{10}$ second in good light, especially with an ultra-fast (f/4) Voigtländer portrait lens.

Most cameras were custom-made by local cabinetmakers, and the few full-time manufacturers made very few cameras; a few dozen, or at most a few hundred, a year. Most of the leading manufacturers of the period (such as Lewis and Lewis,

Photographs of the Civil War, like this one of Confederate bodies on the Wheatfield, provide effective images of the horror of the conflict.

Meagher, Ottewill, and Rouch) are now long-forgotten, except by collectors; original wet-plate cameras now command prices in the thousands. Even lenses might be made by the local optician.

The Civil War was not the first conflict to be photographed — Roger Fenton covered the Crimean War as early as 1855 — but it was the first major conflict to receive intensive photographic coverage. NEVER attempt to clean original Civil War pictures; Daguerrotypes will almost certainly be destroyed, and other pictures are more likely to be damaged than to be improved. Ask a museum (not a camera store) for advice.

Taking "Civil War" Pictures Today

For photographers who want to take "in character" pictures at battle reconstructions, a modern 5×4 inch wooden camera with a Polaroid Land back will look reasonably authentic and is quick to use. For more authenticity, use a 10x8 inch camera with black and white film; the very slow

Fine Grain Positive copying film (ISO 5 or less) is ideal, as it is similar to what a Civil War photographer would have had to handle. Then shoot at f/22 or less.

For photographers who are interested, the majority of modern pictures in this book were taken using Leica M-series (rangefinder) cameras with the following lenses: 21mm, 35mm, 50mm, 90mm, 135mm, 280mm, 400mm.

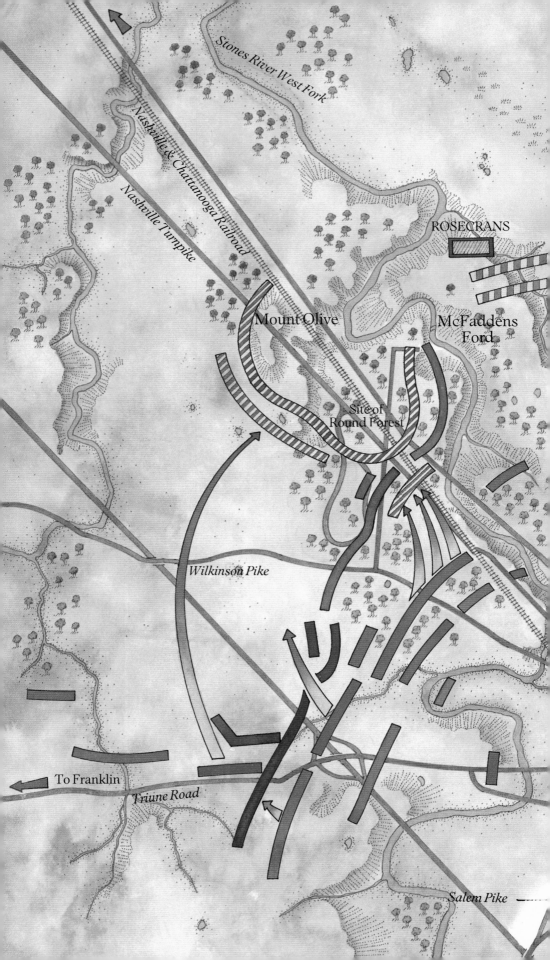

Stones River West Fork

Nashville & Chattanooga Railroad

Nashville Turnpike

ROSECRANS

Mount Olive

McFaddens Ford

Site of Round Forest

Wilkinson Pike

To Franklin

Triune Road

Salem Pike

THE BATTLE OF
MURFREESBORO

Also known as Stone's River
Stone's River, near Murfreesboro, Tennessee
December 31 1862 - January 3 1863

Confederate States	United States
General Braxton Bragg	Major-General William S. Rosecrans
38,000 men	47,000 men
10,265 casualties	13,249 casualties

I n the woods at Stone's River, there are two broken cannon. They lie as if the pounding they received as they were hauled across the stones had been too much for them; the wheels are off, the carriages scarred and battered. They are, of course, carefully arranged by the National Park Service, and indeed secured to prevent theft; but they give a good idea of the battle, and stress the importance that artillery played in it.

The most noticeable thing about the terrain around Murfreesboro is that the shallow soil is frequently broken by

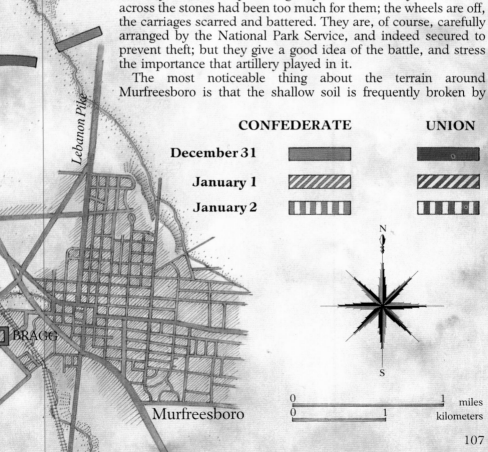

	CONFEDERATE	UNION
December 31		
January 1		
January 2		

Lebanon Pike

BRAGG

Murfreesboro

0   1   miles
0   1   kilometers

outcrops of limestone. Some are like paving-stones, flush with the grass; others are like small tank-traps, ridge after ridge of raised rock anything up to a couple of feet high (though 12-18 inches is more common). These "natural rifle pits" can make excellent defensive positions, though the danger from rock splinters and ricochets when a ball hits is considerable. The whine of ricochets, added to the roar of guns as the Yankees retreated before the initial onslaught, must have been incredible. As terrain to traverse they are deadly. Infantrymen need to be agile if they are to avoid sprained ankles and even broken legs, and pulling artillery across the field is very difficult indeed.

To make life still more interesting, the battlefield consists of a few clearings interspersed with cedar woods. These cedars are typical of this thin, poor soil; the earth between them is covered with a thick, soft duff of debris which can be treacherous; it is easy to see how difficult the trees might make it to maneuver men and artillery.

Few realize how many died there. Look at the casualty figures again. More than 10 per cent of those casualties — slightly over 3,000 men — died during the three days of battle.

THE INVASION OF KENTUCKY

In August 1862, the Confederate army under General Bragg invaded Kentucky. Their intention was partly to scare the North; partly (as they hoped) to rally support in a state whose loyalties were split; partly to encourage European recognition of the Confederacy; and partly to achieve their defensive strategic aims by an offensive tactical approach.

They were remarkably successful. By mid-September, they were well north, and they had beaten the Yankees repeatedly. On September 17, Bragg accepted the surrender of the 4,000-man Union garrison and fort at Munfordville, thereby gaining control of the railroad between Louisville and Nashville, dividing the Union armies and giving himself the choice of fighting the Yankees on favorable terms or of taking Louisville, which was only lightly garrisoned by inexperienced troops.

WILLIAM STARKE ROSECRANS

William Starke Rosecrans, born in September 1819, graduated near the top of his class at West Point in 1842, and was a successful engineer when the War broke out. Together with George McClellan and Jacob Cox, he organized the regiments from Ohio and from Indiana which were raised following Lincoln's proclamation in April 1861, calling 75,000 militiamen into national service for ninety days. He took part in many campaigns but was accused of a "strategy of do nothing and let the Rebels raid the country." He was finally replaced as commander of the Army of the Cumberland in October 1863.

PERRYVILLE — AND POLK'S BLUFF

Perryville Battlefield is a State Park, operated by the State of Kentucky. There is not a lot to see, though there is a good little museum and a well-designed pair of self-guided tours, one on foot and one by automobile. It is, however, an excellent park if you want to try to exercise as much imagination as possible, without an excess of markers, monuments and interpretation.

It was at Perryville that the brave but self-willed Confederate General "Bishop" Polk pulled off an extraordinary bluff. Having formed the mistaken impression that he was being fired upon by his own side, he rode up to the offending battery to make them stop. Unfortunately for him, they *were* Yankees. Upon being asked who he was by the battery commander (it was growing dark, and his uniform could not be clearly seen), he shook his fist and said, "I will show you who I am, sir! Cease firing at once!" He then cantered toward the battery and ordered the men, "Cease firing!" He then rode smartly back to his own corps, "whom he immediately ordered to open fire."

For some extraordinary reason, he did neither, but instead retreated from Munfordville and let Buell's Yankees march unimpeded to Louisville, there to gather reinforcements. He was not afraid to fight, even against long odds, but he seems on this occasion to have had dreams of flanking the enemy and winning "by marching, not by fighting" — though no-one but he could see how he was going to accomplish this.

On October 8 came the Battle of Perryville. It was (as so often) inconclusive, though Union casualties were higher, but Bragg correctly understood that he had been drawn into battle before he had concentrated his forces sufficiently; he retreated to Harrodsburg, there to join the rest of the Confederates under General Kirby Smith.

Then, inexplicably, Bragg ordered a retreat. The army, spoiling for a fight from the general staff downwards, was led back through desolate country on short rations. Bragg was accused of incompetence at best, cowardice and treason at worst. By December, his troops were down in Murfreesborough (as it was then spelled). The Yankees would take the initiative in the next invasion, striking south from occupied Nashville.

TERRAIN

The battlefield may be thought of as a square, about 3 miles on a side, with its bottom right-hand corner at the city of Murfreesboro. Most of the fighting took place towards the upper left-hand corner, well to the north-west of the city; this area, which forms the modern National Battlefield Park, is a few hundred yards wide by little more than a mile from north to south, almost flat, between 550 and 570 feet in elevation.

The river (which is comparatively shallow everywhere) flows northwards with dramatic meanders, about a mile west of the town of Murfreesboro. It falls from about 550 feet at Murfreesboro to about 520 feet at the end of the Yankee lines — a distance of about 3 miles as the crow flies.

The higher land — and this is a relative term — is mostly to the east of the river; the highest point of Murfreesboro is about 630 feet, while north of the town it is as little as 600 feet even a mile east of the river. The west bank is lower still; the Union left flank was on high ground at about 550 feet, 30 feet above the river, while the right flank was at perhaps 620 feet.

Stone's River is shallow, and both Confederate and Union troops crossed it easily during the battle.

The relative flatness of the land meant that there was little real "high ground" to defend or to capture. Nor was visibility normally improved by going for higher ground; the trees obscured everything. Instead, the fighting centered around cover (clumps of trees and woods); around the river, to a limited extent; and most of all, around the Chattanooga and Nashville Railroad and the Nashville Turnpike, essential lines of supply for the Union armies and potentially a way of linking northern Tennessee with the southern part for the Rebels. The old Nashville Pike still exists, roughly paralleling the modern US 70 at this point, but it is south of the railroad tracks instead of north like the newer road. It enters Murfreesboro from the north-west, traveling south-east.

A number of other roads radiate outwards from Murfreesboro, including the Salem Pike (south-west, modern TN 99); Triune Road (due west, the modern TN 96, now bisected by the US 24 for which it is the access road); Wilkinson's Pike (west and slightly north, now known as Manson Pike, TN 604); and Lebanon Pike (north, modern US 231). These may be regarded as the spokes of a wheel, the rim of which (about 2 miles in diameter) was the Confederate line of defense.

THE OPPOSING ARMIES

At dawn on December 31, the Rebel armies were camped along the high ground to the west and north of the city, extending in a broad arc which encompassed about a third of a circle from the south-west of the city to the north. Up to the point where the railroad crosses the river, they were on the west bank of the river, but north of that point they were on the east bank. The country behind them was friendly; they were, after all, resisting a Yankee invasion.

The Union armies were on lower ground in a roughly north-south line which ran from about 300 yards north of the Salem Pike (TN 99) at its southern extremity to Stone's River about a quarter of a mile east of Mount Olive. As so often was the case, there were hardly any Union sentries, pickets or videttes on duty in the area, and those few who voiced any alarm about the possibility of Rebel attack were simply ignored.

The natural rifle pits of Stone's River provided ideal defensive positions.

THE FIRST DAY OF BATTLE

Dawn on New Year's Eve 1862 was much as one would expect dawn to be at that time of year: cold, gray, wet and miserable. In silence, almost like smoke among the trees, the Confederates were gathering. The thick, soft floor of the woods muffled their footsteps; the damp air between the trees swallowed any sound they did make.

In silence they gathered; and at just after six o'clock, they slipped out of the woods, formed line of battle, and charged. Ten thousand men charged forward, still in silence; not until they reached the Union lines did they raise the Rebel yell.

Many cannon carriages must have cracked up in this fast-moving action across very rough terrain.

Their initial success was absolute. As far as any Yankee could see, there were endless lines of Rebels stretching away into the morning mist. Many thought they had been attacked by up to 35,000 soldiers, part of a gigantic army which grew in their minds as they panicked.

The Union forces fell back further and further as their line was rolled up from the southern end, so that their forces were squeezed into an ever smaller area in the north-west corner of the battlefield. At that point, the railroad, the Nashville Pike and Stone's River all come together; the railroad and the Pike were essential to the Union forces both for supply and (if need be) for retreat, so their position was desperate.

The only real delaying action before the Union troops fell back to their final positions (which they were to defend successfully) came from General Phil Sheridan, who repeatedly attempted to form a line at right-angles to the original line. As repeatedly, they were driven back; the artillery duels were frequently at ranges as little as 200 yards. One of

Sheridan's more successful rallying lines is today Stop 4 on the Park Tour, just north of the Manson Pike. At last, lack of ammunition forced them to retreat. As Sheridan led the remnants of his troops past the devoutly Catholic Rosecrans, the senior general remonstrated with him over his swearing. Sheridan replied, "Unless I swear like hell, the men won't take me seriously." Then, pointing to his few powder-blackened men, dragging themselves wearily behind him, he said "This is all that is left, General."

Although this is obviously an artist's interpretation, it does give a very good idea of the relative positions of the road, the railroad and the river.

The Yankees fought bravely, but on that first day at least, they were out-generalled. Individual feats of bravery were almost commonplace; even the supply-wagon drivers on both sides found themselves combatants, the Union wagons hacking a way through the cedars first to escape the Rebels and then to supply Sheridan's troops who were almost out of ammunition, and the Confederates hurrying desperately to keep up with their fast-advancing troops. One Rebel lost track of his men and found himself charging the Yankees "armed" only with two ordnance wagons; the Yankees were so confused, they ran.

On another occasion, the First Tennessee Regiment became convinced that a Union battery was actually one of their own, firing on its own men in error, and did not return the fire — ideal conditions for the Yankees!

PHILIP HENRY SHERIDAN

Born March 6, 1831; West Point 1853; just 30 when the War began. A very short man — just 5′ 4″ tall — Phil Sheridan was brave, aggressive, but hard to get along with unless he had his own way. He fought well in many engagements other than Murfreesboro, and he achieved independent command in 1864 when he was commanded to lay waste the Shenandoah Valley (see pages 213-214). Died August 5, 1888, aged 57, still in the army.

By the afternoon of that first day, the fight centered on the "Round Forest," otherwise known as "Hell's half acre." Almost gone today, the few trees here bear no witness to the fierceness of the fighting, but an extremely hot fire from Union artillery kept the Rebels from overrunning the position. Had they succeeded, "Old Rosy" would almost certainly have had to surrender, with his ammunition trains captured and his route of retreat cut off.

General Samuel Beatty's Brigade, advancing to sustain the Union right near the Nashville Pike.

The Confederate assaults were, however, piecemeal; large in number, but individually relatively weak and unable to take the position. The taking of the Round Forest is one of those turning-points which historians still debate today; many believe that Bragg could have taken it, but there are several different interpretations of *how* he should have gone about it.

By nightfall, sleep on the frozen ground in the beating rain was all the comfort either side could take. No fires were officially permitted on either side (though the ever-anarchic Rebels ignored orders more widely), because of the danger of attracting sniper fire; and these were the days before waterproof materials were readily available to build shelters. Some of the wounded were frozen to the ground with their own blood; that night, many froze to death.

Once again, the night was a turning-point. Many believe that Bragg could have pursued and routed or captured the Union forces, and perhaps he could, but this conclusion is easier to reach in a warm room when you are adequately dressed than it must have been for Bragg and his men, cold, wet, exhausted. In any case, many of the Rebels expected the Yankees to retreat of their own accord. Also, it may have been that Rosecrans wanted to retreat, but believed that he was surrounded and therefore unable to do so — a bitter irony.

THE SECOND AND THIRD DAYS

Although no one realized it at the time, the battle was effectively over. On January 1, there was no heavy fighting; the Union men crossed the river, taking the high ground (up to 580 feet) on the east bank, opposite what is now the Artillery Monument. They crossed by McFadden's Ford, marked as "Very Good Ford" on Rosecrans's map of the action in the *Official Atlas*. Each side was waiting for the other to act.

Then, on January 2, Bragg did what he had done so often before; with a near-victory behind him, and without discussion, he made decisions which were simply wrong, and which his men immediately perceived to be wrong. One officer, who died that afternoon, was in favor of shooting Bragg himself as being the only way of dissuading him from such madness.

In essence, Bragg called for a near-suicidal attack. General John C. Breckenridge's men, coming in from the east, were to dislodge the Yankees from the high ground east of the river that they had occupied the previous day. They drove the Yankees into the river, and even managed to cross in the face of murderous fire, but they could not possibly take the Union position which shelved gently upwards from the river and was protected by no fewer than 58 guns. On occasion, the enthusiasm of the gunners was greater than their discretion; the Chicago Board of Trade Battery fired several rounds of canister into their own men. Breckenridge himself lived, but he took 1,700 casualties out of 5,000 men.

Today, you can follow the path of Breckenridge's attack for yourself. The roaring traffic of the freeway passes over your head on a bridge as you come down the east bank of Stone's River; you splash through the shallow waters (if the water is low, you can jump from stone to stone without getting your feet wet); and then you face the walk up to the Artillery Monument. When you make that walk, it is as if your bones know what happened there. Instead of the terror and exhilaration of (say) Pickett's Charge, which seems still to live in the earth at Gettysburg, a profound weariness comes over you; your body aches with the fatigue the

Stop 8 on the park tour - the Hazen Monument, the first paid-for sculpted monument was erected in 1863.

WILLIAM BABCOCK HAZEN

Hazen was 32 at Stone's River (born April 14, 1830; West Point 1855); he had already distinguished himself at Shiloh. At Stone's River he lost one-third of his brigade in casualties; it was to the memory of the dead that Hazen himself erected the monument in late 1863. His troops were also important at Chickamauga, Chattanooga and the March to the Sea. After the War, he fought the Indians, was an observer at the Franco-Prussian War, and reached the rank of Brigadier-General and Chief Signal Officer. He died on January 16, 1887, aged 66.

Confederates must have felt then; and you know that the battle was lost.

Both sides claimed Murfreesboro as a victory, though it was effectively a stalemate. Because Bragg retreated afterwards, it was at least a strategic victory for the North.

AFTERMATH

Although the result was inconclusive, the cost in terms of lives was high for both sides. Rosecrans commanded 43,400 men and lost a total of 13,219. The Confederates had 33,712 men taking part and sustained losses of 10,266. Bragg's competence had already been urgently questioned before the battle; the President, Jefferson Davis, had traveled by train to Murfreesboro to discuss the situation with him. On January 3, Bragg fell back to Chattanooga, from which he was dislodged six months later by Rosecrans again; the next major trial at arms in the west would come at Chickamauga.

In the 19th century, popular tunes were often written (or sometimes re-named) to commemorate stirring events.

Not all the Confederates were as incompetent. During a Union cavalry raid from Murfreesboro into Georgia, for example, the redoubtable Confederate General Nathan Bedford Forrest captured the whole brigade, 1,600 strong, by persuading them that they were surrounded and outnumbered three to one. He had with him fewer than 500 men.

FURTHER INFORMATION

Maps: USGS 7.5': Murfreesboro and Walterhill
Official Reports Atlas: 30/1; 31/1&3; 32/1
B&L: Vol III: 616

Book: James Lee McDonough, *Stone's River — Bloody Winter in Tennessee* (University of Tennessee Press, Knoxville TN, 1980). Very good: winner of the Jefferson Davis Award.

Park: Keeps very short hours; the gate closes at 5 pm, though pedestrian access is possible later — park by the Hazen Monument. The audio-visual presentation, which uses a number of 1860s images, is much better than the "Magic Marker" artwork slides used by several other Southern visitor centers. The Artillery Monument, by the river, closes at 4:30. There is a picnic area, but alcohol is banned.

Town: Murfreesboro is a sprawling town, well supplied with accommodation and restaurants. The best museum (at least with reference to the War between the States) is at the Park.

INTELLIGENCE

Group at Secret Service Department Headquarters, October 1862. The leader of McClellan's secret service was Allan Pinkerton, America's famous first private detective.

In any civil conflict, total security is impossible; there are bound to be webs of friendship, family ties, and mixed feelings on both sides. Prisoners, too, talk among themselves and with their captors.

On the other hand, reports of troop movements — especially from civilians — are not always reliable, and even if you are reasonably sure where your enemy is, it is much more difficult to guess what he intends to do. Also, the other side can plant "deserters" with stories that they want you to hear — and both sides did. For the most part, military intelligence during the Civil War was as casual as the security it faced; and when, during the Peninsular Campaign, McClellan made a serious attempt to set up an intelligence corps, under Alan Pinkerton of detective-agency fame, the results were arguably less valuable than the commanding officer's guess. Pinkerton and his crew obtained reliable enough information, but for reasons known only to themselves they then interpreted the figures in a way which added whole brigades to the Confederate strength.

Spies and Scouts

The vast majority of military intelligence came either from spies or from scouts. There seem to have been more Southern sympathizers among the Union than vice versa, which is perhaps inevitable when you allow that the Union was the *status quo* while Confederates mostly recruited people dedicated to their cause. Sympathizers for the other side might, however, be anywhere; Lee's famous "Lost Order" (page 73) was less of a disaster than it might have been, because a Southern sympathizer in Pope's camp relayed the news of its discovery to Lee the day it happened. Especially for the South, women did much spying; their wartime role is recorded more fully on pages 220-221.

The Confederates made extensive use of cavalry as scouts; the way the Union army was organized (without a centralized cavalry command) meant that the North was more often in the dark about Southern movements. When Lee was deprived of cavalry intelligence, as at Gettysburg, he fought at a considerable disadvantage.

From time to time, each side would capture battle plans and other orders belonging to the enemy. This was unusual, though, and (for example) Jeb Stuart's capture of Pope's Union battle orders was probably accidental. It seems that Stuart was mainly out to discredit Pope and enhance his own reputation.

Aerial Observation

On June 18, 1861, Dr. Thaddeus Sobieski Constantine Lowe made history by being the first man to essay aerial observation from a tethered balloon connected by telegraph with the ground. At a height of 500 feet, Lowe reckoned he could cover an area about 50 miles in diameter. Like all Civil War balloons, his was an alarmingly inflammable hydrogen model, the gas produced by the action of sulfuric acid on metal filings.

The Corps of Balloonists was tiny, with seven trained aeronauts and half a dozen balloons at its peak, and it was disbanded in June 1863 after it had failed to produce any very worthwhile results. One major problem, of course, was the difficulty of interpreting aerial views. Although photography from a balloon had been shown to be possible by Nadar in France in 1858, wet-plate aerial photography was never really feasible, and the difficulties of getting an aeronaut and a skilled observer (to say nothing of telegraphic equipment and telegraphists) for on-the-spot work were insurmountable.

The Confederates, always poor, always flamboyant, always willing to make any sacrifice for the Cause, made a balloon from silk dresses willingly donated by Southern ladies; it was a patchwork of beautiful multi-colored fabrics. Intended for use in the Seven Days campaign, it was captured while inflated, *en route* to its intended destination. The Confederate General Longstreet wrote, "This capture was the meanest trick of the War and one that I have never forgiven."

Professor Lowe inflating his balloon at Gaines's Hill.

Confederate States
General Robert E. Lee
60,000 effectives
17,287 casualties*

United States
Major-General Joseph Hooker
134,000 effectives
12,764 casualties*

*Losses for campaign, April 27 — May 11, 1863.

N
O
S

0   1   2   miles
0   1   2   kilometers

HOOKER

Rapidan River   Elys Ford

US Ford

The Wilderness

Wilderness
Tavern

US Ford Road   Scotts Ford

Wilderness
Church

CHANCELLORSVILLE

Hazel Grove

Orange Turnpike

Brock Road

Orange Plank Road

Unfinished Railroad

LEE

THE BATTLE OF CHANCELLORSVILLE

Near Fredericksburg, Virginia.
May 1-4 1863

	CONFEDERATE	UNION
May 2		
May 3		
May 4		
Retreat 5 - 6 May		
Site of old road		

To all but the student of military history, the Chancellorsville campaign is inclined to be confusing. The Wilderness, in which much of it was decided, was to become much more prominent in the Battle of the Wilderness almost a year later; and of course Fredericksburg had been fought over in December the previous year.

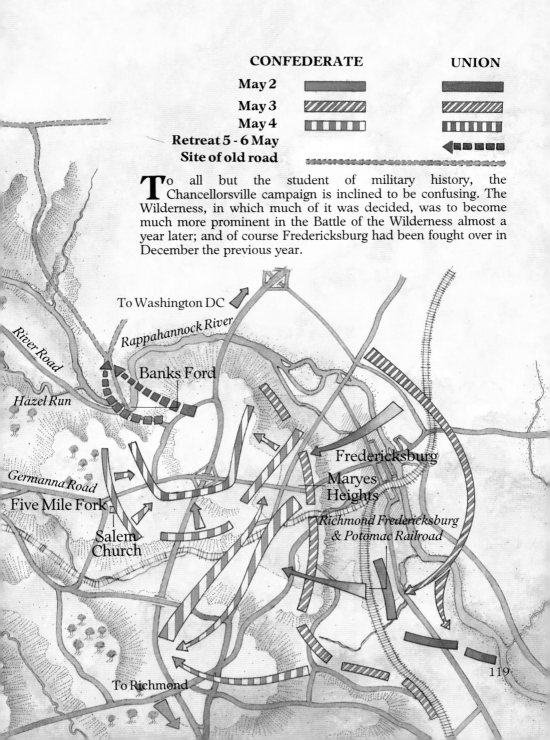

To Washington DC

Rappahannock River

River Road

Banks Ford

Hazel Run

Germanna Road

Five Mile Fork

Salem Church

Fredericksburg

Maryes Heights

Richmond Fredericksburg & Potomac Railroad

To Richmond

119

Even so, it is a crucial campaign. It marked the destruction of yet another of Lincoln's generals; it cleared the way for the second Confederate invasion of the North, leading ultimately to Gettysburg; and it was the last battle led by the seemingly invincible Lee-Jackson partnership, a stroke of staggering military genius overshadowed by Jackson's death.

A number of poignant images cling to the Chancellorsville campaign. One is the road which Jackson took on his historic march around the Union army — historic ground indeed, which can still be traversed today. Another is an old photograph, taken just after the Union had carried the Sunken Road at the foot of Marye's Heights; Confederate dead lie all along that road, which Burnside had been unable to take less than five months previously. A third image is the house where Jackson died, but we shall return to that later.

Confederate dead lying in the trenches at the foot of Marye's Heights, photographed only twenty minutes after the storming of the stone wall.

THE OPPOSING ARMIES

After Fredericksburg, there was something of a stalemate. Lee dug his army in so that it was even more secure; Burnside's army stagnated. Lee reorganized, acquired more small arms (about ten thousand stand) and dug a system of trenches which foreshadowed World War I. He was not worried about resisting an attack; later, outside Petersburg, several Union officers were to comment on the complexity and strength of Confederate trenches, compared with their own relatively simple fortifications.

Early in January, Burnside decided to march along the north of the Rappahannock in an attempt to attack and turn Lee's left (western) flank. An unseasonable thaw turned the attack into what is now known as the "Mud March;" icy rain and freezing mud stalled the Union utterly in a couple of days. Dispirited, they returned to winter quarters. On January 25, Lincoln made yet another change of command; after much politicking in Washington, "Fighting Joe" Hooker took over from Burnside. It was a popular appointment with the rank and file, though some senior officers in the army viewed the change with misgivings.

By April, "Fighting Joe" had reversed the decline in morale; set up a military intelligence network; improved the health and rations of the men; and built what he called "the finest army on the planet." He had almost 135,000 men in the Army of the Potomac, outnumbering Lee's forces better than two-to-one, with a three-to-one superiority in artillery. He had enforced excellent security by the simple expedient of telling no-one his plans, and he had grasped the point that "time is as valuable... as Rebel corpses."

THE CAMPAIGN

Hooker's plan was initially to disrupt the Confederate lines of communication using Stoneman's cavalry, thus luring Lee out and trapping the Confederate army between the Union cavalry and infantry.

Heavy rain put an end to that idea — the Union cavalry could not reliably cross the fords of the swollen Rapidan — so the revised plan was to use three corps to stage a demonstration below Fredericksburg, then throw the main bulk of the Union forces (under Meade, Howard and Slocum) on the Confederate left flank after crossing both the Rappahannock and the Rapidan. Kelly's Ford, on the Rapidan, is about 16 miles upstream of the confluence; Meade, Howard and Slocum were to cross there, and then to split so that Howard and Slocum crossed the Rappahannock at Germanna Ford (about 10 miles upstream of the confluence) while Meade crossed at Ely's Ford, just over 4 miles upstream of the confluence. Sickles's men then joined them by crossing the Rappahannock at U.S. Ford, about a mile downstream from the confluence.

Astonishingly, Hooker succeeded in outmaneuvring Lee. By April 30 he had 54,000 men concentrated on Lee's left flank; he had fooled Jeb Stuart's ever-watchful cavalry into thinking the Union forces were heading for the Shenandoah Valley; he had placed the Union cavalry behind Lee; he had got Sedgewick across the river at Fredericksburg; and he had secured all the crossing points.

On the night of May 1, Union troops were drawn up along a 6 mile front from the Rappahannock on their left flank to Talley's Farm, well beyond Wilderness Church, on their right. There was a strong salient on Fairview Hill (up to 350 feet) about half a mile south-west of Chancellorsville and in Chancellorsville itself. The Union position looked good.

The old Chancellor House, Chancellorsville, burned during the fighting.

Catharine Furnace, stop 8 on the Fredericksburg/ Spotsylvania park tour - one of the few landmarks of the Wilderness. Confederate munitions were manufactured here during the War.

TERRAIN

The terrain surrounding Fredericksburg has already been discussed, but Lee's lines were now more than 20 miles long, from Port Royal (on a bend in the Rappahannock over 3 miles west of Fredericksburg) almost to Banks's Ford (about 20 miles downstream). Chancellorsville is just under 10 miles west of Fredericksburg, about 4 miles south of the junction of the Rappahannock and the Rapidan. In 1863, Chancellorsville was noted chiefly for a large and flourishing inn. Now, even the ruins are barely visible.

Both the Rappahannock and the Rapidan flow roughly south-eastwards through fairly steep valleys; the Rappahannock and the Rapidan are about 120 feet above sea level where they join, but the river falls quite rapidly; ¾ mile downstream from the confluence, the river is at 110 feet, and it falls about 6 feet per mile thereafter. On either side of the river, there are steep bluffs or banks; slopes of 50% (45°) are commonplace. Banks's Ford is a relatively easy crossing, but the road on either side is steep and on the northern side the old road is now a mere trail.

This is typical of the Wilderness; a sudden clearing represents an occasional opportunity for the long-range artillerist.

From the river banks to Chancellorsville, and indeed for a mile or more to the south of Chancellorsville, the ground is very thickly wooded. After that, the south and east is rolling, cultivated land with some timber, but the area around Chancellorsville is known as the "Wilderness."

The Wilderness is dense, wooded country. The ground is still mostly rolling, but it is often steeper than it is to the south, lying mostly between 200 and 300 feet. It is swampy and intersected with many streams and rivulets; oak, maple, ash, cedar and fir grow in low, tangled profusion, sometimes linked together with dense networks of creepers and vines. In the spring, when this campaign was fought, the Wilderness is far from impenetrable but moving an army through such woods, where there are thickets big enough to conceal whole companies, is another matter. In General Warren's words, "a man could not march through it with musket in hand, unless he trailed it."

For such a sparsely-inhabited and uninviting area, the roads were surprisingly comprehensive. On the other hand, roads were effectively the *only* possibility for travel; blazing a trail through the Wilderness is difficult almost to the point of impossibility.

The "Plank Road" between Fredericksburg and Chancellorsville was made of planks 2 inches thick and 16 feet long, nailed to a parallel row of logs. It was not in good condition; some planks were missing, while others were broken or collapsed under the weight of military traffic. About 5 miles from Fredericksburg, going west, the Plank Road splits at Fivemile Fork; the Plank Road itself curves down to the south-west before going up to Chancellorsville, while the Turnpike is slightly more direct. The Pike ran across swampy terrain (where it was corduroyed and gravelled), but in good weather it was a faster road. Like the Plank Road, it was 16 feet wide. The VA 3 follows the Plank Road and the Turnpike.

The two roads united at Chancellorsville, ran west for a couple of miles, and then split again at Wilderness Church; the Turnpike was the right fork, running north-west to Wilderness Tavern, while the Orange Plank Road (now the VA 20) ran south-west towards Orange.

The other road of note was the River Road; a turning from the Plank Road about a mile before Salem Church led to Bank's Ford and then across the high ground (260-290 feet) which roughly parallels the south bank of the Rappahannock. Once again, the road terminates in Chancellorsville. This is now the VA 618.

The "Jackson Trail" is not a state road for most of its length, but it is well maintained in roughly the same condition as it was in 1862 (though much better surfaced, with graded gravel) and it is well signposted. From just east of Chancellorsville (a couple of miles west of Chancellor School, on the modern VA 5), it takes a great loop, first south-west and then north-west. It is open to automobiles.

The Jackson Trail. Jackson took this road to outflank the Union army during the campaign. The road is now well-graded gravel; in Jackson's day, it would have been mud and this ford churned to a morass by his 10-mile column.

DAY 1: MAY 2, 1863

Hooker was not ready, in his own words, "to undertake the impossible." Handicapped by poor knowledge of the terrain, he wanted a crushing majority to be sure of victory, and waited for reinforcements. Unfortunately for the Union, this delay allowed Lee and Jackson to formulate a breathtaking plan. Hailed by many as Lee's greatest victory, and by all as the highest point of the Lee-Jackson partnership, it was daring beyond belief. With the army already split

Lee and Jackson: the last conference.

(part in Fredericksburg, part marching to meet the Yankees), they split it yet again. Lee remained in place with fewer than 20,000 men, while Jackson's 26,000 marched all the way around the Union army so as to be to the rear of their right flank. When Jackson attacked, so would Lee.

The suspense must have been terrifying. Lee's army faced four times its own strength, and Jackson would be unable to come to his aid if the Union attacked; Lee would be wiped out. With a 10 mile column, 6 miles of soldiers and 4 of supplies, it seemed inconceivable that Jackson could get through without being seen; and if Union scouts spotted him at any point, and correctly divined what was happening, it would be the end of the campaign and indeed the War. In fact, Union scouts did *spot* Jackson, and Sickles's men attacked; but they only attacked the rearguard, and probably never realized at the time how close they came to ending the War. It took about six and a half hours to cover the 12 miles of roads, and about another three hours to deploy in the Wilderness.

At something before six o'clock in the evening, after percolating through the trees of the Wilderness, the Confederates charged the Union camp. It was an extraordinary sight. The Wilderness played host to a tremendous amount of wildlife and the animals and birds that lived among the thickets had been retreating as the Confederates advanced through their cover. Now, before the Confederates came into view, their charge was presaged by wildly leaping deer, the strange clockwork whirring of flushed pheasant, and a veritable tide of rabbits leaping like deranged mechanical toys out of the undergrowth. To the Union soldiers, many of whom were imbued with old-time religion, it must have looked like the very Day of Judgement.

Troops in the Wilderness were often cold, wet and uncomfortable but the diligent forager could generally find some food.

What was worse, they were utterly unprepared. Their muskets were stacked; many had relaxed for the evening, and were playing cards or lounging about. Their commanding officer had been warned at about noon that he might be attacked, but he had never really believed that the Wilderness was penetrable, and he disregarded the warning. His men broke and ran; Jackson's troops pressed them to within ¾ mile of Chancellorsville, an advance of about 3 miles. It was

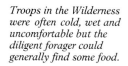

FORAGING IN THE WILDERNESS.

The tangled profusion of trees and undergrowth makes the Wilderness difficult terrain.

nightfall, as much as stiffening Union resistance, which halted the Confederate wave.

There was, however, a terrible price to be paid by the Confederacy. At about eight that evening, Jackson was wounded, and two of his aides were killed outright. The shots came from his own side, fighting in the "fog of war;" the general was in front of his own lines, making a reconnaissance. Jackson's wounds were far from mortal, but they were serious; one ball was lodged in his right hand, a second passed through his left wrist, and a third had also hit in the left arm: "The large bone of the upper arm was splintered to the elbow-joint."

Jackson himself ordered the fact that he had been wounded to be concealed from his men; he did not want them to lose heart. But as he was being carried on a rough stretcher to the nearest road, one of the stretcher-bearers tripped and dropped the general on his wounded arm. Even when they got him to an ambulance, the journey was agony. His last command on the field, before he was loaded onto the ambulance, was, "You must hold your ground, General Pender; you must hold your ground, sir!"

When Lee heard about the incident, he is reported to have said that Jackson had lost his left arm, but that he (Lee) had lost his right arm. In his letter to Jackson, he said, "Could I have directed events, I should have chosen, for the good of the country, to have been disabled in your stead. I congratulate you upon the victory which is due to your skill and energy." When this was read to Jackson, he turned his face away and said, "General Lee is very kind, but he should give the praise to God."

He was never to fight again. The arm was amputated, but Jackson had driven himself too hard for too long; he succumbed to pneumonia, and died on the afternoon of May 10, at about a quarter past three. His last words were, "Order A.P. Hill to prepare for action — pass the infantry to the front rapidly — tell Major Hawks —" He broke off for a moment, and then said, "No, no, let us pass over the river, and rest under the shade of the trees."

"Stonewall" Jackson's arm is buried in the family churchyard of the Lacy House, Ellwood, which later served as a headquarters for Union troops during the Battle of the Wilderness.

DAY 2: MAY 3, 1863

The Rebel armies were now divided in three. Jackson's men (about 26,000 in number, now under Stuart) were just west of Chancellorsville; Anderson's and McLaws's men (17,000 in total) were no more than a couple of miles away, to the east; and a relatively tiny force of 10,000 men under Jubal Early was prepared to defend the same positions that the Confederates had held at the Battle of Fredericksburg in December. Arguably, Hooker should have been able to destroy them piecemeal but he allowed Lee to call the shots all through the campaign.

The Confederates around Chancellorsville renewed their attack at dawn, driving the Yankee salient back towards the north; by the afternoon, the Rebels were north of the River Road and the Plank Road between Chancellorsville and Wilderness Church.

The Yankees had, however, reached a strong position. Their right flank was anchored on the Rapidan, their left on the Rappahannock. There was no real prospect of dislodging them, the more so as they controlled an excellent line of retreat via the U.S. Ford which Sickles had so recently crossed. On the other hand, they were surrounded, they were beaten, and they knew it.

Meanwhile, Early's lines at the foot of Marye's Heights had been far too thin to withstand the Union attack for long, although it was not until the fourth attack that the Union forces broke through. The Confederates then fell back in an orderly manner, fighting a rearguard action.

Lee, realizing the strength of his own position, detached McLaws's men from the Confederates encircling Hooker and sent them towards Fredericksburg. At Salem Church, the reinforced Rebel army halted the Union advance. As with the earlier battle that day, it was a dogged fight without any special characteristics; brave men just fought one another to a standstill.

DAY 3: MAY 4, 1863

Hooker was no longer "Fighting Joe." Lee had stopped him, reversed him, and bottled him up. Stuart, with 25,000 men, held Hooker's 75,000, but Hooker did not even attempt an attack. Instead, he seemed to hope that Lee would make the supreme mistake of attacking him, while all that Lee had to do was to wait. Lee improved upon waiting; understanding Hooker's defensive turn of mind, he ordered Early's men to join McLaws's and to attack not Hooker, but Sedgewick's Union forces.

THE JACKSON SHRINE

One of the most moving memorials of the entire War is the house where Jackson died, now maintained by the Park Service. Originally just an out-building to the main dwelling, which is now long gone, it was used to house Jackson for fear of cross-infection with the wounded in the main house. The room where he died, with the original bed, is preserved. On the mantelshelf, the same clock ticks away the minutes as ticked away Jackson's life. He died a few days after seeing his baby daughter for the first time.

The Jackson Shrine.

Sedgewick, near Salem Church, was well placed to fall back in such a way that both of his flanks were anchored by the river. When Lee's army finally attacked in the afternoon, he was able to withstand the attack. This was the last battle of the campaign; the Union held the Confederates off until nightfall, withdrawing in good order across the Rappahannock (via Scott's Ford) under cover of darkness. Nothing happened on May 5; that night, Hooker's men also withdrew, via the U.S. Ford.

THE AFTERMATH

Lee and Jackson had learned by their mistakes at Seven Pines and during the Seven Days; but on the other side, Washington wanted a scapegoat, not a general who learned by his mistakes. Hooker was ready to fight again by mid-May, but he was summoned to Washington by Lincoln who effectively forbade him to fight. Lee commenced an invasion of the North, crossing the Potomac in late June; Hooker and Halleck (the latter safely in Washington) differed on how to handle things, and as so often, the man in the field was overruled by the man in Washington. On June 28, after being accused of vacillation, Hooker was replaced with Major-General George Gordon Meade.

FURTHER INFORMATION

Maps: USGS 7.5': Chancellorsville; Mine Run;
Fredericksburg;
Salem Church; Brokenburg; Spotsylvania
Official Reports Atlas: 41/1; 93/2; 135/6
B&L: 155; 158; 191; 201

Park: The main Park Center can be reached quickly from Fredericksburg. It is small, with a modest orientation program which is somewhat given to purple prose. The staff are helpful and knowledgeable. Several sites are unmanned; the house where Jackson's arm is buried requires special permission (readily given) to visit. Supervisor: Fredericksburg and Spotsylvania National Military Park, PO Box 679, Fredericksburg, VA 22404.

Town: see FREDERICKSBURG, page 103.

MEDICINE

Because so much about the Civil War seems familiar — because, indeed, many of our readers may have met or known Civil War veterans personally — it is easy to forget the many areas in which the 1860s were closer to medieval times than to our own. An example is medicine.

Sulfa drugs were not introduced until the 1930s; antibiotics did not appear until 1941. Even anesthesia was in its earliest days; ether and chloroform had been known for almost 20 years, but cocaine as a local anesthetic was still in the future; opiates were used more for recreation than for medicine, and although morphia was a recognized anesthetic it was often used in conjunction with whisky. Many surgeons on both sides had no formal qualifications, but had learned medicine via a formal or informal apprenticeship to doctors who might have learned their business in the eighteenth century.

An infected wound often meant either amputation (if practicable) or death; over 60 per cent of Union soldiers with gunshot wounds to the chest died, and for abdominal wounds (where peritonitis was a virtual certainty), the figure was close to 90 per cent. Even getting to the field hospital, staggering on a comrade's arm or bounced on a crude litter or hospital wagon, was agony; there are many

Field hospital with graves; according to the original caption, this is a field hospital at City Point. Most of the graves here would be the result of disease, not wounds.

Interior of a US hospital ship, from a wartime sketch. The goat cannot have been conducive to hygiene or to fresh air, though goats' milk might have been welcome.

accounts of wounded men begging to be put out of their misery as they lay on the battlefield.

Amputation was meant to stop the spread of infection, but it was often dangerous in itself; surgeons never formally "scrubbed up" for an operation, and indeed wore old clothes crusted with dried blood and pus as operating gowns. They habitually used the same instruments repeatedly with no more attempt at sterilization than a cursory wash. One reason why Confederates sometimes survived better than Union soldiers was that a shortage of supplies required Confederate surgeons to clean wounds (which were often infected) with scraps of cloth, which were washed before they were used and then thrown away. Union surgeons used sponges to mop up blood and pus, then squeezed them out a few times in water between patients. Amputations were best performed around the battlefield; if they waited until the patient got to hospital, he normally died anyway.

Sickness and Disease

You did not need to be wounded in order to be at risk. Most soldiers lived in filth, some from lack of opportunity to wash and others from sheer indifference — young farm-hands in their teens and twenties were by no means uniformly persuaded of the virtues of bathing. Lice and vermin of all kinds perpetuated disease, but their bites were regarded as more of a nuisance than as carriers of disease. Few accurate figures exist, especially for the Confederates, but most authorities agree that for every man who died as a result of battle, two or three died of disease.

Dysentery, prevalent because of contaminated water supplies, was often treated with oil of turpentine; typhoid and paratyphoid, which claimed many more, were lumped together with malaria as "typhomalarial fever." The use of quinine as an antimalarial agent was known, though it was far from regularly administered or even regularly available; the Union blockade was designed to stop such drugs from reaching the Confederates.

Pneumonia killed almost 20,000 Union troops and an unknown number of Confederates; others died of smallpox and even measles. Tuberculosis, then called "consumption," was commonplace; over 20,000 Union soldiers were discharged suffering from the disease. Many deaths in prisoner of war camps were attributable to malnutrition. There were also times when scurvy was a real problem, especially after the Burning of the Valley or the March to the Sea.

To Chambersburg

Blacks Turnpike

Oak Ridge

Carlisle Road

Rock Creek

To Harrisburg

Oak Hill

Barlow Knoll

Western Maryland Railroad

Chambersburg Turnpike

Herr Ridge

McPherson Ridge

GETTYSBURG

Gettysburg & Hanover Railroad

York Turnpike

Benners Hill

Millerstown Road

Confederate Avenue

Observation Tower

Culps Hill

LEE

Seminary Ridge

Spanglers Spring

Willoughby Run

Cemetery Ridge

Powers Hill

Peach Orchard
Observation Tower

MEADE

Wheatfield

Little Round Top

Emmitsburg Road

Devils Den

Big Round Top

Taneytown Road

To Washington DC

Plum Run

To Taneytown

THE BATTLE OF GETTYSBURG

Gettysburg, Pennsylvania
July 1-3 1863

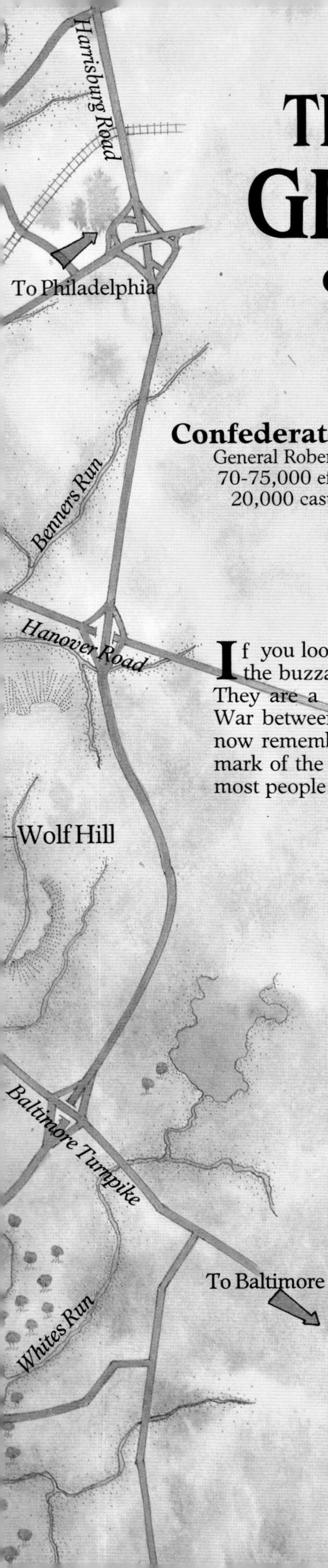

To Philadelphia

Confederate States
General Robert E. Lee
70-75,000 effectives
20,000 casualties

United States
Major-General George G. Meade
85,000 effectives
23,000 casualties

Harrisburg Road

Benners Run

Hanover Road

Wolf Hill

Baltimore Turnpike

Whites Run

To Baltimore

If you look down from Little Round Top at dawn, you will see the buzzards sunning themselves in the first rays of the sun. They are a chilling reminder of the most famous battle of the War between the States. What is more, although Gettysburg is now remembered as a great Union victory and the "high-water mark of the Confederacy," it was a far closer-fought battle than most people realize.

CONFEDERATE		UNION	
July 1	▬		▬
July 2	▨		▨
July 3	▥		▥

| 0 | | 1 | miles |
| 0 | | 1 | kilometers |

THE CONFEDERATE INVASION OF THE NORTH

On June 19, Ewell's Confederates crossed the Potomac to begin the second Confederate invasion of the North, a desperate attempt to gain recognition from the European powers. Longstreet and Hill followed on June 24. For the first week or so, Lee's advance was substantially unchecked. The former Union commander, Major-General Hooker, had been content to march the Army of the Potomac on a course roughly paralleling Lee's, keeping between Lee and Washington; his caution was why Lincoln made yet another change of command and replaced him with Meade on June 27, though Major-General Hunt (of the Union army) refers to Lee's "belief that the chronic terror of the War Department for the safety of Washington could be safely relied upon to paralyze his (opponent's) movements."

Gettysburg was not chosen as a battlefield by either side, but the accident of geography seems quite understandable in retrospect. The town is at the junction of a surprising number of roads; it was a virtual certainty that one army, or both, would march through the little town. As it was, A.P. Hill's Confederate forces were looking for Union supplies — including shoes — when they ran into Buford's men; it was Buford's request to Meade for support which determined the site of the battle.

THE ROADS TO GETTYSBURG

The roads leading into Gettysburg are known by a variety of names. In the list below, the main names are taken from Gouverneur Warren's map which accompanied the *Official Reports*; the names in brackets are alternatives, either contemporary or modern. They begin with the road which runs due north: Carlisle Road (Middletown Road, PA 34 North), Harrisburg Road (Heidlersburg Road, US 15 Business North), York Turnpike (Lincoln Highway, US 30 East), Bonaughton Road (Hanover Road, PA 116 East), Baltimore Turnpike (US 140), Taneytown Road (PA 134), Emmitsburg Road (US 15 Business West), Millerstown Road (Hagerstown Road, Fairfield Road, PA 116 West), Chambersburg Turnpike (US 30 West), Black's Turnpike (Mummasburg Road).

The Gettysburg and Hanover Railroad also runs east-west through the town, though in 1863 it stopped just to the west; the unfinished and partially graded rail bed ran on to the west.

THE OPPOSING ARMIES

Lee had lost Stonewall Jackson in May, and at Gettysburg he was further handicapped by the absence of Jeb Stuart, whose cavalry normally acted as the eyes and ears of the Confederate forces. Stuart had taken a large interpretation of Lee's orders to ride between the Federal army and Washington; an interpretation which a cynic might say was more designed to boost the reputation of Stuart and his cavalry (which had suffered on June 9 at Brandy Station) than to be of any military use, though John Mosby gives a different view in *Battles and Leaders*.

Unsure of the whereabouts of the Union men, Lee had to rely on probing to find them.

On the other side, Meade was ready to fight — that was why he had been appointed — but he naturally wanted to fight on ground of his own choosing. As he advanced, he kept his corps within supporting distance of one another, marching them at a fierce pace reminiscent of Jackson's "foot cavalry."

On June 30, Union troops had occupied the town itself and were extended slightly to the north; Confederate troops were massing to the north and west. Meade himself was not yet present; on June 28, he was still 40 miles south of Gettysburg, and he did not arrive until almost midnight on July 1.

TERRAIN

The battlefield of Gettysburg can best be thought of as a rectangle rather more than 2 miles wide and 4-5 miles long, with its longer axis running roughly north-south; the town of Gettysburg itself is near the top of the rectangle.

The terrain is widely varied. In the north, it is mostly open farmland, though there are small areas of wooded, rugged terrain with thick ground cover intersected with creeks and streams. About ¾ mile east of the center of town is Rock Creek, while Willoughby Run is about a mile to the west. Both flow southwards, diverging slightly as they do so. The town is on relatively flat ground mostly between 520 and 540 feet, though within those limits there are quite marked hills. The lowest ground is at about 500 feet.

The Slaughter Pen at the foot of Round Top, seen here on the day after the battle.

Cemetery Hill, where the Union troops regrouped on the evening of July 1, after being routed by Jubal Early's men.

To the south of the town, there are two roughly parallel north-south ridges, Cemetery Ridge and Seminary Ridge, about ¾ mile apart. The Emmitsburg Road runs between them.

Cemetery Ridge, to the east, is slightly higher (mostly 560 feet to 600 feet) and takes its name from the old town cemetery on Cemetery Hill (about 620 feet) to the immediate south-east of the town. Culp's Hill (about 620 feet again) is about ½ mile to the east of Cemetery Hill and slightly to the south. If you follow Cemetery Ridge southwards for about 2 miles, you come first to Little Round Top (650 feet) and then to Round Top itself, 785 feet at its highest point.

Seminary Ridge, to the west, takes its name from the Lutheran seminary which still stands in the town; its cupola was a Confederate lookout post during the battle. Seminary Ridge is lower than Cemetery Ridge, rarely rising above 560 feet and only reaching 580 feet in a few places. Unlike Cemetery Ridge, there are no large hills to command either end of the high ground.

The ground between the two ridges is mostly rolling farmland, with some woods and small clumps of trees; the lowest point is once again at about 500 feet. The hills are mostly fairly smooth, except at Little Round Top. This is a granite outcrop, very craggy and rough, and at the foot of Little Round Top between the two lines is a jumble of huge boulders known as the Devil's Den.

Round Top - Cemetery Ridge is shaped rather like a fish hook, and Round Top forms the extreme stem of the hook.

DAY 1: JULY 1, 1863

The first day's battle began to the west of the town, on the Chambersburg-Gettysburg Pike, as Confederates of A.P. Hill's corps probing for Union forces encountered Buford's dismounted cavalry at about 8 am. It was a cold, drizzling dawn when the first shots were fired.

During the morning, the fighting was mostly a mile or two west of the center of Gettysburg, around the Pike, Herr Ridge (600 feet), McPherson's Ridge (540-560 feet) and Willoughby's Run, a tributary of Marsh Creek. Two divisions of the Eleventh Federal Corps under Howard moved up to Oak Ridge (600-640 feet) to the NNW of the town, but they were hard pressed by Jubal Early's Confederates of Ewell's corps. Neither Union nor Confederate troops could be entirely sure of the other side's strength or position, and the fighting was indecisive. Before noon, both sides were reinforced as forces concentrated around Gettysburg.

In the afternoon of the first day, the Union lines broke after the death of Major-General Reynolds; when Jubal Early's men overran the Union's right flank at Barlow's Knoll, the Union retreat became a rout. They fled through the town to regroup on the first promising bit of high ground, Cemetery Hill.

This is the first place in which the tide of battle could have turned. It is far from inconceivable that Lee's forces could have carried Cemetery Hill that evening, turning Gettysburg into a Union defeat; perhaps if Jackson had been alive, it would have been done. Ewell, on the other hand, did not press the charge; his delay was fatal, as it lost the initiative and allowed the Union to dig in.

What is more, it probably lost the Confederacy's chance to achieve European recognition. It might not have been a decisive defeat — Meade's Army of the Potomac would almost certainly

The cupola of the Lutheran seminary at Gettysburg, which gave Seminary Ridge its name, was used as an observation post by the Confederates.

have survived to fight again — but a victory on Yankee ground might have caused Britain and France to recognize the new nation.

In all fairness, though, it is easy for an armchair warrior to say this. Faced with the task of storming Cemetery Hill, musket in hand, with very little cover, it suddenly looks more forbidding. Imagine yourself bone-weary after fighting all day; a brisk walk up the hill is hard enough work, without anyone shooting at you. The grass is slightly slippery today; in 1863 it would have been muddy, bloody, and even more treacherous. In the absence of miracles — or genius — this is the sort of detail that decides a battle; and miracles and genius did not smile upon the Confederacy at Cemetery Hill.

By and large, the fighting on the first day is considerably more difficult to visualize than the events which would later take place between Cemetery Ridge and Seminary Ridge, but a knowledge of the first day makes the second and third days easier to understand. Images come to mind: the tired but wary Confederates, who had been up since 5 am or so, running into Buford's men; a sudden exchange of fire, a search for cover; the smell of powder hanging in the damp air among the trees in McPherson's Woods and along Oak Ridge; the death of Reynolds; the Union realization "We Cannot Hold!;" the retreat.

Little and Big Round Top - if Warren, the Union general, had failed to capture Little Round Top, the Confederates might have won at Gettysburg.

DAY 2: JULY 2, 1863

The Union army was now drawn up along Cemetery Ridge, facing the Confederates who were mostly on Seminary Ridge. The Union line was shaped like an inverted fish-hook, curving back from Cemetery Hill to Culp's Hill. This gave them the advantage of a short overall line (about 3 miles), while Lee was forced to adopt an exterior line which was effectively 9 miles between flanks.

Meade assessed his position as weak, but not untenable; in any case, there was no possibility of changing it. Fearing a dawn attack, which could have swept his armies off Cemetery Ridge, he had overnight strengthened his right (northern) flank, where he knew the concentration of rebels to be greatest and where he felt an attack was most likely.

The Yankees had hurriedly dug in; both sides had been fighting long enough by now to realize the value of trenches, however quickly contrived. During the previous night, both sides had filled their canteens in the no-man's-land between the two lines at Spangler's Spring, south-east of Culp's Hill. A few shots had been fired, and there had been scuffles, but it is likely that a tacit truce prevented further trouble; the generals were not about to fight a battle there, and the men had enough to look forward to without trying any freelance heroics.

Cemetery Hill

The obvious choice for the Rebels was to try to roll up the Union line from either Cemetery Hill or Little Round Top, and they tried both. The main battlefield was to be between the two ridges, at the left (south) end of the Union line, but there was also a great deal of hard fighting around Cemetery Hill and Culp's Hill. Had the Confederates attacked at dawn, as Meade feared, they might have won; but poor communications and an almost non-existent staff structure meant that the attack did not come until the middle of the afternoon. Cemetery Hill was actually taken by Jubal Early's Confederates in the evening, though they were forced to retreat when they were not reinforced. Culp's Hill was successfully held by Union forces under General George Green.

Little Round Top

Rolling up the Yankees from the other end would have been almost a foregone conclusion if it had not been for the action of Brigadier-General Gouverneur Warren. Because Meade expected an attack on his right flank, he did not bother at first to occupy Little Round Top, but if the Confederates had taken it, the Union position on Cemetery Ridge would have been extremely

GOUVERNEUR KEMBLE WARREN

Warren was 33 at Gettysburg; he was born on January 8, 1830. After graduating from West Point in 1850, he served in the Corps of Topographical Engineers and taught mathematics at West Point. He was appointed Brigadier-General in 1862.

For a man who did more than most — perhaps more than any — to save the Union, his military career subsequent to Gettysburg (where he was wounded in the neck by a piece of shell) was sadly blighted. He was apppointed Major-General in August 1863, but inaccurate and unfair charges of sloth and incompetence were brought in 1865 by Grant and Sheridan. Not for 14 years was a court of inquiry called; when it was, it took almost two years but finally exonerated him from the four principal charges against him (though they still criticized him for sloth). The results were published on November 21, 1882, three months after his death at the age of 52.

difficult. Fortunately for the Union, Warren decided on his own initiative to gather forces to occupy this crucial position; his troops scrambled up the northern and eastern slopes, and almost immediately had to repulse a ferocious attack by Confederates climbing from the south and west. If Warren had failed to secure Little Round Top, then Gettysburg might still have been a Confederate victory.

The Devil's Den, as this area of rugged boulders was known locally, was the scene of the bloodiest fighting of the battle. It was from the cover of these boulders that Confederate sharpshooters fired on Little Round Top.

Sickles and the "Slaughter Pen"

Also without permission, and with considerably less justification, Major-General Daniel Sickles had decided to occupy the Devil's Den and much of the ground between the ridge and the Emmitsburg Road, including a wheatfield and a peach orchard. From the need for Gouverneur Warren's action, and from the way in which Sickles made his ill-considered salient, it is clear that Meade was by no means fully in control at Gettysburg. Meade actually told Sickles that he was too far out, but agreed that it was too late to retreat; the enemy would not permit it.

In savage fighting on July 2, the Union was forced to give up much of this ground; the fighting raged to and fro, with ground being taken and lost, then gained and lost again. By the end of the day, the Confederates held the Devil's Den, the Wheatfield, and the Peach Orchard. The losses on both sides were awful; the area at the foot of Little Round Top became known as the "Slaughter Pen," an image perhaps more telling to the men who fought there than it is today. Many were farm-hands, used to slaughtering cattle and hogs, and now they were being slaughtered themselves; when the Minnesota Regiment counterattacked against Wilcox's Confederate charge — a single regiment of Yankees against a whole brigade of Rebels — they suffered more than 80% casualties. In other words, only one in five survived. The South had no monopoly on courage.

Despite Confederate successes, at the end of the day the Union army was still well placed on Cemetery Ridge, with control of the high ground on either flank. Meade very wisely decided to dig in all along the ridge, rather than to risk the offensive, thereby forcing Lee to attack as fast as possible before the Union position became impregnable.

Stand on Little Round Top in the morning, with the light behind you as you look across to the Confederate lines; the Devil's Den just after sunrise, when the sun has risen over Little Round Top and strikes the rocks, is awe-inspiringly lonely and frightening. Remember: when the battle was fought, none of the roads that you now see was there, except the Emmitsburg road which you cross briefly.

DAY 3: JULY 3, 1863

On July 3, dawn broke on something of an impasse. The Confederates had pressed the Union line hard, and had taken a great deal of ground, especially the terrain which Sickles had so ill-advisedly tried to occupy. The Union line was, however, very strong: they were on high ground, with natural defenses augmented by whatever their engineers could quickly contrive. The Confederates were in hostile territory, and had to take the initiative if they were to accomplish anything.

In the morning, while it was still relatively cool, the Union tidied up its own lines by concentrating on Confederate positions at Spangler's Spring on the Union's northern (right) flank. They succeeded in driving the Rebels off, but the battle was not to be decided until the afternoon. The heat, actual as well as metaphorical, built steadily.

Pickett's Charge

Having failed to gain either Union flank, Lee took the momentous decision to launch a charge against the very center of the Union lines. He ordered a massive artillery barrage commencing at 1 pm — most of the morning was spent deploying artillery — followed by an infantry charge. The charge was to be spearheaded by the only fresh division available to him, 4,500 men under the command of Major-General George E. Pickett.

The artillery lines were about 750 yards apart at their closest point, and the men were several hundred yards behind the Confederate artillery. At Lee's command, the thunderous barrage ceased and something between 10,000 and 15,000 Confederates advanced on the Union lines, into withering small-arms and cannon fire. They erupted from positions spread across a mile and a half, and although they converged as they began to approach the Yankees, they still advanced as a mile-wide army. Dressed in their ragged grey, many barefoot, many hungry, they advanced as if they were on a parade ground; they even paused to reform ranks after they crossed obstacles.

Pickett's famous charge reached as far as a copse of trees known as The Angle before it was repulsed. This achievement is marked by the High Water Mark, and, indeed, the Battle of Gettysburg is itself known as the High Water Mark of the Confederacy.

GEORGE EDWARD PICKETT

George Pickett was born on January 28, 1825, and graduated from West Point in 1846. At 38, he led the charge which was to bear his name, "with his jaunty cap raked well over on his right ear and his long auburn locks, nicely dressed, hanging almost to his shoulders."

It was his only real moment of military glory but the charge was hopeless; he did not have enough men. He became an insurance salesman after the War and died on July 30 1875 aged 50.

Pickett's Charge impressed everyone who saw it. Men were cut down first by exploding case, then by solid shot, then by canister, and finally by the awesome double canister, like a monster sawed-off shotgun; small-arms fire, at first at maximum range but eventually point-blank, mowed down more. Still they came on in perfect order. Southern battle-standards fell, and were lifted again by willing hands, only to fall once more — and be lifted again. It was as if the colors were more valuable than life itself.

As it was, they reached the Union lines; but as the Confederate General A.R. Wright put it, "It is not so hard to go there as it looks; I was nearly there with my brigade yesterday. The trouble is to *stay there*. The whole Yankee army is there in a bunch."

The fighting around the little clump of trees — now immortalized as "the angle" — was tremendous; the Confederate General Armistead was killed as he led 200 men to silence the Yankee batteries. Then, Union flank attacks drove the Confederates back, and Lee waited for the counterattack — which never came. Next day began the retreat to Hagerstown.

FURTHER INFORMATION

Maps: USGS 7.5': Gettysburg and Fairfield
Official Reports Atlas: 28/4; 40/2; 43/1,2; 73/6; 95/1,2
B&L: 246; 257; 262 (5); 264 (3); 266 (2); 272 (4); 282; 292; 299; 308; 344; 381 (7); 382 (2); 394; 400 (2)

Book: Jay Luvas and Harold W. Nelson, *The U.S. Army War College Guide to the Battle of Gettysburg* (South Mountain Press, Carlisle, PA, 1986; paperback edition Harper and Row, 1987). Extremely detailed but very informative. Several excellent pamphlets are available at the Visitor Center.

Park: A superb park; the Park Museum is the best on any battlefield, and the Electric Map (for which there is an admission charge) makes the action clearer; there is no orientation film or slide/tape show. In the picnic areas, alcohol is not specifically prohibited. Superintendent: Gettysburg National Military Park, Gettysburg, PA 17325.

Town: Gettysburg is the most intensively promoted battlefield of the War. The best museum is at the Park Visitor Center.

MONUMENTS

The very first monuments — stone cairns or upended cannon — were erected during the War. The first paid-for sculpted monument, to Hazen's Union soldiers at Murfreesboro, was built late in 1863.

For well over half a century after the War, monuments were erected commemorating armies, regiments, batteries, individuals and events. At first, the rich North put up far more and to this day, there are far fewer Southern memorials than Northern. Many Southern monuments were built with funds raised by the United Daughters of the Confederacy.

Stone Monuments

These range from simple slabs and modest memorials no larger than an ornate tombstone to huge obelisks and indeed pseudo-mausolea. The quality varies widely, but some are very immediate. Riflemen are often depicted; there are some cavalrymen; and a draped cannon may sound like rather obvious symbolism, but you may be surprised to feel your eyelids pricking.

Of the pseudo-mausolea, the Illinois monument in Vicksburg is probably the most impressive, a massive work of white marble built in the early years of the twentieth century.

Bronzes

Especially memorable are the Rhode Island monument at Vicksburg and some of the Confederate monumental bronzes at Gettysburg. In the latter, the sculptor has captured magnificently the half-starved, wild-eyed Confederate soldier with his broken shoes, fighting against impossible odds.

Other Monuments

Piles of cannonballs mark the sites of headquarters or important events at a number of the more Southern battlefields, especially Shiloh and Stone's River. At Fredericksburg, one of the original rough cairns has been cemented together and is now known as the Meade pyramid; it is beside the railroad tracks, visible from Stop 4 of the self-guided tour. At Antietam, upended cannon mark many important places.

Historical Markers

Cast-iron markers found by the roadside all over the country were erected in the 1930s and cover not only Civil War events. These markers can be hard to spot and even harder to park near. So exercise extreme caution when stopping!

The National Parks Service uses similar markers in cast light alloy rather than cast iron; these are rather easier to read, and are often coded with a blue background (for the Union) and red (for the Confederacy). The Park Service also uses more modern plastic markers.

The Mississippi monument, which was paid for with Confederate funds. Most Confederate monuments date from later than their Union counterparts and the majority were financed by small-scale fundraising activities.

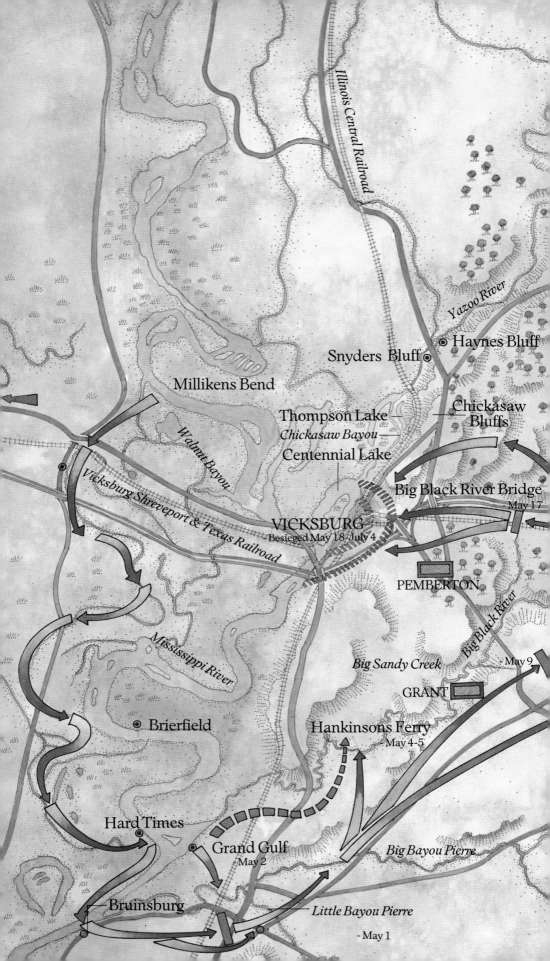

Illinois Central Railroad

Yazoo River

Haynes Bluff

Snyders Bluff

Millikens Bend

Thompson Lake

Chickasaw Bluffs

Chickasaw Bayou

Centennial Lake

Walnut Bayou

Big Black River Bridge
May 17

Vicksburg Shreveport & Texas Railroad

VICKSBURG
Besieged May 18-July 4

PEMBERTON

Big Black River

Mississippi River

Big Sandy Creek

May 9

GRANT

Brierfield

Hankinsons Ferry
May 4-5

Hard Times

Big Bayou Pierre

Grand Gulf
May 2

Bruinsburg

Little Bayou Pierre

May 1

THE SIEGE OF VICKSBURG

Vicksburg, Mississippi
December 27 1862 - July 4 1863

Confederate States
General Ulysses S. Grant
45-70,000 men*

United States
Lieutenant-General John C. Pemberton
20,000 men*

*The Union was constantly reinforced throughout the campaign; the Confederate figure is a good estimate. In view of the length of the campaign and the number of Confederate prisoners taken, meaningful casualty figures are not feasible for either side.

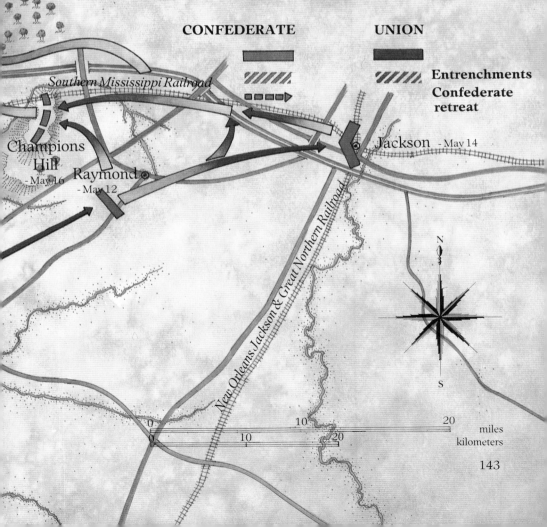

CONFEDERATE   UNION

Entrenchments
Confederate retreat

Southern Mississippi Railroad

Jackson - May 14

Champions Hill - May 16

Raymond - May 12

New Orleans Jackson & Great Northern Railroad

N
S

0   10   20
0   10   20
miles
kilometers

Vicksburg in the 1860s, when its prominent position on the Mississippi made it a center of commerce and industry.

The images of Vicksburg that you carry in your head and your heart are quite different. Modern Vicksburg is a very attractive city, seemingly little bigger that it was in the 1860s; the downtown area is full of attractive buildings, and there are some very fine shops. The battlefield is now one of the most beautiful of the National Military Parks, a marvelous combination of tangled, almost impenetrable woodland and superbly tended grass. There are extraordinary vistas, both man-made and natural.

And yet, as you walk around either the city or the park, there is always another image in the back of your mind — or, as we have said above, in your heart. It is the image of raw earth covered with crude tents and pocked with bombproofs; of the people of Vicksburg growing hungrier and hungrier, until the soldiers ate their mules and horses and begged to be allowed to scrape the bowls a few fortunate citizens still had the corn-meal to fill; of life in caves hollowed from the hillsides; of children with unnaturally rosy faces and bright eyes, permanently running a fever; of screaming shells and bursting bombs, landing on soldier and civilian alike.

THE IMPORTANCE OF VICKSBURG

Vicksburg in the 1860s controlled the Mississippi. In those days, the river followed a different course from today's; the town was on a great bluff, commanding the river absolutely. Guns on the water batteries were in a position to permit or deny passage of the river. As long as the Confederates held Vicksburg, they held the Mississippi, which meant not only that they had access to the rich farmlands (and industrial production) of the West; they could also deny the Union the chance of moving supplies.

What was more, Vicksburg was of great symbolic importance. It is hard to realize nowadays how small most cities were in those days; Vicksburg was no backwater, but a commercial and

144

even industrial center. It was also well fortified; the river and the surrounding wetlands of the Yazoo Delta protected most of it, so the only real possibility for the Union was to get "behind" the city and try to attack it from the south and east — inside territory either held by, or friendly to, the Confederacy. If Vicksburg fell, it would be a huge blow to morale, a great loss to the Confederacy.

The USS Cairo, *as she was at the time of the War.*

THE *CAIRO* **AND THE** *ARKANSAS*

The USS *Cairo* was a City-class ironclad or "Pook Turtle" used in several Mississippi engagements including Fort Henry and Fort Donelson as well as at Vicksburg. She was sunk on December 12, 1863, by an "infernal machine" or "torpedo" — what we would now call a mine — and sank without loss of life. The salvaged *Cairo* is now on display at the National Military Park, together with an excellent museum.

The CSS *Arkansas* was a patched-together ironclad, armored with railroad iron. On July 15, after Vicksburg had fallen, she ran the gauntlet of the entire Union fleet stationed at Vicksburg — odds of more than thirty to one. She damaged a number of Yankee ships, at least one (the USS *Lancaster*) seriously. During the engagement, the steam pressure in the boilers of her rickety engines fell from 130 pounds to 20 pounds (psi), barely enough to move her, but she was never defeated. She was abandoned and burned by her crew on August 4, 1863, to prevent capture by the Yankees; her engines had given out completely. At the time of writing, plans are afoot to build a replica.

The Confederate ram Arkansas *running through the Union fleet at Vicksburg, July 15, 1862.*

TERRAIN

This view from the bluffs north of Vicksburg shows first, how high the bluffs are, and second, the old course of the Mississippi.

Matters are somewhat confused by the fact that the Yazoo Delta is a flatland of constantly changing bayous and rivers. Even the great Mississippi changes its course periodically, and in 1863 it followed the course of what is now the Yazoo River and Centennial Lake. Now, of course, it flows due east for several miles towards Vicksburg, then swings south-west again at the southern extremity of the city. In geographical terms, the new course created what is known as an ox-bow lake over 2 miles long from north to south and perhaps a mile between the open parts of the hairpin.

Even so, the overall elevations remain very similar. The river is (and was) at about 50 feet above sea level; Vicksburg, at its highest point, rises some 240 feet above sea level, almost 200 feet above the river. Even the low areas of the town are typically 20-40 feet above the water level, and within 500 yards of the banks the ground is at an elevation of 200 feet or more (150 feet or more above the river).

To the north and east of the town, steep hills and bluffs of up to 350 feet are intersected by deep bayous, and the ground cover is awesome; when the vines and creepers are at their thickest, in the summer, they make the so-called "impenetrable" Wilderness of Virginia look like a well-kept orchard, and whole copses of trees are welded into huge amorphous green masses.

To the south, on the river, a high ridge of up to 200 feet rises beside the river, but less than a mile inland there is Stout's Bayou (which becomes Hennesy's Bayou further south); this is at a maximum elevation of about 90 feet near the town, so the terrain is very broken.

The steep hills around Vicksburg are thickly carpeted with almost impenetrable vegetation during the summer months.

THE BATTLE OF CHICKASAW BLUFFS

Grant's "First Vicksburg Campaign" took place from December 27, 1862, to January 3, 1863. It was a conventional attack, with safe lines of supply — and it failed. It was, however, the only attack practicable at the time; the Mississippi was unusually high in late 1862, and Grant reckoned that the northern route was worth trying. As he put it, "We will lose 5,000 men before we take Vicksburg, and may as well lose them here as anywhere else."

Chickasaw Bayou runs through the marshy land almost due north of Vicksburg (in fact, it is a little to the east as well). In its present form, it runs from the Yazoo River in a gentle reverse-S for some 2 or 2½ miles and terminates in a marsh on the north-western side of the Illinois Central railroad and the US 61 (which are very close together at this point) about 2¼ miles north-east of town. The modern US 61 roughly follows the "Country Road to Yazoo City" which Grant mentions and which is shown on old maps. There are relatively steep bluffs beside the bayou, often 50% (45°) and sometimes steeper. The water, like the river, is at about 50 feet; the vast majority of the area is marsh at about 85-90 feet. Thompson's (now Thompson) Lake roughly parallels the bayou, about ⅓ mile to ⅔ mile further east. Nowadays, two very minor roads run into the area, one along the south shore of the bayou and one along the south shore of Thompson Lake. You are not tempted to walk far from these roads into the hot, oppressive, murky, wet undergrowth.

In 1862, it turned out to be a slaughter-pen. In the words of Brigadier-General Morgan (to whom the attack was entrusted):

Our troops not only had to advance from the narrow apex of a triangle, whose short base and sharp sides bristled with the enemy's artillery and small-arms, but had to wade the bayou and tug through the mucky and tangled swamp, under a withering fire of grape, canister, and minie-balls, before reaching dry ground. Such was the point chosen for the assault by General Sherman. What more could be desired by an enemy about to be assailed in his trenches!

Union losses were 208 killed, 1,005 wounded, and 563 captured or missing; the comparable Confederate losses were 63 killed, 134 wounded, and 10 missing, for an overall ratio of 1,776 Union losses to 207 Confederate. The Union would have to wait until the new year to try their next attack.

Hovey's Approach. This trench, dug from Union lines, used a zig-zag design to minimize the effect of Confederate fire from Fort Garrott, the sappers' objective.

GRANT MOVES HIS ARMY

The only practical approach to Vicksburg that was left open to Grant, therefore, was from the south and south-east; and that, of course, lay in enemy hands. Even if he could fight his way through the opposing armies, he knew the ground would not be easy. It is still well broken, with elevations varying, often dramatically, from 140 to 250 feet, as well as being steamy, wet, and covered with a most unpleasant assortment of poisonous plants, insects and rattlesnakes, except along a few ridges where the roads beat the earth flat.

It must have been a miserable trial for those soldiers in their thick, scratchy, hot, woolen uniforms.

It was not until April that the Mississippi subsided far enough to allow an army to be marched across the peninsula opposite the city; until then, Grant tried all kinds of tricks, including a fruitless attempt to dig a canal which would simply allow Vicksburg to be bypassed. Also, even with the troops to the south of Vicksburg and on the western shore, the Union needed transport to ferry the men across the river; and this meant a passage, by the Union ships, of Vicksburg.

The Blackhawk, *Admiral Porter's Union flagship, Vicksburg 1863.*

On the night of April 29, Admiral Porter's ships successfully ran the batteries; on April 30, they began to ferry men across to Bruinsburg almost 10 miles below Vicksburg. Fighting and building, fighting and building, the Yankees began their slow progress toward Vicksburg while harassed by Rebels who were covering their colleagues' retreat. On May 1, they won the Battle of Port Gibson; on May 2, there was a skirmish on Bayou Pierre; on May 4 and 5, skirmishes at Hankinson's Ferry on the Big Black River; on May 9, near Big Sandy Creek; May 10, Caledonia and Bayou Macon; May 12, Raymond (a small battle); May 14, Jackson; May 16, Champion's Hill; May 17, Big Black River; and by May 18, Union forces were close enough to Vicksburg to call it a siege. Defeated and demoralized, Confederate troops streamed into the riverside city.

The Assaults of May 19 and 22

On May 19, in the middle of the afternoon, Sherman attacked the fortifications of Vicksburg. It was a straightforward frontal attack, aimed at preventing the Confederates from consolidating their defenses. He was soundly repulsed, with over a thousand casualties. Confederate figures are not available, but they were apparently tiny compared with the Union losses.

Three days later, at 10 am on May 22, Grant ordered a full-scale attack on a 3 mile front. About 45,000 Yankees were engaged; casualties were 3,199. On the Rebel side, losses were under 500.

Like a few other engagements of the Civil War, this one was a harbinger of World War I; it clearly showed the folly of a frontal

JOHN CLIFFORD PEMBERTON

Born in Philadelphia on August 10, 1814, Lieutenant-General Pemberton was 48 when he supervized the defense of Vicksburg. He had been a Southern sympathizer since his West Point days (class of 1837), and resigned from the Union army to fight for the South. After the Battle of the Big Black River, he was reported as saying, "Just thirty years ago I began my military career by receiving my appointment to a cadetship at the US Military Academy, and to-day — the same date — that career is ended in disaster and disgrace."

When nothing befitting his rank could be found for him after Vicksburg, he resigned and served as a colonel of artillery. After the War, he took to farming, first in Virginia and then back in Pennsylvania. He died on July 13, 1881, aged 66.

attack against well-entrenched troops. The deep, narrow ravines which surround the city had been well reinforced by fortifications, and despite incredible bravery and "human wave" numbers which allowed the Yankees to reach the Rebel lines and even take some positions, the attack was doomed. As so often, when looking at the ground over which these men charged, one can only marvel that they attacked at all.

The dead and wounded were still lying there three days later when, in the words of the Chief Engineer of the defenses, "The dead had become offensive and the living were suffering fearful agonies." A truce was arranged, and men of the two armies met; Grant took the opportunity to hand some mail over to the Confederates, "from Northern friends of some of your officers and men." There were still some civilized amenities.

The Mine

On June 25, the Yankees exploded a mine and according to Andrew Hickenlooper, Chief Engineer of the 17th Army Corps:

> it appeared as though the whole fort and connecting outworks commenced an upward movement, gradually breaking into fragments and growing less bulky in appearance, until it looked like an immense fountain of finely pulverized earth, mingled with flashes of fire and clouds of smoke, through which could occasionally be caught a glimpse of some dark objects, — men, gun-carriages, shelters, etc.

The fight in the crater created by the mine of June 25th.

149

Although entry into the crater was easy, the Union troops soon found that they had not created anything resembling a breach in the lines. The Confederates fired down into the hole, protected by a parapet of debris, and rolled short-fused shells down to explode among the milling Yankees. Subsequent mines were dug, and so were countermines (which were usually exploded too early, because the counterminers could hear the miners so closely they judged them to be only a few feet away), but none was used as a serious attempt to breach the lines. The other big mine, of July 1, destroyed the Rebel fort under which it was dug but the crater was raked with fire to prevent rebuilding; there was no assault.

The caves hollowed from the Vicksburg hillside provided welcome shelter for soldiers and civilians alike during the punishing bombardment of the town.

Life in the caves

The same soil which made mining so easy also made possible one of the best-known features of the Vicksburg siege: the caves. The soil is a light yellowish-brown clay or lias, tight-packed and easy to cut with any digging tools. It also hangs together very well, so that any room excavated in it will survive for months or even years; there is reputedly still one wartime cave in Vicksburg, though it is on private land and the entrance is completely obscured by kudzu. Many were filled in after the siege.

Some caves were quite extensive, consisting of two or three or more rooms. They were mostly dug by blacks who hired themselves out for the business. They were remarkably effective against anything except a direct hit, though they also induced claustrophobia and proved attractive to rattlesnakes. Of course, in the event of a direct hit, there was the nightmare of being buried alive; some children were said to have been lost this way. Most people used them only for sleeping, preferring to take their chances during the day.

SURRENDER AND AFTERMATH

By the beginning of July, it was becoming obvious to the Confederates that they would not be relieved by General Johnston. Surrender negotiations were commenced on the third; the formal surrender took place on July 4, 1863. Independence Day was not celebrated again in Vicksburg until 1945.

Coming almost simultaneously with Gettysburg, the loss of Vicksburg was a hammer-blow to the Confederacy. The nation was divided in half by the Union-controlled Mississippi, and their greatest general had just failed in his attempt to invade the North. Their only real hope, from then on, was to prolong the War in the hope that the North would decide that the South was more trouble than it was worth. That they survived for another year and a half was extraordinary; that the final outcome of the War was ever in dispute again (which it was) is almost incredible.

Vicksburg has a particularly attractive battlefield park, offering scenic views of the surrounding countryside.

FURTHER INFORMATION

Maps: USGS 7.5': Vicksburg West Miss-La, Vicksburg East Miss, Redwood Miss.
Official Reports Atlas: 27/2; 31/6; 32/4; 35/4; 36/1,2,6,7; 37/1; 67/2; 132/8; 153-C/2,3
B&L: Vol III, 465; 494; 506; 512; 516

Book: Peter F. Walker, *Vicksburg: A People at War 1860-65* (University of North Carolina Press, 1960; reprinted Broadfoot Press, 1987). The classic on Vicksburg, covering much more than just the Siege.

Park: The park is one of the most beautiful in the country; there are several places where one could take a picnic; and (for once) there are no objections to alcoholic drinks with a picnic, provided you don't get drunk. Superintendent: Vicksburg National Military Park and Cemetery, 3201 Clay Street, Vicksburg, MS 39180.

Town: Vicksburg is an attractive city, with plentiful accommodation and good restaurants. The City Museum is excellent, and "The Vanishing Glory" — a privately-run multi-projector audio-visual presentation in the city, rather than at the battlefield — is superb. Duff Green Mansion, an ante-bellum house now operated as a bed-and-breakfast, has a ceiling cutaway in one room to reveal a beam splintered by cannon-shot.

NAVAL OPERATIONS

Naval operations were of great importance in the Civil War. For obvious reasons, though, there is little to see in the way of battlefields; this is why naval operations only warrant a brief section in this book.

The Blockade

The Union made a major strategic error at the beginning of the War by declaring a "blockade" of Confederate ports — in fact, they tried to close the ports of North Carolina and Virginia even before those States had declared for the Confederacy. A "blockade" can only be applied to the ports of an enemy nation (declaring the ports "closed" would have been the proper action); this technicality effectively recognized the legitimacy of the Confederate States of America.

With 69 wooden ships, only half of them steamers, the Yankees tried to blockade something between three and four thousand miles of Confederate shoreline; during the course of the War, they would build 200 more steamers, including 74 ironclads. Blockade-running was easy at first — the Union only captured one ship in ten in 1861, and one in eight in 1862 — but by 1865 they were catching one in two. The contraband was cotton out, and guns, food, medicine and luxuries into the Confederacy.

Other Naval Battles

Apart from blockade-running, most naval battles on the Eastern seaboard were fought around the mouth of the James (and in the river itself), at the bottom of Chesapeake Bay. The famous battle of the ironclads (the USS *Monitor* and the CSS *Virginia*, formerly USS *Merrimack*) on March 9, 1862, took place in Norfolk Roads, between Norfolk and Fort Monroe. Strange as it may seem to a European, many "naval" battles were fought on the Mississippi River; the balance was again with the Union.

The Confederates' greatest successes at sea were achieved with individual ships — almost privateers — which roamed the seas taking Yankee prizes in much the same way that submarines would be used in the next century. The CSS *Shenandoah* took her last prizes in the Bering Sea in June 1865; the captain learned that the War was over on August 2, and he finally surrendered at Liverpool on November 6, just under seven months after Appomattox.

Amphibious Operations

The Union made good use of combined land/water operations, both on the rivers (notably the Mississippi) and from the open sea. Examples of the former include the Two Rivers campaign (Forts Henry and Donelson) and the Siege of Vicksburg, both of which are covered in this book.

Left: The USS Monitor. *The odd-looking structure on top of the turret is an awning.*

Right: Section of a sea-going Monitor.

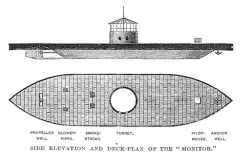

SIDE ELEVATION AND DECK-PLAN OF THE "MONITOR."

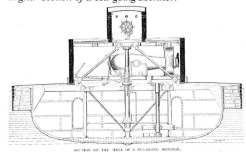

SECTION OF THE HULL OF A SEA-GOING MONITOR.

The CSS Virginia *was built on the salvaged hull of the USS* Merrimack.

Among the Confederate ports which fell as a result of Union naval action, the best known was New Orleans (April 25, 1862). The Union Admiral Farragut's passage of the Confederate forts below New Orleans is a tale of daring and bravery – and also of success. There were many other major Union naval victories in 1862. However, it was not until January, 1865 that the last Confederate fort fell when the Union took Fort Fisher. Here forty seven Confederate big guns had been attacking any Union warship attempting to prevent Confederate blockade runners from reaching Wilmington with vital supplies.

Submarine Warfare

The Confederate privateer submarine *Hunley* was propelled by a hand-cranked screw. She killed several men during trials (including her inventor, Horace Hunley) and the first time she saw action, she was lost with all hands. She did, however, sink the USS *Housatonic* on October 15, 1863, the first-ever militarily successful use of a submarine. The Union's *Alligator*, propelled by oars (!), never saw action but was lost at sea while under tow.

A replica of the Confederate privateer submarine H L Hunley *stands outside the Charleston Museum in South Carolina.*

153

To Chattanooga

Missionary Ridge

Fort Oglethorpe

Battlefield Parkway

ROSECRANS

McFarland Gap

McFarland Gap Road

Park
Headquarters

Reeds Bridge Road

Snodgrass
Field

Brotherton

Snodgrass Hill

Jays Mill Road

Wilder Tower

Viniard Field

Viniard Alexander Road

Wilder Road

Lafayette to Rossville Road

Lee & Gordon Mills

CHICKAMAUGA

To Lafayette

THE BATTLE OF CHICKAMAUGA

Chickamauga Creek, Georgia, near Chattanooga, Tennessee
September 19-20 1863

To Atlanta

Confederate States
General Braxton Bragg
66,000 effectives
18,454 casualties

United States
Major-General William S. Rosecrans
58,000 effectives
16,170 casualties

Reeds Bridge

"Chickamauga" is said to come from the Cherokee, and to mean "River of Death." Many fanciful explanations are advanced for the name, but one of the most persuasive is that the Cherokee used to bathe in its waters to cool their fever —the fever the white people had brought. The whites called it "smallpox."

	CONFEDERATE	UNION
September 20 - am		
September 20 - pm		
Advance		
Retreat		
Site of old road		

West Chickamauga Creek

BRAGG

0   1   miles
0   1   kilometers

155

Today, the black waters of the Chickamauga run under the shade of trees, somewhat to the east of the modern battlefield park. It is an unremarkable stream, and this is the key-word for the rest of the battlefield; there is astonishingly little to see, and the National Park Service has to work hard to think of names for the various stops on the Park Tour.

And yet, among these trees and clearings, a great battle was fought; thousands of men died; many thousands more were wounded, some to recover, some to die later, and some to be crippled for life; and a great Confederate victory, a tribute to the ordinary soldier and his tactical commanders, was to be thrown away by the Confederate generals. The battle commands fascination both for the scale of casualties, and for its importance to the Confederate war effort.

THE TULLAHOMA CAMPAIGN

The Union Army of the Cumberland, under Rosecrans, drove down from Murfreesboro with the intention of overwhelming Bragg's Confederate forces and striking as far as Atlanta. The campaign is named after Tullahoma, to which Bragg had withdrawn after Murfreesboro; the town is about 55 miles north-west of Chattanooga on the Nashville and Chattanooga rivers.

Rosecrans initially conducted a brilliant campaign of maneuver, repeatedly deceiving the Confederate general and causing him to withdraw strategically in order to preserve his lines of supply and retreat. Bragg retreated from Tullahoma within a few days of the beginning of the campaign on June 23. Little more than a month later, Bragg's position in Chattanooga became equally untenable, and on September 9, the Union occupied the town. By mid-September, a battle to halt the Union advance was inevitable; the only question was when and where.

The Snodgrass farmhouse, the Yankees' last defensive position before the retreat.

Crawfish Springs near Chickamauga, the only abundant source of good water near the battlefield.

TERRAIN

The battlefield of Chickamauga is roughly in the shape of an inverted triangle. The point is the intersection of the Lafayette Road (modern US 27) and Chickamauga Creek; the east side is bounded by the creek itself; and the west side is ½ mile to a mile west of the Lafayette Road. Most of the action took place along 3 miles of the Lafayette Road, between Viniards in the south and what is now the Park Headquarters.

The Lafayette Road is mostly at about 720-740 feet; at Lee and Gordon's Mills, where the old road crossed the river, the water is at about 715 feet. The highest ground in that area is only at about 790 feet; the highest ground around which there was fighting (Snodgrass Hill, ½ mile west of the road) was at about 900 feet.

The ground cover then was much as it is today, though not necessarily distributed in exactly the same way. That is, there were and are some fields, some clearings, and a great deal of woodland. From the 86 foot Wilder Tower (Stop 6 on the Battlefield Tour), the "excellent view" which the Park Service brochure promises turns out to be no more than an aerial confirmation of what you already know: there are woods and clearings all over the battlefield.

Because of the thick woodland, the higher ground affords far less of a commanding position than the topography might suggest; only around Snodgrass Hill are there extensive clear lines of fire, although of course the woodland was somewhat cleared in places both to build fortifications and (as the battle progressed) by shot and shell. Generally, though, the description applied by a contemporary St. Louis paper is accurate: it was a soldiers' battle, in that the generals were rarely sure exactly what was going on, so that the actual fighting consisted to a large extent of savage encounters between relatively small groups, often of less than regimental strength.

The woods themselves are thick, often comparable with the Wilderness, and as so often, there are additional discomforts in the shape of poison oak and poison ivy, and a good number of substantial and irascible wasps. The weather at the time of the battle was unusually cold by all accounts; after the heat of a Tennessee summer, the lack of overcoats and blankets on both sides must have been all the harder to bear.

The sink, Chickamauga's answer to the Bloody Pond.

To finish off the unattractiveness of the spot, it was (and still is) very poorly supplied with water. On what was to become the battlefield, there were only a few weak wells and springs, and the only good source of clean, fresh water was at Crawfish Springs, about 3 miles to the south-west. After the battle, the wounded would be so thirsty that as at Shiloh, they would crawl to a mired pond to suck up the half-mud, half-water that spread over a few square yards. "The Sink," as this pond was known to the locals, again became known as "the Bloody Pond;" but it has long since dried up.

THE BATTLE

At dawn on September 19, the Confederates were mostly camped along the west bank of the Chickamauga, though at the south end of the battlefield there were three divisions on the east

The Chickamauga, "River of Death."

Snodgrass Hill, where General George H. Thomas's men temporarily halted the Confederate advance.

side. The Union forces were camped about 1½ miles to the west, near the Lafayette Road. The lines roughly paralleled the Lafayette Road to the south, though at the northern end the Yankee lines ballooned out towards the Rebels and the east. At their nearest points, the armies were only yards apart.

From the very beginning, the battle was confused. On the morning of the 19th, Rosecrans sent out a division to capture what he believed to be a stray Confederate brigade just near Reed's Bridge at the northern end of what was to become the battlefield (Reed's Bridge Road effectively marks the northern limit of the modern Park). Unfortunately they ran into a whole division of Rebels, plus Forrest's redoubtable cavalry. The Union commander inquired ironically of his superiors just *which* part he was supposed to capture. But the fight was on.

The battle that followed is impossible to describe in clear military terms. Both sides marched their men up from the south, throwing them into the battle as soon as there was someone for them to fight; which, given that both sides were following the same tactics, generally meant fairly soon. The battlefront grew in length, and extended steadily southwards. Cannon on knolls thundered canister into the forest, but trees and the risk of hitting their own men diminished their usefulness. Yankees and Rebels fought as divisions rather than as corps; as brigades rather than as divisions; as regiments rather than as brigades; as individuals, and packs and gangs, rather than as regiments. It was blind, brute fighting; you never knew whether friend or foe might suddenly come crashing at you out of the forest, and many must have fallen from shot and shell discharged by their own side.

The Yankees gave a little ground at first; the Union center was somewhat dented, and the Rebels even crossed the Lafayette Road. But the Yankees rallied and repulsed them, so that by nightfall the battle was still completely undecided.

159

CONFEDERATE LINE OF BATTLE IN THE CHICKAMAUGA WOODS.

THE SECOND DAY

This picture illustrates why the Union sentry failed to perceive his compatriots in the dense Chickamauga woods.

During the night of September 19, the Confederate general Longstreet arrived. General Bragg now had at his disposal three lieutenants-general: Longstreet, Hill and the sometime-Bishop Polk. The four of them mostly disliked and mistrusted one another to varying degrees, but Longstreet, Hill and Polk were united in their low opinion of Bragg; and, as we shall see, their opinions were amply borne out.

Because of this animosity, Bragg's very reasonable plan for an early-morning attack failed utterly; when he sent to find where Polk was, the ecclesiastic was apparently discovered at breakfast, reading a newspaper, though an account by Polk's son predictably denies this. Whatever happened, Polk's attack did not take place until ten o'clock, some five hours late.

Thus, for much of the morning, the battle was the same kind of messy, inconclusive, desperate affair in the woods that it had been the previous day. Then, just before eleven, the Union general made his mistake, and gave victory to the Confederates.

LEONIDAS LAFAYETTE POLK

"Bishop" Polk, as his soldiers called him, was born on April 10, 1806. He graduated from West Point in 1827 and was just 55 when the War began. Resigning his commission just after graduation, he pursued his theological studies and he became Bishop of Louisiana in 1841. When he rejoined the (Confederate) army in 1861, he was appointed to high office because he was a close friend of Jeff Davis, not because of his skills in military leadership. An unimpressive soldier, though personally brave, he was killed by a cannon-shot on June 14, 1864, on Kennesaw Mountain (see pages 201 and 202).

What happened was simple. General Rosecrans was informed — quite incorrectly — that there was a gap near the middle of his line. In fact, there was no gap; Brigadier-General Brannan's men were where they should have been, but the Union scout had been unable to see them because of the wood. Unfortunately for the Union, "Old Rosy" did not check the report, and ordered another brigade (under Brigadier-General Wood) to move to the left to close the gap. This created a real gap, which by another stroke of ill luck for the Union was expoited by General Longstreet. The Confederates smashed straight through the Union center; despite the politicking of the Confederate generals, the bravery of the Confederate fighting man (and his leaders, at a tactical level) would win the day.

So dramatic was their charge — they continued unchecked for something like a mile — that the Union line was cut completely in half. The Union right wing simply dissolved, most of the men running to save themselves. By a quarter past two, Longstreet said, "They have fought to their last man, and *he* is running." Rosecrans, and many of his generals, were swept from the field with their men; that they were not captured was lucky.

Even so, the Union defense was not finished. General George Thomas managed to re-form a Yankee line on Snodgrass Hill, a small eminence in a large cleared area. With artillery on the top, and no more cover than a rail fence, he managed to halt the Rebels' headlong advance and to fight them to a standstill. Even at that, he knew he could not hold out indefinitely; his orders, when he finally received any, were to hold the hill until nightfall and to retreat in good order. That he did so is a tribute not only to his powers of leadership, but also to the bravery of his Yankee troops who had to put aside thoughts of defeat (which they had already experienced) and to face men who thought only of victory (which they in turn had already felt).

Left: The Breakthrough, Chickamauga, where Confederates smashed through the Union center.

Right: Snodgrass Hill.

The Lee Gordon House near Chickamauga.

Throughout this battle, Bragg seems not to have had the faintest idea of what his Confederates were achieving; indeed, he appears to have found it difficult to believe that he had won at all. A recurring flaw in his character seems to have been an excessive fear of the consequences if anything went wrong. His planning was usually excellent, but when things went awry, he immediately cast around for someone to blame and, because of his very poor relationships with his staff, this was a common occurrence. This weakness was compounded at Chickamauga by his failure to get onto the battlefield to see how the battle was running, and to make sure that his orders were being followed. Instead, he sat at headquarters miles from the front and issued written orders.

Even so, victory was not merely within the Confederates' grasp at Chickamauga; it was achieved. The Union army was demoralized and running, and if he had had the slightest interest in pursuit, he could probably have destroyed them "in detail," picking off parts of the army almost at his leisure.

ON TO CHATTANOOGA

Despite the entreaties of almost all his generals — including Nathan Bedford Forrest, who excitedly urged him that "every hour is worth ten thousand men" — Bragg did not pursue Rosecrans. Not until the next morning was he convinced of the value of the idea, and then he lost all sense of urgency when mistaken intelligence and false information (possibly deliberately given by Yankee deserters) led him to believe that his opponents were retreating and abandoning Chattanooga. Worried by his lack of horses, the result of terrible losses in the fighting, he decided not to march around the back of Chattanooga and threaten the Union supply lines and thereby force a Union

withdrawal. By not repaying Rosecrans in his own coin, Bragg lost a golden opportunity and (in the opinion of some historians) the Confederacy. His attempt at siege, culminating in the battles described in the next chapter, would be a disaster.

A display of cannon at Chickamauga Visitor Center.

FURTHER INFORMATION

Maps: USGS 7.5': Fort Oglethorpe, GA/TN; East Ridge, TN/GA
Official Reports Atlas: 30/6; 46/1&2&4; 47/2&3&7; 96/4; 97/3; 98/2; 101/20; 111/9
B&L: 640; 648 Tullahoma Campaign: 636

Books: Glenn Tucker, *Chickamauga, Bloody Battle in the West* (Bobbs-Merrill, 1961; 1984 paperback edition, by Morningside Bookshop/ Morningside House). Slightly dated writing, but still the definitive work against which others are rated.

Park: The Chickamauga National Military Park is unusual in two ways. For a start, as already discussed, there is very little to see. Second, it has an appalling orientation slide/tape presentation: uninformative, and dripping with Reconstruction-style propaganda. There is a picnic area near the stop for the Bloody Pond, where alcohol is banned. Superintendent: Chickamauga and Chattanooga National Military Park, P.O. Box 2128, Fort Oglethorpe, GA 30742.

Town: Chickamauga is not a major town; most visitors will do better to stay in Chattanooga and to study the whole sequence of campaigns (Tullahoma, Chickamauga, Chattanooga) as a single entity. More information is given in the next chapter on Chattanooga.

TRANSPORT

Supply lines are a constant concern to armies; and when you look at the figures, you can see why. A full-strength regiment (1,000 men) could easily get through 1½ tons of food a day, and 40 rounds for each man's musket (the standard issue) was another 1½ tons. Artillery guns weighed up to a ton each; a hundred rounds for a 12-pounder Napoleon weighed another ton or so with their packing; and a hungry horse could easily shift 20 pounds of hay.

The net result was that an army of (say) 100,000 men required literally hundreds of tons of supplies *every day*, and that a great deal of *matériel* which was non-consumable (such as artillery) added still more to the baggage trains. For example, even such a notoriously light traveller as Stonewall Jackson had 6 miles of wagons to back up 4 miles of soldiers when he made his celebrated march around the Yankees at Chancellorsville; and during the Wilderness campaign, according to Grant's own memoirs, the supply train for his 115,000-man army would have stretched for 65 miles had it all been on one road.

Although a horse or mule can pull extraordinarily heavy weights on a smooth, level road, most wartime roads were neither smooth nor level — and

Above: United States Military Railroad engineers worked near-miracles in reconstructing bridges that had been destroyed by the Confederates. Often, the bridges were rebuilt in days or even hours.

often there were no roads at all. Many wagons could carry no more than a ton or two; and, of course, horse-drawn transport is deadly slow. At the height of the War, with cavalry and transport losses, the Union armies typically required 500 new horses a day, and during the War the average price of a horse rose from $125 to $185. This was hard enough on the North, but at least the government was paying; Southern cavalrymen supplied their own horses, at their own expense.

Riverboats

Riverboats were not much faster in miles-per-hour terms than horses, but they could carry very much greater quantities of

This was the first war in which the railroad took a key rôle in the movement of troops, weapons, medical and food supplies.

goods. Also, unlike the horse, the steam-driven riverboat did not tire and did not need to be exchanged at regular intervals.

This is one of the reasons why control of the rivers (as typified by the Fort Henry/Fort Donelson campaign, and the Siege of Vicksburg) was so important.

Even more important, in some cases, was the way in which men can be moved by riverboats. A marching army is usually hard pressed to average a couple of miles an hour, even for a few hours a day. A riverboat can average 6 or 7 miles an hour for as long as the pilot is sure of his navigation channel.

Railroads

For maximum speed, though, railroads have it all. They can operate 24 hours a day (though a steam locomotive typically requires an hour of maintenance for every hour of travel), and they can average 20 or 30 or more miles an hour. In the time a riverboat or a mule-train can make a 100 mile trip, a train can make a 300-400 mile trip — or several 100 mile trips.

Although the Confederacy enjoyed "internal lines," their railroad network was thinner on the ground, less interconnected, and (usually) less well maintained than that of their Northern counterparts. Even so, they made the first-ever use of rail in transporting troops to a battlefront (First Manassas), a practise which was to be followed by both sides whenever possible.

As the War progressed, the increasingly rickety state of the Confederate railroads led to their being feared almost as much as battle itself; while the risks were exaggerated, high-speed travel could certainly be hazardous. On the Union side, by contrast, Yankee engineers worked wonders of railroad-building with the US Military Railroads.

CONFEDERATE   **UNION**

November 23

November 24

November 25

Site of railroad

Site of old road

N

S

GRANT

Raccoon Mountain

Moccasin Bend

Union cracker line

Broad Street

To Nashville

Lookout Creek

Point Park

Lookout Valley

To Birmingham

Lookout Mountain

THE BATTLE OF
CHATTANOOGA

Chattanooga, Tennessee
November 23-25 1863

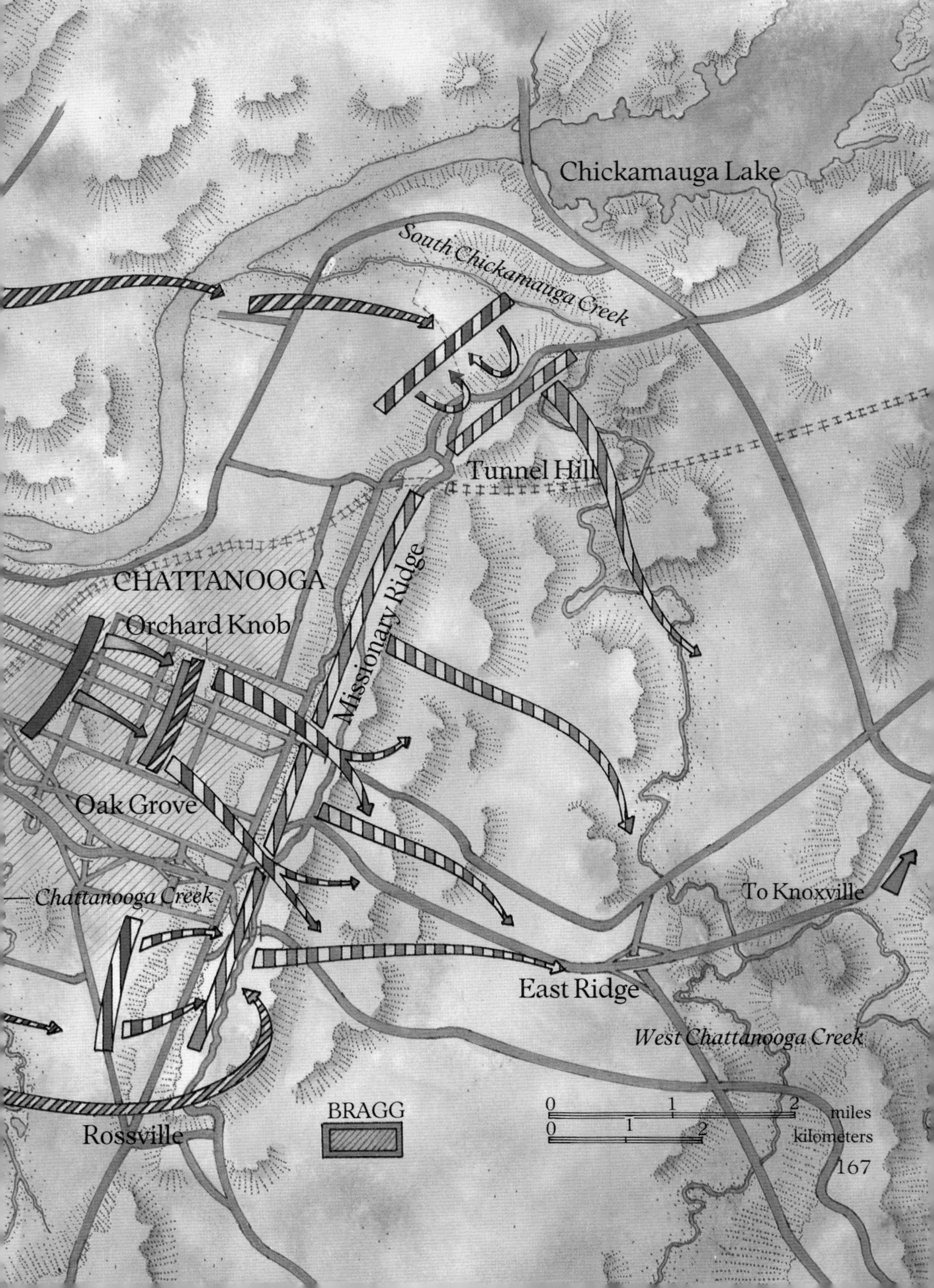

Chickamauga Lake

South Chickamauga Creek

Tunnel Hill

CHATTANOOGA

Orchard Knob

Missionary Ridge

Oak Grove

To Knoxville

Chattanooga Creek

East Ridge

West Chattanooga Creek

Rossville

BRAGG

0   1   2   miles
0   1   2   kilometers

"The battle above the clouds" is the name that legend gave to the action on Lookout Mountain; and once you have been there on a hazy day, let alone in the kind of fog which obscured the battle on November 24, 1863, you can see why. The pedant can argue about whether the battle was truly "above the clouds" (or even "in the clouds"); the evidence of your own senses is sufficient.

Chattanooga, seen here from Lookout Mountain.

Of the other two actions which made up the battles around Chattanooga, Orchard Knob (also known at the time as Indian Hill) is comparatively easy to appreciate, while Missionary Ridge is royally confusing. This is as it should be; the whole Battle of Missionary Ridge was a catalog of mistakes on both sides, misapprehensions as to the terrain, and blind chance.

It is true that Grant's staff was not riven by the dissent and personality conflict which ruined Bragg's Confederates, but the battle itself was still to a large extent a matter of luck.

AFTER CHICKAMAUGA

Bragg's failure to pursue the Union forces after Chickamauga has already been discussed in the last chapter (page 162).

Admittedly, the Union forces in Chattanooga (to which they had fallen back) were in dire straits; their supply routes were menaced by the Confederates, and the one route they could use was steep, hazardous, and still subject to Confederate cavalry raids. Before Grant was appointed to the Union armies, the supply route was apparently littered with dead animals and broken wagons; the Union could barely transport food, let alone ammunition; and the Union soldiers were reduced to quarter-rations, even to making gruel out of hooves and hides. Guards had to be posted when the horses and mules were fed, to stop the soldiers stealing the animals' feed. Reinforcements were on the way — but would they arrive in time?

Grant's appointment changed all this. He reached Chattanooga on October 23, still on crutches as a result of his horse falling in New Orleans in August; he had to be carried over places where it was not safe to cross on horseback. By the end of the month, the daring action of Brown's Ferry had opened a new "cracker line" for supplies, running almost due west from the city. The ferry is long gone, but a small road in Lookout Valley, on the west coast of the Tennessee, leads to where it used to be. Food now flowed in at a vastly increased rate, together with ammunition — and the Confederates were apparently unaware of the importance of the line.

Although the Confederate forces seemed to be well placed all around Chattanooga, it was now only a matter of time until Sherman arrived with Union reinforcements, and they would have to fight for their positions.

TERRAIN

Modern maps of the Chattanooga area, compiled with the aid of aerial surveys, tell a very different story from the maps available to the opposing forces in 1863. The most important difference is that Missionary (or Mission) "Ridge" is only a ridge in its southern extremities; in the north, as it approaches the river, it breaks up into a sprawling complex of high ground which has variously been described as resembling a malformed starfish or (less poetically) as "a series of hills."

What is more, no map tells the full story, especially where Lookout Mountain is concerned. The sheer rock faces of Lookout Mountain have to be seen (even if only in photographs) to be believed.

Chattanooga itself lies at around 640-700 feet; the river is shown on the maps at 634 feet, with virtually no fall, while some of the knobs and knolls exceed 700 feet. Orchard Knob, which was to become important in the fighting, is rather over 2 miles due west of the old town; it is surrounded by the modern city.

The old city was largely contained in a loop of the Tennessee River, on a promontory which bulges northward and is surrounded by the river. Ever fickle, the Tennessee River reverses its direction on the west side of the town and carves through the Cumberland Escarpment to form the gap which makes Chattanooga so important. At this point, it is flowing more or less westwards, though the meanders make this confusing.

The city is dominated by Lookout Mountain to the south-west; this dramatically-shaped carved escarpment is over 2,100 feet high at its highest point, and the modern Point Park (the highest point at which there was fighting) is just under 2,000 feet, so the whole rises more than 1,300 feet above the town. The steep edge of the mountain points north-east, though there are sheer faces of considerable height on both the north-western and south-eastern sides. Lookout Creek runs along the west side of the mountain, and Chattanooga Creek along the east side.

As this original photograph, taken from Lookout Mountain, shows, the town of Chattanooga was once confined to this loop in the Tennessee River; but the modern town has since sprawled South Eastwards.

To the south and east of the city is Missionary Ridge (also known as Mission Ridge). This is extremely uneven, rising and falling by 50 feet or more along its spine, which is very narrow indeed for most of its length. The maximum height of the ridge is about 1,100 feet.

Just about due east of the city, however, it loses its continuous ridge-like character and breaks up into a series of isolated hills, and peaks separated by ravines, to become very much less distinct. Maximum altitudes remain much the same, but the dips between the high ground become much more pronounced.

During the siege, the Union army was bottled up in the city while the Confederate forces were dug into breastworks which ran from the foot of Lookout Mountain almost due west of the city, straight across to Missionary Ridge, then up Missionary Ridge to a point almost due east of the city. They also occupied the Ridge itself; Tunnel Hill (named, presumably, for the railroad tunnel which ran though it) to the north of the Ridge, just before South Chickamauga Creek; and of course Lookout Mountain.

A wartime photograph of General Joe Hooker on Lookout Mountain, from which he had driven the Confederacy on November 24th, 1863.

DAY 1: ORCHARD KNOB

This was the closest Confederate outpost to the east of the city, a small knoll less than 200 yards in diameter which rose not 100 feet above the surrounding terrain. A line of rifle pits, improved with logs and stone, stretched north and south close to the railroad. The Yankees played a spectacular and heroic trick.

General Thomas marshalled his Union troops in what appeared to be a grand review and display: flags flying, fixed bayonets polished, 25,000 men in perfect parade-ground order. Apparently, not a few Yankee soldiers also believed that they were merely on brigade drill, as the bugles sounded and they marched and countermarched. The Confederates admired the sight — until two o'clock. Then, the soldiers charged. There was virtually no battle; the vastly outnumbered Rebels were overrun in short order. The main fascination of visiting this site is the realization that the Union managed to launch a surprise attack, using 25,000 men, in full view of the enemy!

DAY 2: LOOKOUT MOUNTAIN

On the face of it, Lookout Mountain seems impregnable — and the Confederate forces evidently thought the same thing. Terrifying rockfaces, some with overhangs, tower 50 and 100 feet or more high. Grassy ridges suddenly split to reveal great cracks and ravines; even with the modern guard-rails, going too near the edge can induce vertigo. About half-way up, there is a fair-sized plateau farmed in the 1860s by Robert Cravens; his original house was badly damaged in the attack, and the modern Cravens House (maintained by the Park Service) is an improved version which he built on the same foundations.

Hooker's Yankees came up the west side of the mountain, having surprised and overcome the Rebel pickets at about eight o'clock and crossed Lookout Creek. They scrambled up the "steep, rocky, ravine-seamed, torrent-torn sides of the mountain" until they were at about the same height as the Cravens House; they then turned north, towards the point of the mountain, and came around the side. This part of the mountain is only readily accessible today by trails and footpaths; the motor road runs up the east side of the mountain. Take the time to walk along these trails — you will find it hard to believe what the Yankees achieved.

At first, the Rebels did not take the attack seriously. The Union artillery support could not even reach up the mountain; they yelled derisively at the gunners as the shot fell short.

They were, however, reasonably well prepared for defense. The first line ran parallel to the Cravens house, and the second line was about a quarter of a mile behind this. It is important to realize that these defenses faced west, or "uphill," rather than east towards Chattanooga; it is easy to forget this when approaching the mountain from the east yourself, and in view of the fact that the main Union forces were east of the Confederates.

The attack was inevitably funnelled through the narrow

Lookout Mountain; Confederate troops controlled communications at Chattanooga by occupying the surrounding mountains and blocking the river, roads and railroads.

Umbrella Rock, a favorite location for wartime photographs, is no longer readily accessible.

passage around the mountain, but there were simply not enough Confederates to halt the Union onslaught. The Confederates fought like heroes, retreating slowly as the Union forced them back, but the Yankees were no less heroic; frequently, the order to fall back would not be given to the Confederates until the Union men were ten paces away.

To make matters worse, they were fighting in a thick mist which made it, in the words of one general, "almost impossible to distinguish any object at a distance of 100 yards." As one side advanced, and the other fell back, each had to take the location of friend and foe on faith.

Running low on ammunition, pushed hard by the Yankees, and knowing that Lookout Mountain was not where the main battle would be (the bulk of the army was on Missionary Ridge), all the Rebels could do was to hold the mountain according to their orders: "as long as possible."

That they did so until nightfall — they withdrew, under orders, at two in the morning — is greatly to their credit; that the Union men attacked them at all, let alone managed to dislodge them, is equally to the Yankee credit.

DAY 3: MISSIONARY RIDGE

So far, the battle had been a matter of first-class generalship on the Yankee side. The third day was to be characterized by equally first-class fighting on both sides, though the generals would not emerge looking so clever — unless you read their own memoirs.

On the Confederate side, the errors of leadership came from the way that Missionary Ridge was held. The soldiers were spread too thin, the terrain was such that men could not be switched rapidly from one part of the battle to another, and worse still, they were perched along the very crest of the ridge. A

Missionary Ridge. Under Grant's orders, Union troops assaulted Confederate emplacements at the foot of Missionary Ridge, going on successfully to dislodge the Confederate stronghold at the summit.

PAT CLEBURNE

Patrick Ronayne Cleburne was born in County Cork, in Ireland, on St Patrick's Day (March 17), 1828. After serving three years in the British army, he emigrated to the United States in 1849, working first as a pharmacist and later qualifying as an attorney. He 'listed as a private in 1862, and was elected captain. His subsequent promotion was meteoric: Colonel almost immediately, full Brigadier in March, 1862, Brigadier-General in December, 1862. A non-slaveholder who advocated freedom as a reward for blacks who would fight for the Confederacy, he was killed at the head of his troops at the Battle of Franklin on November 30, 1864. In Jeff Davis's words, "a vacancy was created which will never be filled." He was 36.

skilled general would have placed them lower, on the west side, along the "military crest." This is the first high position which gives a clear field of fire across the lower ground, while providing good protection for the soldiers themselves. In the event of a successful enemy charge, the actual crest can then be used as a second line of defense. If the troops are stationed along the actual crest, of course, they can only spill down into the valley on the other side in the event of an enemy breakthrough.

To make matters worse, Bragg's extremely poor relations with his fellow generals meant that no one was too keen to exercise any initiative, as Bragg would countermand their orders quite cheerfully and would then do his best to use their "disobedience" as a means of explaining his own shortcomings to Richmond.

On the Union side, Grant displayed that same mixture of military genius and butcher-like shortsightedness which has left him with such a mixed reputation. To make matters worse, poor maps would leave the Union unsure of exactly what they had captured, and what they still had to do.

Unlike the previous day, the early-morning haze soon burned off and the day was bright and clear. The action began with an attack by Sherman on Confederate positions on Tunnel Hill; the aim was to turn the Rebels' right (north) flank and cut them off from their lines of supply and their best route of retreat.

Unfortunately for the Yankees, they came up against Pat Cleburne's men. Cleburne, of Irish extraction, was not only a natural fighter himself; he also fired the fighting spirit of his men. No great strategist, he was one of the best tactical fighting leaders of the Confederacy. A countercharge from behind the Confederate breastworks repulsed the first Yankee charge; the second was broken by enfilading fire, with brief countercharges further breaking up the Yankees. So many Rebel artillerymen were killed that some batteries were manned by infantrymen. In one, command devolved upon a corporal as all the officers and sergeants were killed.

For something under two hours the battle raged; and then there was a lull. Soon, charge and countercharge resumed, but by mid-afternoon the Yankee attack had been decisively repulsed. Many Confederates must have believed that they had won.

Then, the battle turned abruptly around. As Sherman's attack was failing, Grant ordered fresh troops to take the rifle pits at the foot of Missionary Ridge, in the center, so that Bragg would (with any luck) feel that his center was threatened. Grant hoped that this might relieve some of the pressure on Sherman by distracting Bragg and possibly by draining some of the soldiers from the north of the ridge to the center.

As it turned out, the order would have been little short of murder if it had been carried out correctly. While the Yankees could and did overrun the Confederate rifle pits, in doing so they exposed themselves to a hellish fire from both sides as well as the front; the Confederates had placed their artillery well. The Union men therefore had three choices. They could retreat from the ground just won; they could stay where they were, and be cut to pieces; or they could continue the charge up the hill.

Still burning with the fire of success, they chose the last course — and astonishingly, they succeeded. They were aided by the unwillingness of the Confederates to shoot, lest they wounded their own retreating men, but it was still an extraordinary feat. Up the steep hill they struggled, pausing for breath and to shoot at the Rebels, until they were at the top of the hill, having cloven the Confederate lines in two. In fact, the Confederate line was pierced almost simultaneously at up to half a dozen points; the battle was effectively over.

Because Missionary Ridge is now the most desirable housing area of Chattanooga, it is not really practicable to re-create that charge. There are houses at the foot of the ridge, and houses at the top, but the slopes and ravines are so steep that they have not been built upon. At the few stopping-places available along the top of the ridge, you can get out of your automobile and look down into those ravines up which they charged, and marvel. Puffing, blowing, red in the face, displaying incredible bravery, the Yankees made a successful attack which even a Confederate would have to acknowledge as heroic. The Delong reservation (marked on the park map) is a good point to stop and try to work it all out, especially if you can go there in winter when the trees are bare and the view is unimpeded.

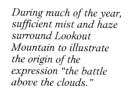

During much of the year, sufficient mist and haze surround Lookout Mountain to illustrate the origin of the expression "the battle above the clouds."

AFTER THE BATTLE

The only parts of
Missionary Ridge which
have not been built upon
are the steep sides and a
few reservations, of
which the Sherman
Reservation at the north
end is the largest.

The Union army harassed the retreating Rebels, but were unable to destroy the army. Knoxville was relieved by the Yankees, breaking Longstreet's siege of the city, then the armies of both sides went into winter quarters. The next year (1864) would see the Union achieve very little with Banks's Red River Campaign (correctly dismissed by Grant as almost irrelevant), but the subsequent Union march to Atlanta and on to the sea would confirm Yankee military supremacy.

FURTHER INFORMATION

Maps: USGS 7.5': Wauhatchie TN, Chattanooga TN, East Chattanooga TN, Hooker GA/TN, Fort Oglethorpe GA/TN, East Ridge TN/GA
Official Reports Atlas: (Lookout Mountain) 50/4; (Missionary Ridge) 45/8; 49/1&2; 50/2&3
B&L: 686

Book: James Lee McDonough, *Chattanooga — A Death Grip on the Confederacy* (University of Tennessee Press, 1984). An excellent account, and rather more entertainingly written than his book on Stone's River (see page 115).

Park: Point Park is open from early morning to mid-evening, though the Visitor Center (where there is a giant painting of the battle, with taped exposition) keeps shorter hours. The sites on Missionary Ridge and Orchard Knob are effectively open all the time, though they are in theory closed at night. Superintendent: as for Chickamauga.

Town: Chattanooga is a pleasant town, well supplied with accommodation and adequately supplied with restaurants. The Park Service maintains an excellent bookshop at Point Park on Lookout Mountain, but the main interpretative display is at the Chickamauga park to the south. Both Chattanooga and Chickamauga run on Eastern time, not Central.

The Chattanooga Museum of Regional History puts no special emphasis on the War, though it has an excellent range of general exhibits. The Confederama, a 480-square-foot model of the battlefield with over 5,000 model soldiers, is greatly superior to the National Park Service presentation at Chickamauga, though still a popularized explanation.

RATIONS

After the Battle of Chattanooga, a young Rebel boy lay dead. He was one of many, though younger than most; the Union officer who found his barefoot body estimated that he was 15. In his haversack were a day's rations: "A handful of black beans, a few pieces of sorghum, and half a dozen roasted acorns."

Although some Union troops on some campaigns went short, and although army food was as universally despised then as has been in subsequent wars, the Union by and large did not suffer as the South did. Large numbers of civilians also suffered real hunger for the sake of the Confederacy. In all fairness, many civilians on both sides lost cattle and hogs to soldiers eager to supplement their rations; the usual excuse was to challenge the beast, and when it failed to give the proper password, to shoot it for having enemy sympathies.

Rations "from the stalk" were a welcome addition to army food for Rebels and Yankees alike.

Union Rations

The Union Surgeon General boasted that his men had the most abundant food allowance of any soldiers in the world, and the official rations (which were often exceeded) bore him out. The *daily* allowance was 12 oz of pork or bacon or 20 oz of fresh or salt beef and 22 oz of soft bread or flour, or 20 oz of corn meal or 16 oz of hard bread; and in addition, every 100 men shared 15 lb of peas or beans, 10 lb of rice or hominy, 8 lb of coffee (10 lb if unroasted, or 20 oz of tea if coffee was unavailable), 15 lb of sugar, 3 lb 12 oz of salt, four quarts of vinegar, 4 oz of pepper, and (when practicable) 30 lb of potatoes and a quart of molasses.

On the down side, this food was very often prepared amateurishly and unhygienically, fried in a sea of grease (which killed most of the bugs!) and probably accounted for more illness than wounds and exposure put together. Although the meat ration looks good, it was often fatty and of poor quality; and the hard bread (also known as hardtack or biscuit) constituted the original "iron rations." But at least they did not starve.

Confederate Rations

Confederate rations started out at Union levels, but it rapidly became clear that these targets could not be met; they were cut, as they were to be cut and cut again throughout the War. In 1863, on the eve of Chancellorsville, Lee's men had been living on a daily ration of 18 ounces of flour and four ounces of bacon or raw salt pork, and at the end of the War, at the retreat to Appomattox, no food was issued to at least one battalion for an entire week. Molasses was normally reserved for the sick and wounded, and luxuries such as coffee and sugar were hardly ever seen.

Even when the food was available (which was rarely), Confederate commissary organization was very bad, and to make things worse, there was an acute shortage in the South of salt, vinegar and other preservatives, which meant that food could not be transported without spoiling. Union control of the Mississippi also meant that the meat, sugar and molasses produced in the west were denied to Confederate soldiers. One celebrated story tells of a Confederate of Irish extraction urging his comrades on with "Charge 'em, boys! They have cheese in their haversacks!"

Water was a perennial concern, and there were many skirmishes even for scummy ponds like this, Doctor's Creek at Perryville.

Confederate Shortages

As early as April 1863 there were "bread riots" in Richmond; in February, bread was selling for 50 cents a pound in Charleston, South Carolina, and flour was $65 a barrel. Even this was nothing next to what happened in Richmond at the War's end: hens were $50 each, butter was $20 a pound, and flour eventually exceeded $1,000 a barrel. An army private was paid $11 a month in 1863.

But what is the use of writing about the pangs of hunger? The words are utterly meaningless to persons who have never known actual starvation, and cannot be made otherwise than meaningless. Hunger to starving men is wholly unrelated to the desire for food as that is commonly understood and felt ... It is a horror which, once suffered, leaves an impression that is never erased from the memory, and to this day the old agony of that campaign comes back upon me at the mere thought of any living creature's lacking the food it desires, even though its hunger be only the ordinary craving and the denial be necessary for the creature's health.
(Sergeant-Major George Cary Eggleston, CSA)

Small mammals provided a supplement for hungry soldiers.

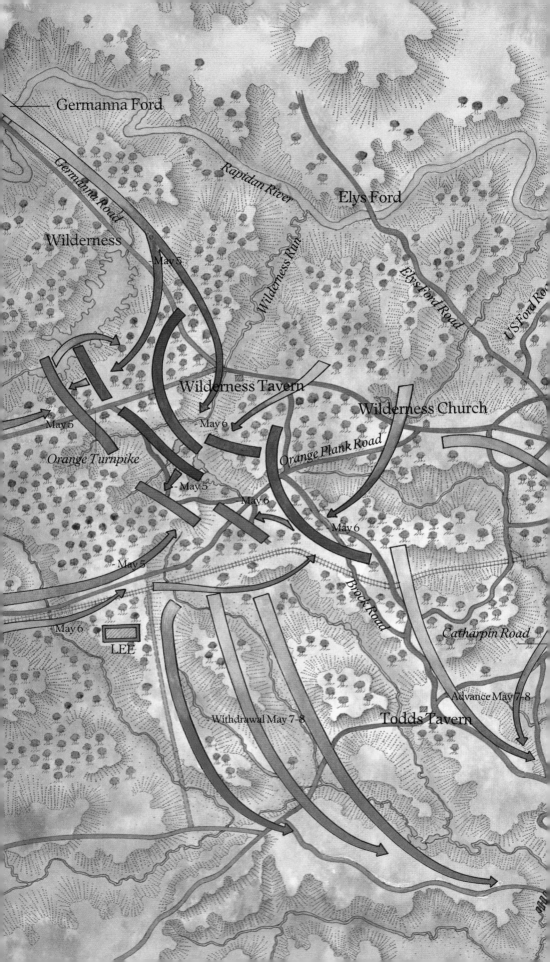

Germanna Ford

Germanna Road

Rapidan River

Elys Ford

Wilderness

Wilderness Run

Elys Ford Road

US Ford Road

-May 5

Wilderness Tavern

Wilderness Church

May 5

-May 6

Orange Plank Road

Orange Turnpike

-May 5

May 6

May 6

Brock Road

-May 5

Catharpin Road

-May 6

LEE

Advance May 7-8

-Withdrawal May 7-8

Todds Tavern

THE BATTLES OF THE
WILDERNESS
AND
SPOTSYLVANIA
Around Chancellorsville and Spotsylvania, Virginia
May 5-19 1864

Confederate States
General Robert E. Lee
62,000 effectives*
20,000 casualties*

United States
Lieutenant-General Ulysses S. Grant
110,000 effectives*
34,000 casualties*

*For the Wilderness and Spotsylvania together; all numbers are approximate, and Confederate casualties are only guesswork.

	CONFEDERATE	UNION
May 5 - 10		
May 12		
Entrenchments		

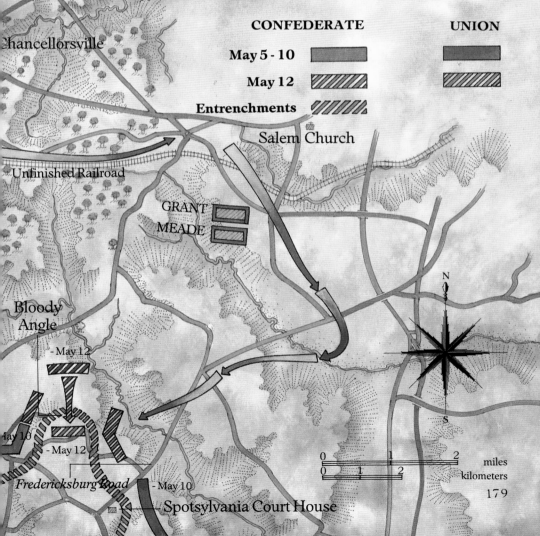

Rappahannock River

River Road

Chancellorsville

Salem Church

Unfinished Railroad

GRANT
MEADE

Bloody
Angle

- May 12

- May 12

May 10

- May 10

Fredericksburg Road

Spotsylvania Court House

N
S

0   1   2   miles
0   1   2   kilometers

The most immediate feeling, when walking over the battlefields of the Wilderness and Spotsylvania, is disbelief that there was ever a battle here. The Wilderness seems altogether impossible terrain for a fight, while the insignificant village of Spotsylvania Court House seems to offer so little advantage to either side that there is little to fight about.

The original Spotsylvania Court House. It was severely damaged during the War and has now been completely rebuilt.

THE VIRGINIA CAMPAIGN OF 1864

The Virginia Campaign of 1864 was a clash of Titans: Ulysses S. Grant, newly promoted to Lieutenant-General on March 9, against Robert E. Lee. The basic strategy was another Union "Drive to Richmond," and like the others, it would fail; but it only failed because of an incredible feat of generalship by Lee and an equally incredible feat of bravery by his heavily outnumbered, hungry, barefoot soldiers. As Major-General McLaws said,

> I recall an instance of one hardy fellow whose trousers were literally "worn to a frazzle" and would no longer adhere to his legs even by dint of the most persistent patching. Unable to buy, beg or borrow another pair, he wore instead a pair of thin cotton drawers. By nursing these carefully he managed to get through the winter.

If ever there was cause to hang on to your Confederate money, because the South will rise again, this is it.

Even so, it marked another stage in the steady attrition of the South. To call the South brave is not to belittle the North; under Grant, the Yankees showed what they could do, and for the first time the Army of the Potomac advanced after a defeat instead of retreating. Both sides lost a third of their armies, but the Union could replace both men and *matériel*, while the Confederacy could not.

THE OPPOSING ARMIES

There were two armies on each side. The Union fielded the Army of the Potomac (about 110,000 men), under Meade of Gettysburg fame, while the the smaller Army of the James (35,000 men) was under Major-General Benjamin F. Butler. General Ulysses S. Grant was in overall command.

The Wilderness Tavern, on the Orange Turnpike. The remains are now negligible, just a few foundations.

For the Confederates, General Beauregard headed an *ad hoc* army of about 25,000 men who had been brought together to protect Richmond while Lee (as ever) commanded the Army of Northern Virginia, about 62,000 strong. As usual, the number of "effectives" was significantly lower than the sizes of the armies would suggest.

Grant's plan was to march swiftly through the Wilderness and to engage Lee somewhere between there and Richmond, smashing the weakened Confederate army and going on to take the Confederate capital. Butler, meanwhile, would move on Richmond from the south.

Butler was essentially a political appointee, and his army was mostly irrelevant; during most of what is described below, he was maneuvring into place with agonizing slowness, and on May 16 he finally encountered General Beauregard at the short, sharp battle of Drewry's Bluff. Butler's men were smartly bottled up between the James and Appomatox rivers — not just bottled up, but in Beauregard's own words, "strongly corked." This was as well for the Confederacy; had Butler prevailed, he might easily have penetrated a lightly-defended Richmond.

TERRAIN

The terrain of the Wilderness and Fredericksburg is described on pages 98 and 181-182, but the Battle of the Wilderness took place somewhat to the west of the previous year's engagements. Also, it was not fought along the roads; it was mostly fought between the Orange Turnpike (now the VA 20) and the Orange Plank Road (now the VA 621), a mile or two to the south and west of Wilderness Tavern. Wilderness Tavern itself is just over

The Orange Plank Road, along which some of Lee's troops progressed on the way to the Wilderness.

Ellwood (the Lacy House) served as a Union headquarters before the Battle of the Wilderness. At the time of writing, it is not open to the public.

3 miles north-north-west of Wilderness Church; it is the modern village of Wilderness, where the VA 3 (the Germanna Road) and the VA 20 diverge as you travel west.

A chain of three lakes (Wilderness Run Lake, Lee Lake and Grant Lake) marks the approximate center of the battlefield; they are modern reservoirs, but they show how swampy and wet the terrain was, even then. They are at 289 to 337 feet; the highest ground, to the south-west, is at 422 feet and other high points are typically around the 400 foot mark. Drainage is by many small runs and rivulets, rather than broad streams. The terrain is mostly rolling, though there are some quite steep ridges; in places, there are slopes of 50 per cent. There are a few clearings, but in most places, visibility is severely limited by thick vegetation.

To the south, the terrain around Spotsylvania is slightly more open, and marked with rather fewer steep slopes, though overall elevation is similar. The Battle of Spotsylvania actually took place about 1½ miles north and west of Spotsylvania Court House, again on ground which was then trackless but which is now served by a loop which leaves the VA 613 (the old Brock Road, which existed at the time of the battle) about 1¼ miles north-west of modern Spotsylvania.

THE INITIAL ATTACK

Germanna Ford is about 5½ miles north-west of Wilderness Tavern; Meade's men crossed this on the night of May 3-4 and made for the Tavern on the Germanna Plank Road. They then left the road and struck out south through the thick, tangled

Wilderness, moving in the valleys in order (Grant hoped) to escape detection.

Although the Wilderness was a terrible place to fight, Lee realized that unless the Confederates launched an attack, Grant's men could advance rapidly on Richmond via Hanover Junction. He also realized, though, that Grant's army would be strung out on line of march, and that a flank attack could prove devastating.

At 7:15 am on May 5, Gouverneur Warren warned Meade that the Confederates were gathering on the Orange Turnpike, a mile or so to the West. Meade ordered Warren to attack.

Initially, the Union attack was very successful; the Confederates fled in front of Hancock's Federal troops for almost a mile before regrouping. Both sides, though, found that they were engaging with only a part of their armies; thick smoke made the already poor visibility worse, and men fought at incredibly close distances. Every tree might conceal a sniper, and impromptu ambushes were the main tactic.

The horror of fighting under these conditions is hard to imagine. Flashes of flame, whether single rifles or volleys, might come from anywhere; and to add to the terror, the thickets sometimes ignited. A comparatively mild sprain might be enough to stop a man fleeing; a temporarily incapacitating wound was a death sentence, as men burned alive in the undergrowth. Their screams mingled with the crash of musketry and the yells of the troops; the unmistakable stench of roasting and burning flesh combined with the smell of powder. The first day's battle ground to a halt at about eight in the evening.

During the night, Lee ordered Longstreet to make a night march, so as to arrive on the field at daylight the next morning. Unfortunately, they did not make it fast enough. The troops they were supposed to reinforce were "thoroughly worn out. Their lines were ragged and irregular. In the expectation that they would be relieved during the night, no effort was made to rearrange and strengthen them to meet the gathering storm.""

The storm broke at dawn, with a Yankee attack; and once again, the Confederates fell back. Then Longstreet's corps arrived in double column and Lee himself spurred his horse as if to join Gregg's Texan troops who were about to counterattack. They yelled at their general: "We won't go on unless you go back." When they were sure that "Marse Robert" was safe, they charged, "eight hundred Texans, regardless of numbers, flanks or supports ... In less than ten minutes one-half of that devoted eight hundred were lying upon the field dead or wounded; but they had delivered a staggering blow and broken the force of the Federal advance."

Thereafter, the battle ebbed and flowed in the Wilderness, but in rather more organized military form than the previous day. To quote a Confederate report,

The Wilderness as it is today; the thick undergrowth which hampered the troops is still evident.

"Law's brigade captured a line of log breastworks in its front, but had held them only a few moments when their former owners [Webb's Brigade] came back to claim them ... the storm of battle swept to and fro, in some places passing several times over the same ground, and settling down at length almost where it had begun the day before."

Using Longstreet's fresh troops, Lee turned Hancock's left (southern) flank and began to roll up the Union line, but Longstreet himself was wounded and the attack faltered. A subsequent attack on the unguarded Union right (northern) flank was launched too late in the day. The Battle of the Wilderness had exacted plenty of casualties on both sides (about 17,000 Union and 7,500 Confederate), but it had decided nothing.

SPOTSYLVANIA COURT HOUSE

On the morning of May 7, Grant found that Lee's men had withdrawn into trenches. Both sides surveyed one another more or less warily; it was on May 8 that the Union General John Sedgwick made his celebrated remark that "They couldn't hit an elephant at this distance," only to be shot in the head a few seconds later, and killed.

Knowing that it would be difficult to get the Confederates out to fight, the Union general ordered his men to march south around Lee's right flank in an attempt to isolate the Confederate army from Richmond, but Lee was not to be fooled.

Somewhat tangled marching by the Yankees gave the Rebels time to anticipate them. By the time Grant's men arrived at Spotsylvania Court House on May 8, they found that Lee's men were already entrenched in a great jagged line from just south of Spotsylvania Court House itself, then 1½ miles north to some woods, then south and west for another 2½ miles.

For the next two weeks, the Union hurled attack after attack at the Confederate lines, and none broke through. The attack on the "Mule Shoe" was the one that lives in popular memory as the "Bloody Angle."

Warren's Confederate fifth corps distributing ammunition whilst under fire - May 6, 1864.

THE BLOODY ANGLE

This sketch of the Bloody Angle shows the chaos and horror of the battle.

The woods to the north of Spotsylvania Court House provided a natural salient for the Confederates; with the woods behind them, and a wide, open clearing in front of them, they were in a very strong position. Its shape gave this salient the name of "The Mule Shoe."

The Union commanders did not believe, however, that the Rebel position was an impregnable one. On the morning of May 12, just before 4:30 am, a short artillery barrage preceded a tremendous attack by Union infantry. The density of the attack was incredible: two dozen Federal brigades attacked a few hundred yards of Rebel lines, in General Johnston's words "in great disorder, with a narrow front, but extending backwards as far as I could see." The ground was soggy from storms the previous day, but the weather had now turned "raw and disagreeable;" many on both sides had had no sleep, lying in the open with no protection, but the Yankees charged and the Rebs fought back.

The Wilderness, from an original photograph.

Musketry was so heavy that whole trees were chopped down by the steady whittling of musket balls; after the engagement, pairs of balls would be found that had collided in mid-air. Soldiers could not reload fast enough, and even when they could, the black-powder deposits fouled the guns so badly that on both sides, guns sometimes exploded when they were fired. When men reached the log barricades — now just gentle undulations in the Virginia earth — gun-butts smashed teeth and skulls, bayonets were poked through chinks in the fortifications, and slashing, carving wounds from the broad knives carried by both sides laid open bones and put out eyes. One Yankee lieutenant leapt three times onto the breastworks themselves to fire a musket down into the Confederates; the third time he fell, shot through the head.

The Union initially captured something between two and four thousand Confederate soldiers, to say nothing of two generals (including Johnson), large numbers of small arms that the South could ill afford to lose, and 20 Rebel guns. It was a heroic charge, or rather series of charges, and it appeared to be succeeding; but when the Union hit the Confederates' second line of defense, the advance was halted.

Grant tried to get Warren's corps to attack, in order to pressure the Confederates elsewhere, but for some reason Warren was unable to organize this initiative. Grant ordered him replaced in the field with Major-General Andrew A. Humphries, but it was too late. Although the "Bloody Angle" raged on until past midnight, the Battle of Spotsylvania ground to a halt. By May 19, Grant had decided to abandon this unprofitable "siege of nowhere" and instead to try to move around Lee's troops on the way to Richmond.

THE AFTERMATH

Both Grant and Lee now had the measure of their opponents. Grant was used to Confederate retreats in the West; Lee was used to Union retreats in the East. Facing one another, they both fought like tigers.

Grant made the extraordinary (but almost certainly correct) decision that he had *too much* artillery, and sent a hundred guns back to Washington; they slowed him down, he said. Yankees and Rebels alike called him a "butcher," because of the number of men he had lost. Undeterred, he would continue; and it is not unfair to say that if earlier Union generals had been as willing to risk their men, they would in the long run have saved thousands of lives by the simple expedient of ending the War earlier.

The Bloody Angle as it is today, in its peacetime tranquillity.

FURTHER INFORMATION

Maps: USGS 7.5': Brokenburg VA, Mine Run VA
Official Reports Atlas: Wilderness: 55/1; 83/1&2; 94/6; 96/1. Spotsylvania 55/2&3; 81/1&2; 83/3; 94/7; 96/3
B&L: Wilderness: 120; 131; 153; 155; 159; 166. Spotsylvania: 167

Park: The Visitor Centers at Fredericksburg (see page 103) and Chancellorsville (see page 127) also cover Spotsylvania and the Wilderness. Wilderness Battlefield and Spotsylvania Court House Battlefield both have gates on the Park Service roads, and may be closed during the hours of darkness. Superintendent: PO Box 679, Fredericksburg, VA 22404.

Town: See Fredericksburg, page 103.

Confederate cemeteries, like this one in Spotsylvania, are much rarer than so-called National (i.e. Union) cemeteries. Many Confederates were buried in common graves.

ATROCITIES

What happened in the Wilderness was atrocious by any standards; but it did not qualify as an "atrocity:" a deliberate act by which one side exceeds the admittedly lax and hazy bounds of the "Rules of War" and arouses universal indignation on the other side. On the other hand, what did happen was sufficiently awful to encourage still further the "Peace Democrats" in the North.

During the War, both sides accused one another of atrocities. Civilian "massacres" seem not to have taken place, though the Confederates (under Nathan Bedford Forrest) were accused of a "massacre" at Fort Pillow and the shooting of ten Confederate prisoners at Palmyra in 1862 is often known as the Palmyra Massacre.

At Fort Pillow, Forrest's men allegedly "massacred" black soldiers, but the facts are unclear; however, they are not inconsistent with a hard-fought battle and extreme bravery on the part of the blacks, who sold their lives dearly. Given that Confederates were actually accused of "massacring" black soldiers during the

"Battle of the Crater," one may detect the hand of the propagandist here.

At Palmyra, the local Provost Marshal (Strachan) ordered the execution by firing squad of ten prisoners of war, who had been captured in uniform, because the local inhabitants would not or could not deliver up a Yankee quisling about whose safety he was concerned. Only three were killed outright by the firing squad; the rest, including one who had not even been hit, were despatched like dogs, with a revolver. One had to be shot seven times.

The Hanging Matches

In late 1864, the Union's Phil Sheridan attempted to treat Mosby's Confederate Raiders as bandits, hanging or shooting seven of them *after* they had been captured (in uniform) and affixing to the bodies placards which read "Such Will Be The Fate Of All Mosby's Men." Mosby

A bird's eye view sketch of Andersonville Prison, seen from the southeast.

later chose six men by lot from Union prisoners he had captured, and returned the compliment. The hanging match stopped immediately.

This tactic was to be tried a number of times, usually at Union instigation, but in no other cases does it appear to have been carried to its obvious, barbaric conclusion: Confederate threats of retaliation prevented the executions.

Prisoner of War Camps

The Southern prison camp of Andersonville is a by-word for the horrific treatment of prisoners, and indeed thousands died there and elsewhere. However, in proportion to the numbers engaged, and to the numbers of prisoners of war on both sides, *more* Southerners died in Northern camps than vice versa. Rations for Union prisoners in the South were admittedly poor, but everyone was starving. In the North, by contrast, the reduction of prison rations to the same level as was reported in the South was an act of calculated cruelty; there was no shortage of food, and well-fed guards stood over starving prisoners.

Copperheads

While the South was always fairly solidly behind the Confederacy, there was a strong Peace Movement in the North throughout the War; they saw no reason

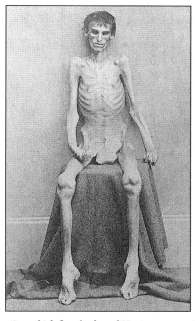

Starvation which foreshadowed Nazi concentration camps characterized several prisons. Prisoners on both sides testified to the brutality, hardship and privations endured for long months.

to fight, either initially or as the War progressed. These Peace Democrats were especially strong in the Midwest, and although they were mostly sincere and honest men, they were reviled as "copperheads" — a reference to the copper pennies they were alleged to wear as a badge of their allegiance to the Peace Democrats. Several of them suffered imprisonment, the closing of their newspapers, and other indignities.

A photograph of August 17, 1864, showing Andersonville Prison, Georgia, seen from the main gate, during the issue of rations to 33,000 prisoners.

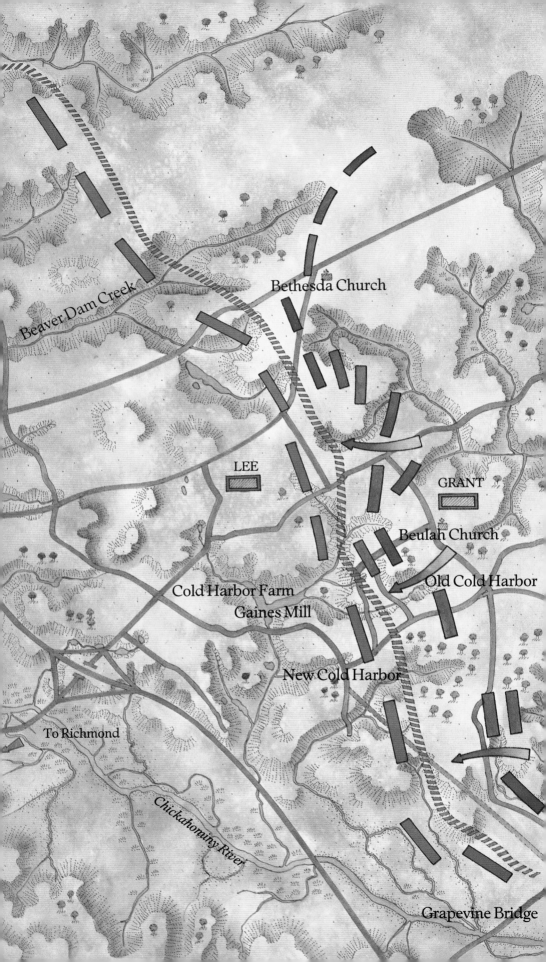

Beaver Dam Creek

Bethesda Church

LEE

GRANT

Beulah Church

Cold Harbor Farm
Gaines Mill

Old Cold Harbor

New Cold Harbor

To Richmond

Chickahominy River

Grapevine Bridge

THE BATTLE OF
COLD HARBOR

Cold Harbor, Virginia
June 3 1864

Confederate States
General Robert E. Lee
30,000 engaged out of 59,000
1,500 casualties

United States
Lieutenant-General Ulysses S. Grant
50,000 engaged out of 117,000
5,000-7,000 casualties

At dawn on June 3 1864, one of the most terrible charges of the Civil War was made. About 50,000 Union troops charged something less than 30,000 Confederates: a straightforward, all-out attempt to smash through the well-entrenched Rebels. The roar of artillery and musketry could be heard in Richmond, about eight miles to the south-west. The Yankees were cut to pieces. By noon, Grant had called off the Union attack.

CONFEDERATE	UNION
▬▬	▬▬

Entrenchments ////////

Site of old road ----------------

N

S

| 0 | | 1 | miles |
| 0 | | 1 | kilometers |

This one brief, deadly charge — a precursor of World War I — changed war for half a century or more. It showed that an infantry charge against a well-entrenched position, faced with entrenched guns, was doomed. Grant learned his lesson, and also learned the lesson that men would fight all the more bravely against a frontal attack on their capital. His next plan was an attack on Petersburg, 20 miles south of Richmond — a sort of back-door attack. When that failed, the Siege of Petersburg (pages 227 and 230) was what would finally decide the War in the East.

There is little to see at Cold Harbor, and the scale of the carnage is almost impossible to relate to that few acres of scrubby woodland and abandoned fields. Nevertheless, it deserves a place in this book for three reasons. First, it was such an appalling slaughterhouse. Second, it was a pivotal battle in the development of Grant's understanding of tactics. And third, it served notice to the Confederates in the East of the kind of man they had to face. To quote Sergeant-Major Eggleston, CSA, of Lamkin's Virginia Battery:

We had been accustomed to a program which began with a Federal advance, culminated in one great battle, and ended in the retirement of the Union army, the substitution of a new Federal commander for the one beaten, and the institution of a more or less offensive campaign on our part ... But here was a new Federal general ... so ill-informed as to the military customs in our part of the country that ... instead of retiring ... he had the temerity to move by his left flank to a new position, there to try conclusions with us again. We were greatly disappointed with General Grant, and full of curiosity to know how long it was going to take him to realise the impropriety of his course.

Cavalry charge at Cold Harbor

Old Cold Harbor House, now long gone.

PREFACE TO COLD HARBOR

After Spotsylvania, there had been inconclusive skirmishes and battles between Lee's troops and Grant's. Grant had constantly been trying to slide by Lee's right flank, and Lee had constantly been stopping him from accomplishing this easily. The Battle of the North Anna took place on May 23-26, and the Battle of Totopotomy (primarily a cavalry engagement) on May 28.

The Federal army arrived in the vicinity of Cold Harbor on June 1, but although the battle is sometimes described as lasting from the evening of that day to noon on the third, it was the great Union charge of the final day which should be regarded as the true Battle of Cold Harbor.

Meade, with 108,000 men, was deployed across a front something more than 5 miles long, from beyond Bethesda Church in the north-west almost to Grapevine Bridge in the

After Cold Harbor, as after many other battles, the dead were gathered for re-interment.

193

south-east. Lee, with something under 60,000, faced him; the two armies were closest in the south-east, as much as a mile apart in the north-west. Lee's armies were well dug in, as befits a defending army.

TERRAIN

Broadly, the terrain across which Cold Harbor was fought rises from the swampy Chickahominy River valley to heights of about 200 feet; the river bed is between about 60 feet in the north-west, and 50 feet in the south-east. The slopes are mostly fairly modest, though there are a few which are a bit of a scramble even unencumbered; with a musket to be carried as well, they would indeed be hard work.

The main battle, on June 3, was centered between Old Cold Harbor and New Cold Harbor (in fact, the two are little more than a mile apart) beside what is now the VA 156; the field slopes up to the north-west of the road, rising from about 120 feet to 160 feet. It is less than 10 miles from the center of Richmond, which lies to the south-west of the battlefield.

Woods now cover the site of Cold Harbor.

THE BATTLE

In the opinion of a majority of its survivors, the Battle of Cold Harbor should never have been fought. There was no military reason to justify it. It was the dreary, dismal, bloody, ineffective close of the Lieutenant-General's [Grant's] first campaign with the Army of the Potomac. (Martin McMahon, Brevet Major-General, USV)

There is little else that can be said. The attack began at 4:30 on the morning of June 3. It was a straightforward frontal charge, across the whole front (with apparently no plans for reserves) against well-prepared earthworks. The frontal fire was withering, and Lee had planned the defenses so well that the Confederates could (and did) deliver enfilading fire with equal ease, in support of the next section of line. It was just a matter of advancing, and being shot to pieces. Eight Union colonels died in about as many minutes; in less than an hour, anything up to 7,000 Union men had fallen, compared with a total loss for the Confederates of perhaps 1,500 at most; 14 per cent casualties for the Union, a maximum of 5 per cent for the Confederacy. If casualties for June 1 and 2 are included, Union casualties rise to 12,000; Confederate figures are not available, but were vastly lower.

THE AFTERMATH

Across open terrain such as this, the Yankees advanced - and were cut to pieces. Taken from the Union lines.

For ten more days, the Yankees and the Rebels faced one another in the stifling 100-degree heat. Both were dressed in wildly unsuitable uniforms — summer issue uniforms were an innovation which had yet to come — but at least the Yankees were well fed; the Rebels grew hungrier every day. At last, Grant realized that this last Drive to Richmond had failed. On June 12-14, he moved his great army away from Cold Harbor, across the James downstream from Richmond, and on towards Petersburg.

FURTHER INFORMATION

Maps: USGS 7.5': Seven Pines
Official Reports Atlas: 97/2
B&L: 140; 214; 216

Park: This is an outlying part of the Richmond Battlefield Park (see page 67). There is a small unmanned shelter with an ingenious "electric map" of the movements of the armies before the battle which is extremely informative when it is working properly; which is by no means invariably.

Town: See RICHMOND, page 67.

LIVING HISTORY

At a battlefield such as Cold Harbor, where there is very little to see (in terms of relics, landmarks, etc.), reconstructions and "Living History" make the battlefield much easier to understand.

One of the best "Living History" sites is at Vicksburg. The soldiers who man it stay perfectly in character, as if they were Rebels of 1863 defending their city against the Yankees.

Most of the time, they just sit around in their bomb-proof behind a stockade, like so many soldiers in so many wars. Then, at prearranged times, they give musket or cannon demonstrations. They explain what they are doing for the benefit of the bystanders, prefacing their remarks with the observation that things must be pretty bad in the city for so many people to have come up to the front lines. Even the infrequency of their firing is explained as reflecting the need to conserve powder and shot. If you engage them in conversation, they will tell you how they fought at the Big Black River before falling back to Vicksburg. And at the end of their demonstrations, they finish with a plea to bring some food up from the city, "cause there ain't much of it on the front lines."

Most parks organize similar "Living History" displays throughout the summer months, usually during weekends or on public holidays. The programs typically run from around Memorial Day to around Labor Day, though they may start or finish either earlier or later, and the precise timetable varies from year to year. Check with individual parks before you go.

The great advantage of "Living History" displays is that they show you what the fortifications were like at the time of the

Firing cannon at a "Living History" display, Vicksburg.

War, before time and weather softened them; they give you some idea of the practical details of life during the War; and they show you just how much smoke was generated by black-powder firearms.

As an example of "practical details," it is one thing to see a leather artillerist's pouch; it is quite another to see a modern replica of that pouch being used to keep the powder dry on a damp, drizzling day. Again, a reconstructed Sibley tent or hut — or even pup-tent — gives you some idea of the discomfort of the War, though it is perhaps surprising how homey some huts were made (Fort Donelson has some good examples). As for smoke, a single round from a cannon, or a single volley of musketry, generates a lot of smoke which sticks to the ground. After several shots (which is rarely practicable in a "Living History" display), the "fog of war" must have been literal as well as figurative.

Like their forebears, the "soldiers" who take part in Living History's remarkably evocative re-enactments, cannot restrict their soldiering to fair weather. Here at Chickamauga, cold, wet Rebels huddle together under authentic waterproofs of the 1860s. In this way, twentieth century visitors are able to appreciate the difficult conditions in which this War was fought.

Re-enactments

Whereas "Living History" displays are held on a regular basis, various kinds of re-enactments are held at different locations during the year, many, of course, being held on the anniversaries of specific battles. The best way to keep track of these is via such magazines as *Civil War Times Illustrated*. At these, you can see cavalry, artillery, musketry, bayonet drill, re-enactments of the battles themselves, and even US Sanitary Commission tents and other improbable reconstructions.

197

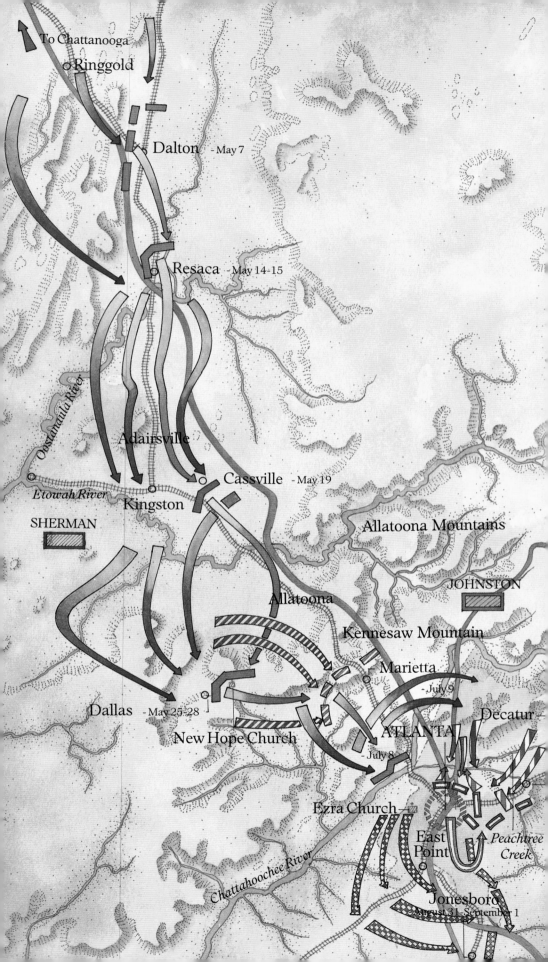

To Chattanooga

Ringgold

Dalton - May 7

Resaca - May 14-15

Oostanaula River

Adairsville

Etowah River

Kingston

Cassville - May 19

SHERMAN

Allatoona Mountains

JOHNSTON

Allatoona

Kennesaw Mountain

Marietta

- July 9

Dallas - May 25-28

New Hope Church

- July 8

Decatur

ATLANTA

Ezra Church

East Point

Peachtree Creek

Chattahoochee River

Jonesboro

- August 31 - September 1

THE FALL OF
ATLANTA
AND THE
MARCH TO THE SEA

Fall of Atlanta, Georgia
September 2 1864

Confederate States

General Joseph E. Johnston
Lieutenant-General John B. Hood
35,000 effectives*
13,500 casualties†

United States

Major-General William T. Sherman
98,000 effectives*
8,000 casualties†

*May 1864, at the gates of Atlanta

†For the battles of Kennesaw Mountain, Peachtree Creek and Atlanta

By the time you get to Atlanta, you can feel the War winding down. You know what happened: the destruction of the city, the March to the Sea. You know what came next: Reconstruction, the carpetbaggers. No matter what your feelings about the preservation of the Union, a leaden weight settles on you: the

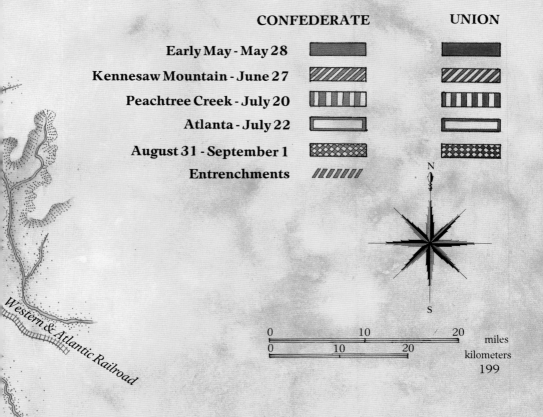

	CONFEDERATE	UNION
Early May - May 28		
Kennesaw Mountain - June 27		
Peachtree Creek - July 20		
Atlanta - July 22		
August 31 - September 1		
Entrenchments		

Western & Atlantic Railroad

N

S

0   10   20   miles
0   10   20   kilometers

waste, the death, the suffering. It is perhaps as well not to dwell too long on the subject.

But unless you face it, either as a Yankee or as a Rebel — or, if you can manage such a feat of detachment, as an impartial observer — you will never really understand the ruthlessness of war and the humiliation of the South.

That is why this campaign, one of the last in the book, is not a single battlefield: it is a great long journey, a day perhaps in Atlanta, a day driving to Savannah, and another day driving up from Savannah to Charleston in South Carolina.

THE ATLANTA CAMPAIGN

Early in May 1864, Sherman set out from Chattanooga. He had with him the Army of the Cumberland, the Army of the Tennessee, and the Army of the Ohio, together with four cavalry divisions.

His orders, from General Grant, were "to move against Johnston's army, to break it up, and to get into the interior of the enemy's country as far as you can, inflicting all the damage you can against their war resources."

Of course, "war resources" is a broad term; and Sherman correctly understood that, in a nation fighting for its life, everything is a "war resource" — even the economic and social structure, the women who support their menfolk while they fight and the children who will grow up to become soldiers. Logically, but horrifyingly, he proposed therefore to carry the War to the women and children.

His Confederate opponent, Joseph E. Johnston, had already realized that he could not hope to prevail against the vastly superior Union numbers. At the end of 1863 and the beginning of 1864, he says, "Instead of a reserve of muskets, there was a deficiency of six thousand and as great a one of blankets, while the number of bare feet was painful to see. The artillery horses were too feeble to draw the guns in fields, or on the march, and the mules were in similar condition."

Even at Resaca on May 14-15, Johnston was outnumbered

The charge of Logan's corps at Kennesaw Mountain.

about 3:2 (100,000 Yankees against 70,000 Rebels), and although he gained a strategic victory there and lost rather fewer men than Sherman (5,000 instead of 6,000) he was forced to make a strategic retreat. A few days later, at New Hope Church on May 25-27, the Confederates also inflicted heavy losses on the Union for relatively minor losses themselves: over 3,000 Union casualties, and probably less than 1,000 Confederate. Once more, Sherman outmaneuvered Johnston, who fell back again, this time to a position 30 miles in front of Atlanta. At the minor engagement of Allatoona, strongly entrenched Yankees fought heroically (and successfully) to preserve the Union supply lines, with losses of 700-800 sustained on each side.

The first pitched battle near Atlanta came at Kennesaw Mountain on June 27; the second was the Battle of Peachtree Creek, and the third was the Battle of Atlanta. The Battle of Jonesborough, on August 31 and September 1, was the last before the Fall of Atlanta on September 2.

Because you can now drive up the park roads, it is easy to forget the difficulties which the soldiers often faced. Imagine trying to haul guns up Little Kennesaw.......

KENNESAW MOUNTAIN

The Confederate defenses based on Kennesaw Mountain were about 2 miles north and west of Marietta, now effectively a suburb of the city. In fact, the Confederate lines extended southwards along a ridge of hills rising up to 800 feet above the surrounding countryside, which is mostly at 1,000-1,100 feet. From north to south they were Big Kennesaw (1,808 feet); Little Kennesaw (just over 1,600 feet); Pigeon Hill (about 1,250 feet); and Cheatham Hill (about 1,200 feet). To the north-west, the direction from which Sherman was advancing, the ground rarely exceeds 1,050 feet. Every ravine, every hollow or gully, was covered with cannon and rifle fire; it was a superb delaying position, but both Johnston and Sherman knew that unless Sherman made some serious mistakes, it was neither a final defensive position nor a base for a counterattack which could destroy the numerically vastly superior Union army.

In those days, the surrounding terrain was much more heavily wooded than it is now, and also very swampy. Heavy rains had turned the roads into mires, so Sherman could not really contemplate a flanking movement; but his men were spoiling for a fight, after all the marching and maneuvring, so he launched a somewhat ill-advised frontal attack on the strongly fortified Rebel positions. First, his cannoneers pounded the Confederate position for days to soften it up, destroying so much tree cover that one Confederate defender said that Little Kennesaw should have been renamed "Bald Mountain." Then, he sent his infantry in on June 27.

While Kennesaw is no Lookout Mountain, it is steep and the surface is rocky where it is not covered with trees and scrub — and the Rebels were well dug in. With extraordinary determination, the Yankees managed to carry the first line of Confederate defenses, but the second or main line was impregnable. If you stand in the fields to the north-west of Pigeon Hill (Stop 3 on the Park Tour), you may find it hard to believe that anyone would even consider charging such a position.

Big and Little Kennesaw Mountains. The Yankees had to contend with soaring temperatures as well as difficult terrain when fighting in this area.

Gun emplacement, Kennesaw Mountain.

The result was predictable. Three or four thousand Union men fell (accounts vary as to precise losses), but Confederate losses were probably only 7-800. Sherman would think twice before he tried such a frontal attack again.

On the other hand, the diversionary movement which Sherman made to distract Johnston was more successful than the Union commander had hoped or (apparently) intended. It captured a road junction which permitted him to cross the Chattahoochee and continue his flanking movement.

Kennesaw is the only part of the battlefields around Atlanta to be designated an official National Battlefield Park, and it bristles with prohibitory notices, especially against alcohol; there are, however, designated picnic areas. There is a bitter humor in the warnings in the Park Service brochure that "The earthworks and mountain ecology are fragile, and disturbing them causes irreparable damage."

PEACHTREE CREEK

After Kennesaw Mountain, Johnston's men fell back to prepared positions on the north bank of the Chattahoochee River on July 4; the drying-out of the roads allowed Sherman to continue his flanking movement. As it turned out, the Confederates were outflanked at the Chattahoochee as well; there were simply not enough men to hold the positions which had been prepared. Accordingly, they fell back on July 8 and 9 to Peachtree Creek about 3 miles north of the center of Atlanta. The Creek is at about 760 feet, with steep sides, and it is overlooked on both sides by considerably higher ground at up to 850 feet within a few hundred yards of the river banks.

Peachtree Creek where Johnston planned to surprise the Union army as it crossed. Bad timing and lack of coordination resulted in huge Confederate losses here.

In response to public alarm about the way in which Johnston kept falling back, but much against the wishes of Confederate soldiers of all ranks, President Davis replaced him with Major-General John B. Hood. Hood was a brave fighter who had lost the use of his left arm at Gettysburg, only to lose his right leg at Chickamauga, but he was no match for Johnston as a strategist. Sherman acknowledged this when he rejoiced at the change in command, saying that Johnston "was equal in all the elements of generalship to Lee" and that "The character of a leader is a large factor in the game of war, and I confess I was pleased at this change."

Johnston's plan had been to fall on the Union army as it crossed Peachtree Creek (which is quite wide and deep) and to destroy it before it had a chance to prepare for fighting; Hood adopted the plan wholesale. Unfortunately, the perpetual Confederate bugbears of poor timing and poor coordination meant that the Confederate attacks were brave but ragged. The Union troops had already crossed on improvised bridges when the Confederates attacked. It was only with difficulty that the Yankees were able to fend off the Confederate attacks, but they still managed to do it, and to inflict terrible Confederate losses in the process. About 20,000 Union troops — the Army of the Cumberland — were engaged under Major-General George Thomas, and they lost 1,779 men. Out of close to 19,000 men in his command, Hood lost 4,796.

Peachtree Creek passes under the modern Peachtree Street (also known as US 19/GA 9), and to the east of the road is a pleasant suburb of Atlanta. West of the road, there is a small park beside the water; still further west, it broadens out into a golf course.

THE BATTLE OF ATLANTA

Only two days after the battle of Peachtree Creek, Hood tried another way to attack the Union forces. He withdrew from his outer defenses, hoping thereby to persuade the Yankees that he was in full retreat and to lure them into the open. The plan then called for a surprise attack against the advancing invaders.

Once again, a mistake ruined things. The Confederate

attackers had not marched far enough east to clear the right flank of the Union line, so instead of a flank attack, it became a frontal attack. Also, appalling timing meant that instead of two simultaneous attacks on the left and front of the Union army, the attacks came one after the other and the Yankees were not overwhelmed; instead, they could attempt to destroy the Rebels "in detail." By nightfall, Hood had lost more than 8,000 men while the numerically superior Union armies had lost less than half that number; the battle was a stalemate.

There is nothing to see on this battleground, which was fought over land now thoroughly incorporated in modern Atlanta; though it is a strange feeling to walk in Crestlawn Cemetery or around Howell School and to realize that in 1864 a great battle was fought on this same ground, and that where men bled and died there is now another golf club — Druid Hills.

Fuller's division rallying to hold its ground after being forced back by the first charge of the Confederates in their flank attack at the Battle of Atlanta, July 22. From a painting by James E. Taylor.

THE MARCH TO THE SEA

After the Union broke the thin Confederate defenses at Jonesborough, almost completing the encirclement of Atlanta, Hood had no option but to withdraw the Confederate army from the city. He did so, and set out to march north and west into Tennessee.

Sherman, on the other hand, sent about a third of his army to Nashville to complete his business with the Confederates there. The other 62,000 men were to march to Savannah, which they did in November and December 1864.

The strictly military objective was to cut the supply lines from the South to Virginia, starving the Confederate armies there of food and *matériel*, but Sherman went far beyond this. Whole towns were put to the torch, along with isolated farms and plantations. The Union armies, which had been sent out without supply wagons, had been instructed to live off the land, and they did so with enthusiasm. Livestock was slaughtered, and

Contrabands marching to the sea in the wake of Sherman's army.

frequently deliberately fouled to prevent the Rebels even salvaging what was left. One Yankee refers to orders "to consume everything eatable by man or beast." Crops and barns were fired. Women and children were turned out into the snow as the Union men destroyed everything they owned; even the children's clothes were burned, rent, or dragged in mud. A swathe of Georgia some 200 miles long and up to 60 miles wide was destroyed. Starvation was widespread among the Rebels afterwards, though Union soldiers remained well clothed and well fed.

While Sherman apparently had no qualms about what he did, he was worried that his orders might be countermanded. Indeed, although Grant supported him, General John A. Fawlins in Washington apparently tried to have him stopped. Sherman himself describes "how free and glorious I felt when the magic telegraph was cut, which prevented orders of any kind coming to delay or hinder us." The horror of those days has not been forgotten yet.

Some idea of the spirit in which the destruction was undertaken may be gleaned from Major-General Slocum's jocular instructions in *Battles and Leaders* (*Vol IV*, page 685) on how to destroy railroads:

Sherman's men cutting the telegraph wires: now, he could not be countermanded.

> ...the men should have a good breakfast ... I suggest roast turkeys, chickens, fresh eggs and coffee, for the reason that in an enemy's country such a breakfast will cause no unpleasantness between the commissary and the soldiers, inasmuch as the commissary will only be required to provide the coffee.

Such a breakfast might well be necessary if (as the writer suggests), "a thousand men can easily destroy about five miles of track per day, and do it thoroughly."

In fairness to Sherman, he did not specifically order the atrocities which were committed by his men, and many of the worst acts were the responsibility of "bummers," freelance looters who had previously been stragglers but now foraged in front of the army. Many Yankees despised these men almost as much as the Rebels did: one wrote, "The 'coffee-coolers' of the Army of the Potomac were archangels compared with our 'bummers,' who often fell to the tender mercies of Wheeler's cavalry, and were never heard of again, earning a fate richly deserved." But it cannot be said that Sherman discouraged the "bummers;" even in Yankees' minds, the distinction between "bummers" and "foragers" was not always clear. Slocum, already mentioned for his railroad-wrecking, refers to "an efficient corps of foragers (vulgarly known in our army as 'bummers')..."

IN SHERMAN'S FOOTSTEPS

To see the land which Sherman laid waste, the blood-red earth of Georgia and the once-rich fields which even now have not regained their former prosperity, stay off I-75 and I-16. Instead, take the following roads:

US 23 south-east out of Atlanta to Jackson, about 30 miles from the city. From Jackson, GA 16 E to Monticello, about 18 miles. From Monticello, GA 11 S to Gray, just under 25 miles. From Gray, GA 18 S and E to Gordon, about 15 miles, then on to the junction with GA 57 (a mile beyond Gordon).
Left/east on GA 57 to Irwinton (12 miles) and Tombsboro (another 20 miles), then on to the junction with GA 68 (about 10 miles from Tombsboro).
Turn left (north) and follow GA 68 to Tenille, about 13 miles. Then take GA 15 N to Sandersville. From there, follow GA 24 E to Louisville (well signposted, about 23 miles).
From Louisville, take GA 17 to Midville, about 20 miles. You now stay on GA 17 through Millen, Scarboro, Rocky Ford, Oliver, Egypt, Guyton and Marlow. About 10 miles after Marlow, 80-90 miles from Midville, you join I-80 about 10-15 miles before Savannah.

This is not exactly the route that the Yankees followed, because some bridges were destroyed, and besides, part of the time Sherman's men corduroyed their own roads; but most of the time, you will be traveling roads which at least part of the Yankee armies also traveled.

SAVANNAH AND ONWARD

Astonishingly, the old town of Savannah escaped widespread destruction. There is still a good deal of the ante-bellum town to

Left: As you follow the March to the Sea, the memorials leave you in no doubt that you are in Confederate territory. This is in Jackson, Georgia.

Right: No doubt, this house burned recently; but during the March to the Sea, such sights were commonplace. Seeing a burned house on this route suddenly lends poignancy to the drive, and reinforces the image of "total war."

see, though Colonial-period relics are hard to find. After Savannah, Sherman's men marched northwards to Columbia in South Carolina, which they destroyed with a thoroughness and vindictiveness that was unusual even for them: "The city was filled with helpless women and children and invalids, many of whom were rendered houseless and homeless in a single night" (Slocum again).

From there, the Yankee troops went on to Fayetteville in North Carolina, then continued north and east to link up with Grant's men in Virginia. If you visit Savannah yourself, it is worth visiting nearby Fort Pulaski which was a Union stronghold for most of the War, even though it was in the heart of the South; the Yankees captured it on April 11, 1862, and then used it to support the blockade.

Fort Pulaski, outside Savannah, Georgia, was captured by the Union as early as April 11, 1862; new long-range rifled guns meant that it was no longer impregnable.

If you are making this tour by automobile, you may find it interesting to make a detour and drive up to Charleston. There, you can see not only the extraordinary, jumbled museum operated by the Daughters of the Confederacy but also the place where the War officially started: Fort Sumter.

THE AFTERMATH

The back of the Confederacy was broken. To be sure, there would be more battles, and some of them would be hard-fought; but with the Confederate States now rent in three pieces (north of Sherman's March, south of Sherman's March, and Trans-Mississippi), it was a miracle that the fight lasted for even a few months more.

FURTHER INFORMATION

Maps: USGS 7.5': Marietta; Atlanta NW; Atlanta NE
Official Reports Atlas: Kennesaw: 43/4; 47/4; 49/4; 56/2;
58/6; 59/1; 60/1; 62/6,10,13,14; 65/2,3,5; 96/5;
101/19. PeachTree Creek: 47/5; 101/7. Atlanta: 45/3;
56/6; 56/7; 59/7; 61/2+3; 61/15; 62/3+8+9; 64/4;
87/6; 88/1; 90/3+5; 131/3. March to the Sea: 101/21
B&L: Vol IV: 251; 295; 300; 304; 312

Park: As might be expected of one of the newer parks, the Kennesaw Mountain Visitor Center is interesting but not yet well developed. Superintendent: PO Box 1167, Marietta, GA 30061.

City: Atlanta is a modern, *big* city: generally more interested in the future than in the past. The City of Atlanta does, however, operate the Confederate Cyclorama at Grant Park (by the Zoo). This is a more interesting cyclorama than the one at Gettysburg, and the presentation is much better. There is an excellent museum attached.

TOTAL WAR

John Mosby, leader of Mosby's Raiders: they were a band of partisans who operated in Virginia for two years.

According to the theory of total war, *any* person on the "other side" is a combatant; and *any* means of prosecuting the war is legitimate. This includes officially sanctioned destruction of homes and food supplies, usually accompanied by looting; the burning of whole towns; the taking of hostages; the shooting of prisoners in "retaliation" for enemy action; "terror" bombardment of civilian targets; and even such barbarisms as marching prisoners through minefields in order to clear them.

Total war differs from isolated atrocities in that it is ordered by the high command, with the intention of frightening people into submission. Its mirror image is guerrilla warfare: the guerrilla fights when he wants, then melts back into the background and becomes an apparently run-of-the-mill farmer or shopkeeper. Set against guerrilla warfare, such acts as the destruction of houses and food supplies sometimes make a kind of vicious sense; similar tactics have since been used (for example) in Burma and Vietnam.

On the other hand, the random destruction of property and the deliberate murder and mistreatment of hostages and prisoners have been universally condemned. There were occasional Confederate acts such as the burning of Chambersburg at the end of July 1864, but Sheridan's Burning of the Valley in September 1864 and Sherman's March to the Sea were something else altogether. At least the burning of the Shenandoah Valley was in large part a military necessity, designed to prevent a Confederate return, but Sherman's behavior on the March to the Sea was terrorism pure and simple. Sherman was simply demonstrating to the people of the South in a peculiarly vicious and despicable way that they had been defeated.

The Confederate destroyed a great deal of Richmond on the night before the Union armies arrived.

Sherman and Total War

Sherman's men forage on a Georgia plantation.

Sherman first formulated his theories of "Total War" in Kentucky and Mississippi. He began by issuing an order that for every Union boat fired upon, ten citizens chosen by lot would be given three days to abandon their houses and remove themselves and their families at least 25 miles from town.

Next came the destruction of the village of Randolph, not because it contained any soldiers, but because it sympathized with the Rebels. Two evil ideas were worked together; first, that the South was "guilty" rather than an honest foe, and second, that "guilt by association" was an infallible principle.

Thereafter, Sherman went from bad to worse. On the way to Atlanta he was bad enough; the destruction of Atlanta was so thorough that reconstruction was to take more than half a century, and from Atlanta to the sea, a swathe 60 miles wide was simply destroyed. His men gorged themselves on the best food, fouling the rest and leaving it to rot. They slaughtered animals and destroyed crops. They burned houses, often driving women and children out into the rain with nothing but the clothes on their backs. They stole mercilessly, and what they could not steal, they burned, smashed or destroyed. Nothing was exempt: beautiful furniture and paintings met the same fate as the clothes and bedding of the very poorest, even of slaves. Treasured silver, much of it pre-Revolutionary, was stolen and frequently smashed for scrap. They burned cotton, and stole cash. Churches, libraries, hospitals, *everything* in their path was destroyed.

Nor did they confine their damage to property. Householders were tortured to make them reveal the whereabouts of their valuables — just casually with bayonets or fire, or by being strung up by their thumbs. Many were killed. The women and children who were the only occupants of many houses, were raped — though this is probably the only atrocity of which Sherman's men did *not* boast. Black women and girls were particularly liable to rape, because they were regarded as sub-human.

Perhaps more than anything else, Sherman's "Total War" perpetuated the bitter memory of the War between the States. Many wounds which might otherwise have healed are still to be found, just under the surface.

A searing indictment of William Tecumseh Sherman can be found in J. B. Walters' *Merchant of Terror: General Sherman and Total War* (Bobbs-Merrill, Indianapolis and New York 1973).

THE BATTLE OF
CEDAR CREEK

Cedar Creek, Virginia
October 19 1864

Confederate States
Major-General Jubal Early
10-15,000 effectives*
3,000 casualties

United States
Major-General Philip Sheridan
Over 30,000 effectives
5,665 casualties

*Figures are disputed and range from 8,800 to 18,000.

The Shenandoah Valley is as idyllic a place as its name suggests. The Blue Ridge Mountains shimmer in the haze; there is rich agricultural land; many of the towns date back to the eighteenth century, when much of the surveying was done by a young George Washington; there are trees, and streams, and woods and pastures.

It was also of crucial importance during the War between the States. It was the breadbasket of the Confederacy after the Union gained control of the Mississippi and denied the South access to the agricultural produce of the west, and it was a

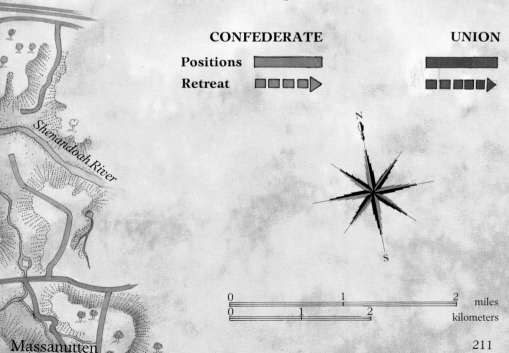

	CONFEDERATE		UNION
Positions			
Retreat			

Shenandoah River

Massanutten
Mountain

| 0 | | 1 | | 2 | miles |
| 0 | 1 | | 2 | | kilometers |

north-south corridor up which Confederate armies could range with impunity, striking either north (as in the Second Invasion of the North) or east (towards Washington) as the mood took them. Many were the battles fought in the Valley — it was where Jackson achieved many of his successes — and when he was appointed Lieutenant-General, Grant ordered Phil Sheridan to lay it waste, in order to deny the Confederacy its comforts.

The Battle of Cedar Creek (also known as the Battle of Belle Grove) is the only battle covered in detail in this book which does *not* have an official Battlefield Park associated with it. The land is still in private hands; there are precious few official markers; and tracing the course of the battle is an interesting piece of detective work, made much easier with the booklet described at the end of this chapter.

This photograph of 1885 is a view, from Kershaw's Ford, of the Valley Turnpike where Sheridan joined his troops before occupying the hills seen in the background, on October 19, 1864.

THE HISTORY OF THE VALLEY

After First Manassas, Jackson was promoted to Major-General and assigned to the Shenandoah Valley in November 1861. His brief was to keep an eye on Union forces in or near the Valley, and to be ready to reinforce Johnston's victorious Confederates who were concentrated around Centreville.

By the end of the year, he had enlarged his original small band of militia to an army of about 10,000 men, and he was ready to play a strategic, rather than a tactical, part in the Confederate campaign. His aim was to occupy Union troops, thereby keeping the Union armies divided and keeping Washington in a perpetual state of nervousness about his capabilities and intentions; this in turn would delay McClellan's Union advance on Richmond, as Lincoln insisted on retaining a substantial garrison in the capital.

By a combination of brilliance and daring, which won strategic victories even when he was tactically defeated, Jackson managed to tie up Union forces several times his own strength. He was defeated at Kernstown on March 23 (outnumbered 3:1); won at McDowell on May 8 (10,000 Confederates against 6,000 Union troops); captured Front Royal on May 23, cutting off Bank's Union troops and narrowly missing destroying them; won at Winchester on May 25 (outnumbering his opponents 2:1); won again at Port Republic (5,900 Rebels against 3,000 Yankees); and royally confused Shields and Fremont in early June.

The reasons he could so often attack with superior forces were his genius for guessing the enemy's movements; his refusal to tell anyone what he was doing, thereby ensuring security hitherto unimagined in most Civil War armies; and his willingness and ability to press himself and his men to the limit, especially by covering large distances in one-half or one-third of the time (sometimes less) that any other general could manage.

Through the latter part of 1862, and most of 1863, the Valley was fairly quiet — though Lee invaded the north via the Valley in June 1863, on his way to Gettysburg. In 1864, there was a good deal of coming and going by both sides, and after the defeat of Jubal Early's Confederate forces in September, Phil Sheridan's Union forces engaged in the "Burning of the Valley," the

New Market. Breckinridge's Confederate victory here on May 15 severely hampered Union hopes of gaining control of the Shenandoah Valley.

NEW MARKET

About 30 miles up the Valley from Strasburg (south — the Shenandoah flows north, remember) there is a unique Battlefield Park which commemorates the last Confederate victory in the Valley. It was the Battle of New Market, fought on May 15, 1864. The park is administered by the Virginia Military Institute (VMI), whose cadets played a special part in the battle.

So desperate was the Confederacy for men that 257 cadets of the VMI marched to New Market from nearby Lexington to join the militiamen and others put together under Major-General John C. Breckinridge. With only 5,000 men, Breckinridge reversed a Yankee army of about 6,500; at his reluctant command, "Put the boys in," the teenage cadets charged the Yankee batteries and took them. Fifty-seven fell, but such are the powers of youthful recuperation that only ten died. Their names are commemorated every year at the VMI: the roll is read, followed by "Dead on the field of honor! Sir!"

213

systematic destruction of barns, crops and anything else that might be useful to the Confederates. The last major battle in the Valley, and the one which marked the end of Confederate power there, was the one described here.

TERRAIN

The Allegheny Mountains and the Blue Ridge Mountains run roughly parallel for hundreds of miles, about 150-250 miles inland from the east coast of North America. The names change locally; to the west of the Shenandoah Valley, the Alleghenies are called the South Mountains, and to the east the Blue Ridge Mountains are sometime called the Catoctins.

At Mechanicstown, some 20 miles north of Harper's Ferry, the mountains are about 1½ miles apart; at Harper's Ferry itself, where the Potomac breaks through both ranges, they are about 9 miles apart.

Cedar Creek, after which the battle is named, is one of the tributaries of the Shenandoah; it joins the South Fork and the North Fork just by Manassas Gap, about 75 miles west of Washington. Strasburg, which played a critical part in the battle, lies between the North Fork of the Shenandoah (which is actually to the west of the South Fork) and Cedar Creek. Middletown is about 4½ miles north-east of Strasburg; Belle Grove Plantation, near modern Meadow Mills on the VA 727 as it approaches the VA 624, is half a mile closer to Strasburg. This was Sheridan's Union headquarters.

The Manassas Gap railroad runs eastwards through Strasburg, going on to the Gap from which it got its name. The main road in 1864 was the Valley Turnpike, which ran north and south; it now corresponds to the US 11, which is paralleled by the modern

The Belle Grove Plantation gives the battle of Cedar Creek its alternative name as a result of its central role in the action. Not only was the Mansion Sheridan's Union headquarters; it also served as a store for captured goods and weaponry and for Confederate prisoners. The Belle Grove Plantation was also the scene of some of the fiercest combat of the battle.

I-81. Cedar Creek Battlefield appears on modern USGS maps as the space between the two roads, about a mile south-west of Middletown.

Strasburg is at about 500-600 feet; the highest point, on the northern edge of town, is at 660 feet or so. Hupp's (or Hupp) Hill is about a mile north of Strasburg, at 712 feet. Belle Grove is at almost 700 feet, while Middletown is on a ridge at 700-730 feet (the Valley Turnpike follows this ridge fairly closely). Cedar Creek runs very roughly north-south in the area which concerns us, with many twists and turns. The sides of the valley are frequently very steep; gradients of 50% are commonplace.

As might be expected in an valley between two ranges of mountains intersected with mature rivers, the terrain generally is very varied; there are some relatively flat areas, especially where the rivers have changed course, and some very steep hills. Where there is not pasture or farmland (which means across most of the steeper grades, and in the narrow river valleys), the ground cover consists of thick woods. The whole is ideally suited for the concealed movement of troops.

To the south and west of Strasburg, however, there is much higher ground. Three Top Mountain, Green Mountain and Massanutten Mountain are all over 2,000 feet; Meneka Peak is at 2,393 feet; and Signal Knob on the end of Three Top is at about 2,100 feet. Unless troops were making a conscious effort to move unobserved, these heights provide an excellent overview of the rest of the terrain.

The Shenandoah Valley, seen from the edge of the New Market battlefield. Following the defeat at New Market which dashed Union hopes of taking control of Shenandoah, Grant gave Sheridan orders to destroy the Valley.

THE BATTLE

Sheridan's forces were on the high ground around the Valley Pike, almost exactly half-way between Strasburg and Middletown. With the aid of field-glasses, Early's men could study the Union camp in detail (remember, camouflage was still a thing of the future); General John B. Gordon and the topographer Jedediah Hotchkiss planned for a night attack.

The battle began at five o'clock in the morning, and the Confederate attack was initially successful. By about seven, the Union had however managed to stem the Confederate rush, and by about nine or ten they were retreating no further. Sheridan's return from Washington at 10:30 put new spirit into the Union troops, and at about four in the afternoon a Union counterattack was extremely successful; the Confederate troops were pushed back to their original position, and suffered severe losses of irreplaceable *matériel*. Even so, Union losses were about twice those of the Confederates.

The Dawn Attack

The trail which Gordon's Confederate troops took along the base of Massanutten Mountain is mostly lost today, but they crossed at McInturff's Ford (about 200 yards downstream from the junction of Cedar Creek and the North Fork) and Bowman's

Bowman's Mill Ford, which was crossed by some of the Confederate troops approaching the Union camp for the dawn attack.

Ford, less than half a mile further downsteam again. They reunited a few hundred yards inland and marched north-east for about a mile until they were within half a mile or so of the Union camps on the right (eastern or southern) flank.

Other Confederate troops moved up the Valley Pike and along what is now the VA 635. The latter crossed at Bowman's Mill Ford (as distinct from Bowman's Ford), about 2 miles upstream from the confluence of Cedar Creek and the North Fork; the modern road crosses via a low concrete bridge. They too came up on the right flank of the Union line.

There was an early-morning fog, typical of the area, which helped both to conceal their movements and to muffle the sound of their marching. Swords and canteens were left in camp, to reduce noise still further. The damp, cold smell of the air on such a day is something that is hard to forget. For the Confederates, it must have been an eerie march; for the Union, it was just another foggy night.

The Confederates were also assisted by the fact that Union posting of sentries and videttes (mounted sentries) was disgracefully lax. Some divisions were not even dressed, and even those which had managed to spot the Confederates had only a few minutes in which to prepare. At five o'clock, the Confederates fired and rushed forward with the blood-curdling Rebel yell. To descend to bathos, an alarm clock or a telephone call at that hour can wake you with your heart pounding; imagine what a Confederate charge might do.

The half-dressed Yankees fought patchily, where they fought at all; the early risers abandoned their breakfasts in the frying-pans. Within 20 minutes, Confederate artillery was on Hupp's Hill, adding to Union discomfiture; Early had delayed bringing it up any earlier, for fear the noise would alert the Yankees. Small knots of men fought at very close quarters — "brawled" is not too inaccurate a word — but the few minutes of time that each brave

Yankee stand could buy were to be decisive in the battle to come, because if all the Yankees had run, the Confederate advance would have gained more impetus.

By ten o'clock, however, the Confederates straddled the Pike at Middletown, in front of the modern VA 627 (their lines were in part on the modern VA 633) while the Union had their backs to what is now the VA 633; all of these roads existed in 1864. The two lines were about a mile apart.

The Confederate attack then faltered and died. By some accounts, Jubal Early called a halt to reorganize; by his own account, he had not enough men left to fight with. As he puts it,

> This was the case of a glorious victory given up by my own troops after they had won it, and it is to be accounted for on the ground of the partial demoralization caused by the plunder of the enemy's camps, and from the fact that the men undertook to judge for themselves when it was proper to retire.

Another crossing employed by troops during the movements on October 19th.

Whatever happened, the Confederates lost the initiative. Early's commanders felt that he should never have paused. The game of "What if...?" is hard to resist. Early is reputed to have said, "The Yankees got whipped, and we got scared."

Sheridan's Ride

Sheridan had been in Washington, conferring with Lincoln and other leaders, though the Confederates thought he was at Belle Grove and indeed planned to capture him there; they would probably have succeeded with this strategy, if their premise had been correct. At Winchester, some 8 miles north of Middletown, he had heard the sound of battle, and he galloped off to be with his troops. "Sheridan's Ride" was the stuff of which legends are made; he thundered down the Pike and then cut along the line waving his hat.

Major General Philip Sheridan.

The sight of their commanding general galvanized the weary and battered Union troops. It was indeed a magnificent sight: a general throwing himself to the fore, genuinely leading his troops instead of directing them from a safe place. As his men rose to cheer him, he yelled "God damn you, don't cheer me! If you love your country, come to the front!"

Under the direction of Sheridan, the Union troops reorganized and formed once more in line of battle. When the Confederates finally launched another attack, the Union troops were able to repulse it without difficulty.

217

An artists's impression of the savage fighting around the Belle Grove Mansion.

The Union Counterattack

At four in the afternoon, Sheridan launched his counterattack. It was a frontal assault concentrating on the center of the Confederate lines, with a cavalry attack on their left (west) flank led by an officer whose name was to be much more famous in years to come: George Custer.

GEORGE ARMSTRONG CUSTER

Custer was already well known before Little Big Horn as a Yankee hero in the War between the States. Born December 5, 1839, he graduated from West Point in 1861; three days later, at the age of 21, he fought at Manassas. In June 1862 he was one of the first soldiers to make observations from a balloon, and at the age of 23 he was promoted from Captain to Brigadier-General after his heroic charge at the Battle of Aldie in June. He led the second brigade of the Third Cavalry Division at Gettysburg. Like many great men, he had the faults of his qualities. Thirsty for personal glory, he never cared much about anyone else, which led to his successes as an Indian fighter. Court-martialed in 1868 for leaving his post without permission, he was reinstated next year, before he was 30. He was 36 when the Sioux took their revenge on June 25, 1876.

Sheridan's use of fighting cavalry was among the most masterful of any general. Jeb Stuart's Confederate cavalry were used for three main purposes: intelligence, screening troop movements, and raiding. Sheridan, on the other hand, used his mounted arm like a modern armored division — with great success.

The flank attack broke the Confederate lines, and the Rebels broke and ran. By evening, they were streaming through Strasburg; and a small mishap there made things even worse. Accounts vary as to what happened, but they all center on a small bridge near Spangler's Mill in central Strasburg. According to some sources, the bridge broke; according to others, a wagon went off the edge. Whatever took place, the result was a bottleneck which prevented the passage of any more wagons or guns. Not only did the Confederates lose the Union guns they had captured that morning; they also lost a good deal of their own *matériel*. The little bridge still exists, though you have to look hard to find it now; it is now very much wider, and forms a part of the well-surfaced main road through Strasburg.

Early regrouped at Fisher's Hill, about 5 miles south of Strasburg, and withdrew during the night. It was the end of Confederate military power in the Valley.

Above: The small bridge, now lost under the main road, caused the Confederate bottleneck during the retreat.

Below: Spangler's Mill, Strasburg. Sheridan's destruction of resources available to the Confederates excluded this mill which provided Union rations during this campaign.

FURTHER INFORMATION

Maps: USGS 7.5': Strasburg and Middletown quadrangles
Official Reports Atlas: 69/3; 82/9; 99/2
B&L: Vol. IV, 517

Book: Joseph W.A. Whitehorn, *The Battle of Cedar Creek* (Wayside Museum of American History and Arts, Strasburg, VA 1987). Somewhat expensive for its size, but a superb little guide with an excellent self-guided tour.

Town: Strasburg is an agreeable small town; there are numerous motels and restaurants in the Valley, of widely varying standards, but usually excellent value.

WOMEN IN WAR

The amateur nurses all stood firm ... One who had no thought of leaving her post desired to send her sister — a mere child — out of harm's way. She, therefore, told her to go to their home, about half a mile distant, and ask their mother for some yellow cloth that was in the house, thinking, of course, that the mother would never permit the girl to come back into the town. But she miscalculated. The child accepted the commission as a sacred trust, forced her way out over the crowded road, where the danger was more real than in the town itself, reached home, and made her request. The house had its own flag flying, for it was directly in range, and full of wounded. Perhaps for this reason the mother was less anxious to keep her daughter with her; perhaps in the hurry and excitement she allowed herself to be persuaded that it was really necessary to get that strip of yellow flannel into Shepherdstown as soon as possible. With streaming tears, she kissed the girl, and saw her set out to go alone, half a mile through a panic-stricken rabble, under the fire of a battery and into a town whose escape from conflagration was at best not assured.

This incident occurred after Antietam and was recorded in *A Womans' Recollections of Antietam* by Mary Bedinger Mitchell. The little girl delivered her yellow flannel, to make a hospital flag; yellow was the color of hospitals then, before the Red Cross became the international symbol. She and her mother and sister had come a long way from the days when Southern girls cheered Secession, and vowed either to marry a soldier or to die an old maid.

In the South, women ran the farms and smallholdings as best they could; thousands of their menfolk never came back, thousands more came back minus a leg or an arm, and most were away for long, cruel years. And yet, it seems, they were no more given to defeatism than their menfolk. There are wistful references to a peace long gone, and occasional condemnations of the War, but most remained solidly Secessionist. They were nurses, they made cartridges and — when propriety and the War permitted — they flirted with the soldiers, and sometimes married them. Teenagers with stars in their eyes married soldiers in their thirties and forties, and were themselves widowed before they were 20.

In the North, things were a little different but not much better. There was food, and their men were paid; but the women still had to take the burden of running many farms single-handed. Grand ladies worked with the Sanitary Commission, some in an ornamental capacity but many more in a sincere attempt to help the poor soldiers. Ordinary women, as in the South, did

Southern women frequently smuggled contraband (often necessities like books, medicines and blankets) through the Union lines, under their skirts. As the attendant at the Petersburg Siege Museum, where this petticoat is on display, said: "Sir, not even a Yankee would search a lady!"

THE SISTER OF CHARITY

HOME TIDINGS

what they could. One of the "firsts" of the War between the States was the way in which women flocked to serve as nurses, inspired by Florence Nightingale's example in the Crimean War and her book *Notes on Nursing*. Previously, nursing had been the province of men, and the few women near the front were either officers' ladies or camp-followers of the lowest kind.

Jennie Hodgers, though, went one step further. Born in Belfast on Christmas Day, 1844, she stowed away to get to America and enlisted as a private in the 95th Illinois Volunteer Infantry on August 6, 1862, aged 17, under the name of Albert D.J. Cashier. For almost three years she fought, and when the regiment returned home, she shared the heroes' welcome. After the War, she earned a living as a handyman. Not until 1911, when she broke her leg aged 66, did anyone realize she was not a man. She was admitted to the Soldiers' and Sailors' Home in Quincy, still as a man, with the connivance of her doctor. In 1913, apparently senile, she was transferred to the Insane Asylum at Watertown, where the authorities refused to keep up the pretense.

She drew a veteran's pension of $70 a month, and when she died on October 11, 1915, she was buried in uniform with full military honors. At 70, the only woman to have completed a fully documented Union army enlistment was dead.

This contemporary illustration shows various images of women during the War - as an incentive to victory, a comfort and support to the wounded and a source of vital supplies: helping the war effort without straying from traditional feminine roles.

Further reading

Curtis Carrol Davis (ed.), *Belle Boyd in Camp and Prison, Written by Herself*, (Thomas Yoseloff, Cranbury, NJ, and London). Intriguing, if self-serving, autobiography (heavily edited and commented upon) of the famous/notorious Southern lady spy.

Bell Irvin Wiley, *Confederate Women* (Greenwood Press, Westport, CT, and London, 1975). Only Chapter 4 could be said to deal with women in general (the first three chapters are biographies of individual women), but still a useful book.

Agatha Young, *The Women and the Crisis, Women of the North in the Civil War,* (McDowell, Obolensky, New York, 1959). An early feminist tract, arguing that the Civil War was as much about the liberation of women as the liberation of slaves — a very Yankee, middle-class book of the 1950s.

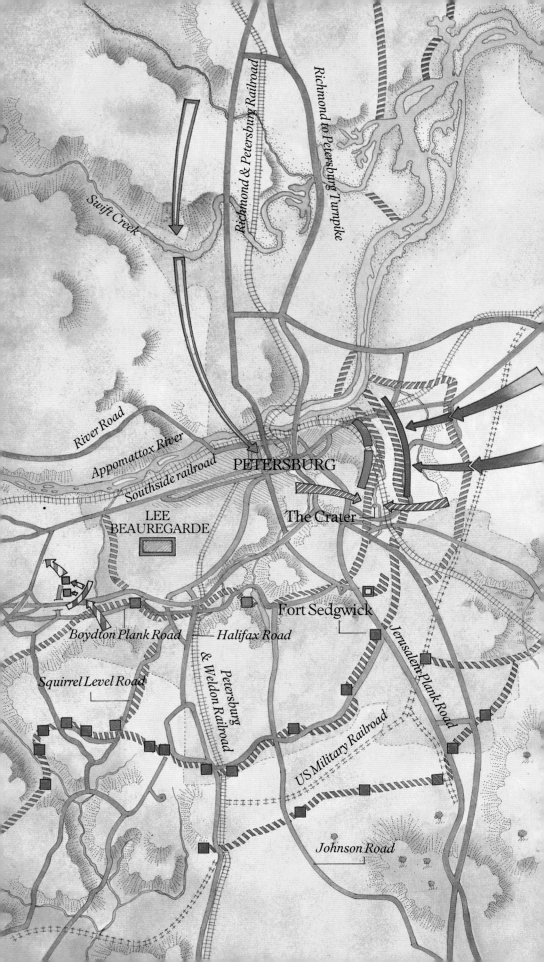

THE STRUGGLE FOR PETERSBURG

Petersburg, Virginia
Assaults: June 15-18 1864
Siege: June 18 1864-April 2 1865

James River

Hopewell

Petersburg & City Point Railroad

Confederate States
General Robert E. Lee
48,000 effectives[*]
28,000 casualties[†]

United States
General Ulysses S. Grant
95,000 effectives[*]
42,000 casualties[†]

[*]On the afternoon of June 18, 1864; Lee had received 28,000 reinforcements around noon. By February 1865, the Union had about 110,000 and the Confederacy perhaps 60,000.

[†]During the Siege itself.

GRANT
MEADE

Petersburg today is a strangely quiet, almost melancholy, town. Before the War, it was a major commercial and industrial center, with mills, foundries, tobacco warehouses, locomotive works and a great deal else. A sense of loss pervades everything; it is an attractive city, but also a haunting one.

More than the other battlefields of the War, the area around Petersburg is eerie, too. The sites themselves are less heavily

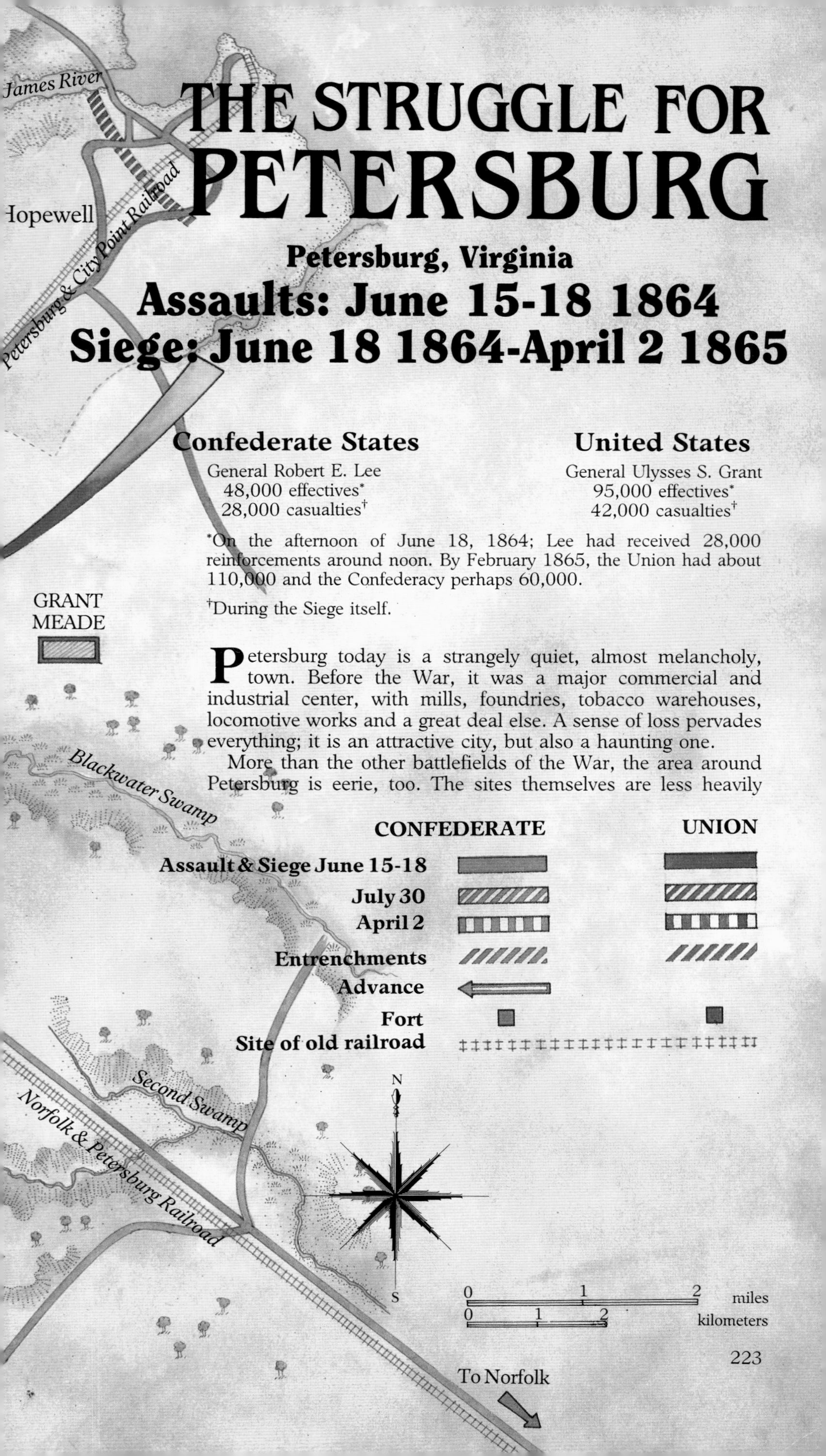

Blackwater Swamp

	CONFEDERATE	UNION
Assault & Siege June 15-18		
July 30		
April 2		
Entrenchments		
Advance		
Fort		
Site of old railroad		

Second Swamp

Norfolk & Petersburg Railroad

N

S

| 0 | | 1 | | 2 | miles |
| 0 | 1 | | 2 | | kilometers |

To Norfolk

223

restored than some others; there is a sense of a slow return to normal, of the earthworks slowly subsiding into the earth from which they were torn. It is like one of those Hollywood movies where, as you stare at an empty landscape, misty figures are slowly faded into view by some optical trick and the ghostly sounds of long-gone trains, sutlers' calls, drill-sergeants' curses and the jingling of spurs are heard.

In one or two places, there are modern reconstructions of the old fortifications, complete with the raw earth, the logs, the water-sodden trench paths and the sutlers' huts. These too are more powerful than the long-fallen-in trenches, overgrown with grass, treated by most people with an almost exaggerated respect. By their very rawness, they re-create the weathered remains, so that we can people them in our imagination with thronging soldiers, the stink of the camp, the long periods of boredom interspersed with moments of terror.

Troops in front of Petersburg.

THE IMPORTANCE OF PETERSBURG

"Drives to Richmond" had repeatedly failed; it took Ulysses S. Grant to see what now seems so obvious in retrospect, that if Richmond could be isolated from its sources of supply, it would wither and die. Petersburg, at the junction of five railroads and the main link with Richmond, was the key.

Even at that, Grant underestimated the tenacity of the South. Repeated assaults in mid-June 1864 failed to carry the town, so the Union settled down to a long siege. Even then, they did not realise how long it would take. By the time Richmond fell nine and a half months later, the Union had built a veritable military city to the east of Petersburg, supplied by a specially laid military railroad which ferried supplies from City Point (modern Hopewell) on the James River.

Until Grant's attack on June 15, Lee still believed that the Union's main force was near Richmond; not until June 18 was he able to get his army down to Petersburg, arriving around noon. From June 15 to 18, the Union army had its chance, as described below. After that, it was an ever more bitter siege.

TERRAIN

Between the James and Petersburg, the land is mostly low-lying; maximum elevations are mostly under 150 feet, and the beds of the streams are at 60-70 feet; the land generally lies at 50-80 feet near the river, perhaps 100-120 feet close to Richmond.

Around Petersburg, the Appomattox River falls quite rapidly from about 60 feet above sea level a couple miles upstream to sea level at the town itself; Petersburg is the tidal limit of the Appomattox. To the west, the valley is quite steep (rising to 50-100 feet in only 100 yards), but the lowest-lying parts of Petersburg are only 10-20 feet above sea level. The highest points of the town, a mile and more south of the river, are at about 160 feet.

To the east of the town, around the modern Battlefield Park, the land mostly lies at 100-130 feet, with maximum elevations around 140 feet. The land is mostly rolling hills, though surprisingly large areas are flat plateaus. As you swing south, below the town, maximum elevations increase; heights of 170 feet and more are not uncommon, with stream beds and low-lying areas at 120 feet or less.

There is a good deal of swampy ground; Blackwater Swamp lies to the east of the town, and Second Swamp to the south-east. The soil is mostly thick and clay-like; drainage everywhere is poor.

During the War, the five railroads converging on the city were the Richmond and Petersburg (headed due N), the Petersburg and City Point (NE), the Norfolk and Petersburg (SE), the Petersburg and Weldon (due S) and the Southside (W). At least traces of all of these can still be seen; some are still in use. A US military railroad, of which there are now hardly any remains, was built during the War; it was about 10 miles long and looped south-west around the town, linking the Petersburg and City Point Railroad with the Petersburg and Weldon Railroad.

The road network was altogether more tangled and of less military and economic significance. Two main roads came in north of the river, the equivalents of the modern US 1/US 301 and the I-95. On the south bank, the River Road (modern VA 600 and 601) came in from the west, the Boydton Plank Road from the south-west (modern US 1), the Squirrel Level Road (modern VA 613), the Halifax Road (modern VA 604) and the Jerusalem Plank Road (modern VA 608, Johnson Road) from the south, and a stage road (modern US 460, becoming VA 406) from the east.

Fort Sedgwick, built in 1864 by Union troops and destroyed a century later. The fort was the scene of heavy and repeated Confederate bombardment.

THE ASSAULTS OF JUNE 15-18, 1864

Grant's headquarters in the grounds of Appomattox Manor, City Point, outside Petersburg.

The Confederate lines around Petersburg were in the shape of a great fish-hook. The line stretched south from Richmond, defending the Richmond and Petersburg Railroad, broken only by rivers, until it looped back on itself by a westward turn; the end of the line was anchored on the Appomattox, upstream (west) of Petersburg, so that the city was surrounded by troops on three sides and by the river on the fourth.

In early June, General Beauregard's left (eastern) flank was about a mile downstream (east) of the railroad bridge in the center of Petersburg, around what are now the Broadway Marshalling Yards. The Confederate lines ran along the high ground (rising to about 150 feet within a mile or so of the river), roughly south for something over 2 miles. The other fortifications were much more skimpily manned, and they were also further from the town center — 2-2½ miles, instead of 1-1½ miles.

On June 15, 14,000 Confederates under Beauregard faced more than three times their strength in Union troops, but the old familiar story of poor staff work, inadequate maps, sloppy supply lines and a remarkable lack of coordination between commanders (this time on the Yankee side) meant that the opportunity to take Petersburg that afternoon was lost. The Confederates had to fight like heroes, and they did, but a victory against such odds (even with the advantage of fighting from fortifications) cannot be ascribed to Confederate bravery alone; Union mismanagement must take part of the responsibility.

There are countless earthworks and forts all around Richmond and Petersburg. Even with old maps and Park Service information, it is often impossible to work out which is which.

On June 16, the Union attacks began in earnest. Facing overwhelming odds, the Confederates inflicted heavy casualties on the Union attackers before falling back to prepared positions on the night of June 17. The carnage was becoming familiar: attacks on entrenched positions invariably led to heavy losses for the attackers. On June 18, Lee's men arrived and more than doubled the numbers available to the embattled Confederates. Faced with odds of just under 2:1 *in their favor*, the Yankees settled down to a siege. So far, they had lost over 8,000 killed and wounded.

It was impossible to aim the shot from "Dictator" class mortars accurately, but their impact was terrifying.

THE SIEGE

By now, the only real hope for the Confederates was that they could keep the Union fighting for long enough for the growing Peace Movement in the North to influence public opinion enough to bring a halt to the War.

From the Union point of view, there were two objectives. One was to cut the railroad lines, especially between Richmond and Petersburg, and the other was to keep up the pressure on Petersburg until it surrendered.

In such a long siege, only a few episodes can be spotlighted. We have chosen two.

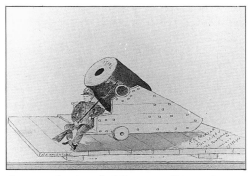

A cartoon drawing of a 13" mortar, "Dictator," in front of Petersburg on September 1, 1864.

The Bombardment of Petersburg

A "Dictator" class mortar outside Petersburg.

One of the most famous photographs of the War shows the Dictator-class mortar mounted on a railroad car. These gigantic mortars had a 13-inch bore, weighed over 17,000 lb, and lobbed a 220-lb shot for almost 2½ miles; with their usual grisly precision, the artillery books quote 4,325 yards at 45° elevation with a 20-lb charge of powder. At least one of these was used at Petersburg, along with several 10-inch guns.

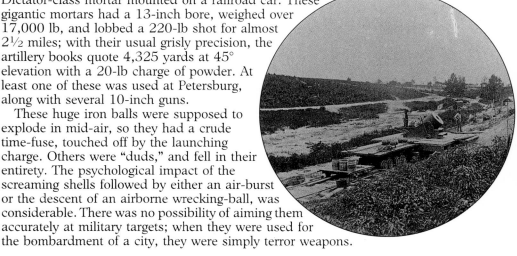

These huge iron balls were supposed to explode in mid-air, so they had a crude time-fuse, touched off by the launching charge. Others were "duds," and fell in their entirety. The psychological impact of the screaming shells followed by either an air-burst or the descent of an airborne wrecking-ball, was considerable. There was no possibility of aiming them accurately at military targets; when they were used for the bombardment of a city, they were simply terror weapons.

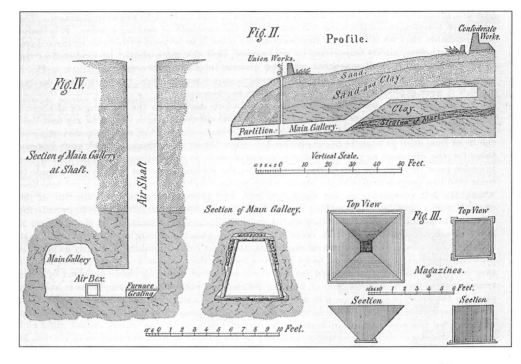

Plans of the mine at Petersburg. The "air box" provided the draft for a fire, which sucked the air through the workings and provided ventilation.

The Mine

At a quarter to five on the morning of July 30, 1864, four tons of gunpowder were detonated under the Confederate lines. A fort, and several hundred feet of Confederate earthworks, suddenly ceased to exist; the men manning them — 278, according to one account — were killed instantly. The hole was 170 feet long, 60-80 feet wide, and about 30 feet deep.

The mine, 586 feet from entrance to chamber, was dug by a party of coal miners-turned-soldiers in the 48th Pennsylvania Regiment; it took rather over a month. The army engineers were sceptical about the possibility of success and would take no part in the operation. They raised the problem of ventilation but the colonel in charge succeeded in providing air by means of a coal-mining ventilation shaft. Perhaps surprisingly, the Confederates suspected what was going on, and dug listening galleries; they probably missed detecting the main tunnel by only a few feet. The Union theory was to blow a huge hole in the Confederate defenses, through which specially-trained soldiers (the Fourth Division, the only black division in the Union army) could pour. As so often is the case, theory and practice did not coincide.

First, the Negro regiment which had been trained for the purpose was held back; the Union did not want to be seen to ask blacks to do their dirty work for them. Then, the regiments which were sent in were untrained, and instead of going around the pit, they poured into it. For the Confederates, it was like shooting fish in a barrel. By the early afternoon, when the attack was called off, the North had lost about 4,000 killed and wounded, as against 1,500 or so Confederates.

The crater left by the mine can still be seen today, though obviously it has rounded with time and it is now considerably shallower and lined with grass. Behind the Yankee lines, you can see a reconstruction of the entrance. Perhaps the most poignant feeling, though, comes from walking along beside the course of the mine. A depression in the grass marks where much of the roof has fallen in; but there are still small sections, in all probability where the duckboarded floor and the ingenious ventilation system (worked by a flue) still exist, unseen since July 1864.

Union artillery at Petersburg, from a wartime sketch.

Mine entrance.

THE END OF THE SIEGE

There is little to see at Fort Gregg now, and Fort Whitworth is still less visible; but once again, they are imbued with the aching sense of loss that characterizes so much of this battlefield. At these two forts on April 2, 1865 — the night before the Fall of Petersburg, which effectively marked the end of the Confederacy — a mere 600 cold, half-starved Rebels held off 5,000 well-fed, well-equipped Yankees for two hours, allowing Lee to withdraw his troops in safety in the hope of fighting once more.

Those 600 men must have known they had lost. So why were they fighting? To keep slavery alive? Most of those men had never owned a slave in their lives. For States' Rights? Yes, but not in those words. They were fighting for the things for which almost anyone will fight, in the last analysis: their homes, their loved ones, their way of life. And they lost.

Petersburg Courthouse, as it was in the 1860s. The cupola was a sighting-point for Union gunners.

Taylor Farm, outside Petersburg. The farm was destroyed during the Siege, but the chimney (amazingly) survived.

FURTHER INFORMATION

Maps: USGS 7.5': Petersburg and Prince George; Hopewell is
  useful, but not essential
  Official Reports Atlas: 65/9; 67/8&9; 77/2; 79/1;
  105/2&7; 118/3
  B&L: 538; 539; 569; 574

Park: A first-class park, with excellent orientation programs.
Because it is so near a city, the main park and the City Point unit
(also manned, and hard to find in modern Hopewell) are closed
from evening to morning. Picnic areas; no alcohol.
Superintendent: PO Box 549, Petersburg, VA 23804.

Town: Petersburg deserves to have more visitors than it does. The
Siege Museum is very human-scaled and attractive. Other sights,
not specifically related to the Civil War, include Blandford Church
(1735), with its 15 Tiffany stained-glass windows and
remarkable graveyard; and Centre Hill Mansion (1823),
headquarters of the Virginia chapter of the Victorian Society in
America. Blandford Church is the site of Confederate Memorial
Day observances on June 9 every year.
  Petersburg has a remarkably go-ahead tourist office and
information center at Petersburg Information Services, PO Box
2107 (VG), Petersburg, VA 23804. Tel: (804) 733-2400.

APPOMATTOX

Petersburg fell on April 2, 1865. That night, the Confederate government evacuated Richmond. As Robert E. Lee said to a subordinate, "This is a sad business, colonel. It has happened as I told them in Richmond it would happen. The line has been stretched until it is broken."

The rest of the story of the War can be told as a brief chronology. On April 4, Lincoln was in Richmond. Grant wrote to Lee about the possibility of surrender on April 7; on April 9, at Appomattox Court House, the Army of Northern Virginia was surrendered. Lee's parting words to his army were:

> I have done for you all that it was in my power to do. You have done all your duty. Leave the result to God. Go to your homes and resume your occupations. Obey the laws and become as good citizens as you were soldiers.

Mobile, Alabama, surrendered on April 12. General Joseph E. Johnston surrendered at the Bennet House near Durham Station, North Carolina, on April 26. The last land engagement on any scale took place in Texas on May 12; the Confederates won. On July 26, Simon Bolivar Buckner surrendered the Army of the Trans-Mississippi at New Orleans.

On June 22, the CSS *Shenandoah* took her last prize, eleven whalers in the Bering Sea. Her captain learned that the War was over on August 2, and she surrendered to British officials at Liverpool on November 6; the sovereign Confederate flag was run down for the last time.

During this time, Lincoln was of course assassinated; he was shot on April 14 and died on April 15. It made no difference to the course of the surrender. He was buried on the 19; four of the alleged conspirators responsible for his death were hanged on July 7.

Reconstruction

"Reconstruction" is still a dirty word in most of the South. Northern carpetbaggers — unprincipled opportunists, often with political pretensions — moved South to feather their own nests. They were aided in this by the scalawags, renegade

"Moving day in Richmond" - a Yankee cartoon from near the War's end.

Southerners who were also out for themselves. The Civil Rights Act of 1866 made everyone a citizen except those who (one might think) were best qualified: Native Americans.

By various maneuvers, those who had fought for the Confederacy were disenfranchised; for example, Article 99 of the Louisiana Constitution of 1868 required all voters to swear that they had never, of their own free will, served the Confederacy in a military or civil capacity, voted for Secession, or even written or published newspaper articles or preached sermons favoring Secession or "treason." On the other hand, their property rights had been "restored," so they could be taxed without representation.

Vote-buying among the remaining voters was easy, especially as many were newly-enfranchised blacks who had no very clear idea of their own rights or of what they were voting for, but literally had nothing to lose by voting for whoever promised them most. According to one source, 144 out of 155 South Carolina state legislators in 1870 were Radical Republicans, with 76 illiterates among that number. Ninety-eight were black; poetic justice perhaps, but hardly calculated to promote real harmony in the state.

Once again, no thought appears to have been given by Northern politicians to the inevitable way in which old hatreds would be worked off and new ones created; it was the same old simplistic "sin and sinner" mentality all over again. Attempting to redress the balance by reversing the positions of rulers and ruled is not a recipe for long-term harmony in the real world.

Unsurprisingly, various secret and semi-secret organizations arose to try to reverse the balance again. These included the Knights of the White Camellia ("A white man's government or no man's government"), the White League, the Red Shirts and an organization formed in Pulaski, Tennessee, in 1866: the Ku Klux Klan. Although they were highly racist, the Klansmen were not the straightforward killers they were to become later, and they actually did some good in kicking out carpetbag/scalawag state governments under the hopelessly corrupt

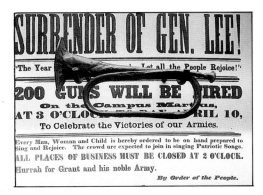

This Union poster, a somewhat threatening exhortation to rejoicing, is a typical example of the propaganda seen during the Civil War.

administration of Ulysses S. Grant, whose political acumen as President proved much less than his military ability.

When Grant left office in 1877, Reconstruction effectively ended and the Klan was officially disbanded. Whether the modern organization of the same name is a true descendant of the original is disputed.

What if ?

Since the end of Reconstruction, the reunification of the United States seems to have been genuine; indeed, it is now hard to imagine two nations (or more) occupying the same territory. Would it have worked? Or would the States have reunited anyway without a war? What would have happened to slavery? It would be gone by now, but when and how would it have ended? With a slave revolt, more terrible than the War between the States, perhaps with a black-dominated People's Republic of America? Or would the Confederacy be another South Africa, with apartheid and white rule?

Who can tell? It is a fascinating, if fruitless, realm for speculation. Almost certainly, the South would not have been the Utopia that so many modern "Confederates" imagine. Equally, it is very unlikely that it would have been the hell that others imagine. That, surely, is the true genius of the American people; maybe the United States of America is not perfect, but at least it wants and tries to be.

233

GLOSSARY

Not all of these terms appear in this book, but an understanding of all of them will be useful when visiting battlefields or when reading National Park brochures. Where fuller definitions are given in the text, the reader is referred to the appropriate page. A very useful book, which unfortunately contains enough errors to make it unreliable as your *only* reference book/encyclopaedia, is *The Historical Times Illustrated Encyclopaedia of the Civil War* (Harper and Row, 1986).

Abatis: Fortification. See page 11.

Aide-de-camp: Confidential secretary and helper for a general.

Bivouac: Sleeping in the open, without tents.

Bomb-proof: Bomb-proof shelter.

Brevet rank: Temporary or limited appointment to higher rank, usually used in recognition of outstanding fighting.

Caisson: Part of cannon-train. See page 68.

Chevaux-de-frise: Fortification. See page 11

Columbiad: Heavy gun. See page 69.

Contrabands: Fugitive slaves under Northern protection.

Corduroy: To build a road of logs laid together transversely.

Detail: An enemy can be destroyed "in detail" when his forces are separated and can be attacked in turn by the other side's whole force.

Effectives: Men available to fight, as distinct from the muster or roll strengths

Embrasure: A gap in fortifications, for firing through.

Enfilade: A "raking" fire, which strikes a column of troops obliquely or from the side as distinct from frontally.

Fascine: Bundle of sticks or twigs used to reinforce earthworks.

Flank: Imagine two lines of 20 men, standing side by side. They can easily attack or defend along the broad side (20 men). If the lines are attacked on the flank or "end on" (against the two on the end), those furthest from the attack will be unable to shoot without hitting their friends in front. Much the same is true, on a larger scale, of whole armies.

Gabion: Cylindrical wicker basket or tube, filled with dirt and stones, used to reinforce and shore earthworks. The protruding top of the basket furnished additional protection. See page 225.

Head log: In earthworks, a log laid above an **Embrasure** (q.v.).

Infernal machine: see **Mine**.

Ironclad: Wooden ship armored with sheet-iron.

Lunette: A semicircular field fort or strongpoint on a battle line, open to the rear. See also **Redan**.

Matériel: Supplies and equipment for prosecuting a war (French).

Mine: In 1860s usage, a tunnel ending in a chamber under the enemy's position; gunpowder would be exploded in the chamber. What we call "land mines" and shipping mines were then called "torpedos" or "infernal machines." A time bomb was a "horological torpedo."

Minnie ball: Misspelling of Minie Ball. See page 56.

Muster strength: Number of men actually available, not all of whom will be detailed off (or available) to fight.

Napoleon: Smoothbore artillery weapon. See page 68.

Picket: Part sentry, part offensive; used to test the position of the enemy. A full-strength picket detail from a single regiment consisted of 47 men.

Pup tent: Basic tent affording minimal shelter.

Redan: A small, pointed outcrop (usually in earthworks, in this War) consisting of "two parapets meeting at a salient angle" (Funk & Wagnall). See also **Lunette**.

Redoubt: Small fortress, often of earthworks; sometimes, an extension or satellite of a larger fort.

Revetment: In fortifications, a buttressing wall.

Rifle: Rifled guns are more efficient and more accurate than smooth-bores. This applies to big guns (see ARTILLERY, page 68 and 69) as well as to pistols and muskets (page 56 and 57).

Roll strength: Number of men on the army "rolls" (books). A proportion would be on leave, wounded, or otherwise missing.

Salient: Protrusion or bulge in a battle-line, either making use of natural features to create a strongpoint or used as a means of attacking an enemy.

Sally port: Small door in permanent fortifications, used for discharging groups of men to attack or harass the enemy, or to escape.

Sap roller: Large wicker basket, often several feet in diameter, full of earth and wood, rolled in front of sappers digging trenches towards the enemy: a sort of movable fortification.

Sibley tent: Large tent named after its inventor.

Torpedo: See **Mine**.

Vidette: Mounted sentry or picket. Also spelled **Vedette**.

Wig wag: Semaphore machine. See page 80.

Zouaves: Colorful volunteer regiments with uniforms based on those of French troops in North Africa. See page 44.

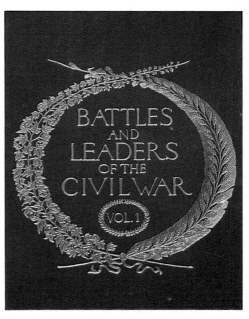

The cover of volume 1 of Battles and Leaders.

FURTHER READING

There are reputed to be over 100,000 books on the War between the States. Only those actually consulted by the authors are listed here, and not all of those are included. The "star" ratings are as follows:

*****	Invaluable general book
****	Good general book, or outstanding account of a particular battle or aspect of the War
***	Standard works with reliable information *or* simply a good read
**	Useful, but outdated, unreliable or otherwise flawed
*	Better than nothing, on a particular subject

Atlas to Accompany the Official Reports of the Union and Confederate Armies ***** See page 12.

Bakeless, John **Spies of the Confederacy** *** (Lippincott, Philadelphia and New York, 1970)

Battles and Leaders of the Civil War ***** (4 vols., first published in the 1880s by The Century Magazine; reprinted by Castle of Secaucus, NJ, in reduced-scale facsimile). Absolutely superb, first-hand accounts of much of the War, often excellently written. Extraordinarily good value in reprint.

Catton, Bruce **The Army of the Potomac** *** (3 vols.: **Mr Lincoln's Army**, 1951; **Glory Road**, 1952; **Stillness at Appomattox**, 1953; Doubleday). A standard work

Craven, Avery O. **Civil War in the Making** **** (Louisiana State University Press, 1959)

Davis, Curtis Carrol (ed.) **Belle Boyd in Camp and Prison, Written by Herself** (Thomas Yoseloff, Cranbury, NJ, and London, England). Intriguing, if self-serving, autobiography (heavily edited and commented upon) of the famous/notorious Southern lady spy

Donald, David (ed.) **Why the North Won the Civil War** **** (Louisiana State University Press, 1960; Collier/Macmillan ed., 1962, used). Five essays by major-league historians. Very interesting

Grant, U.S. **Personal Memoirs of U.S. Grant** *** (Da Capo, 1982). From the horse's mouth, though fairly heavy going

Great Battles of the Civil War *** By the editors of Civil War Times Illustrated (Gallery Book, 1988). Big, slightly dull book for real aficionados

Griess, Thomas E. (ed.) **The American Civil War** *** (West Point Military History Series, Avery Publishing, Wayne, NJ, 1987). With its supporting **Atlas for the American Civil War,** an excellent overview with a predictably strong military bias

Griffith, Paddy **Rally Once Again** **** (Crowood Press, Marlborough, Wilts., UK, 1987). Very readable book on Civil War tactics

Grissom, M.A. **Southern by the Grace of God** *** (Rebel Press, Nashville, TN, 1988). Highly entertaining, extremely biased book aimed at redressing Yankee propaganda

Gross, Anthony **Lincoln's Own Stories** ** (Garden City Press, New York, 1912). Sickeningly hagiographic, but very revealing

Harper's Pictorial History of the Civil War **** (Harper and Brothers, 1866; reprinted by Fairfax Press, n.d.). More than just pictorial; second only to **Battles and Leaders** (q.v.) as a source book. Extraordinary good value in reprint

Historical Times Illustrated Encyclopedia of the Civil War **** (Harper & Row, 1986). A very useful book, though a little marred by a number of errors.

Johnson, Swafford **Great Battle of the Confederacy** ** (Bison, 1985). A highly popularized account

Long, E.B. **The Civil War Day by Day** ***** (Doubleday & Co., 1971; Da Capo paperback ed., 1985, reprinted 1987). An essential book for checking details. A master work

Luvas, Jay and Harold W. Nelson **The U.S. Army War College Guide to the Battle of Gettysburg** **** (South Mountain Press, Carlisle, PA, 1986; paperback ed., Harper & Row, 1987). Very informative self-guided tour

Luvas, Jay and Harold W. Nelson **The U.S. Army War College Guide to the Battle of Gettysburg** **** (South Mountain Press, Carlisle, PA, 1986; paperback ed. Harper & Row, 1987). Very informative self-guided tour

McDonough, James Lee **Chattanooga — A Death Grip on the Confederacy** **** (University of Tennessee Press, 1984). An excellent account

McDonough, James Lee **Shiloh — In Hell Before Night** **** (University of Tennessee Press, 1977). First-class book

McDonough, James Lee **Stone's River — Bloody Winter in Tennessee** **** (University of Tennessee Press, 1980) Excellent account

Mitchell, Lt.-Col. Joseph B. **Decisive Battles of the Civil War** **** (Putnam, 1955; Ballantine ed., 1983). Possibly the best general overview at low cost and small compass (224 pages)

Medicine of the Civil War National Library of Medicine (n.d.). A mere 10-page pamphlet — but superb value

Natkiel, Richard **Atlas of American Wars** ** (Bison, 1986). As its name suggests, covers many other wars also. Very useful 2-color original maps

Nesbitt, Mark **If the South Won Gettysburg** ** (Reliance Publishing, Gettysburg, 1980). Entertaining, but more could have been gotten out of it

Sherman, William T. **Memoirs of General William T. Sherman** *** (Da Capo, 1984). Surprisingly readable and revealing

Smith, G.W. and C. Judah **Life in the North During the Civil War: A Source History** *** (University of New Mexico Press, 1966). A workmanlike compilation of source material

Tanner, Robert G. **Stonewall in the Valley** **** (Doubleday, 1976). Superb analysis of strategy and tactics in the field

Tilley, John S. **Facts the Historians Leave Out: A Confederate Primer** *** (Bill Coats Ltd, Nashville, TN, 1951; 1988 ed. used). As biased as they come, but no worse than many schoolbooks

Tucker, Glenn **Chickamauga: Bloody Battle in the West** *** (Bobbs-Merrill, 1961; paperback ed., Morningside). Dated, but the definitive work

Walker, Peter F. **Vicksburg, A People at War 1860-65** *** (University of North Carolina Press, 1960; Broadfoot reprint, 1987). Classic book on Vicksburg

Walters, J.B. **Merchant of Terror: General Sherman and Total War** *** (Bobbs-Merrill, 1973). A searing indictment of Sherman

Whitehorn, Joseph W.A. **The Battle of Cedar Creek** *** (Wayside Museum of American History and Arts, Strasburg, VA, 1987). Superb guide with self-guided tour

Wiley, Bell Irvin **Confederate Women** ** (Greenwood Press, Westport, CT, and London, 1975). A useful book

Wiley, Bell Irvin **The Life of Billy Yank** **** (Louisiana State University Press, 1952; 1987 reprint used). A follow-up of equal quality to the book listed next

Wiley, Bell Irvin **The Life of Johnny Reb** **** (Louisiana State University Press, 1943; 1978 ed. used). A well-annotated selection of Rebels' own views of the War

Williams, T. Harry **Lincoln and His Generals** **** (Knopf, 1952). Exactly what it says

Young, Agatha **The Women and the Crisis: Women of the North in the Civil War** (McDowell, Obolensky, 1959). Feminist tract

Women sending the soldiers off to fight at Manassas.

INDEX

These two stained glass memorials appear in the Trinity Church at Vicksburg.

Pittsburg Landing.

PICTURE ACKNOWLEDGEMENTS

T=Top, B=Bottom, R=Right, L=Left, M=Middle

United States Military History Institute

7, 13, 16T, 16M, 16B, 17T, 17M, 17B, 18T, 18M, 18B, 36, 40T, 41T, 44, 48, 49, 56, 57, 61, 69, 73, 76T, 79, 80T, 80B, 81, 88B, 93T, 97, 102L, 104, 105, 108, 109, 112T, 112B, 115, 116, 117, 120, 125T, 128, 133, 136, 137, 140, 144, 145T, 145B, 148, 149B, 161I, 164, 165, 168, 169, 172, 180, 181T, 181B, 185T, 185B, 188, 189T, 189B, 193T, 193B, 200, 208T, 208B, 212, 217B, 218B, 224, 225, 227M 227B, 230, 232.

Battles and Leaders

5, 6B, 8, 9T, 9B, 12, 19T, 20T, 20B, 21T, 21B, 24, 25, 28T, 28B, 29B, 30, 32, 33L, 33R, 37, 40B, 41B, 42, 45, 50, 53, 64, 65, 66, 74, 76B, 77, 84, 85, 88T, 89, 92, 93B, 96, 99B, 100T, 101, 102R, 113, 121, 124T, 124B, 129, 149T, 150, 152T, 152B, 153T, 156, 158T, 160, 173, 176, 177B, 184, 201, 204, 205T, 205B, 209, 218T, 228, 229T, 235, 237, 240.

Roger W. Hicks

6T, 11T, 11B, 19B, 26, 27T, 27B, 29T, 31, 38, 39T, 39B, 43, 51T, 51B, 52, 54, 55, 60, 62, 63, 72, 75, 78T, 78B, 86, 87B, 90, 91, 98T, 98B, 99T, 100B, 103, 114, 122T, 122B, 123, 125B, 127, 134T, 134B, 135, 139, 141, 146B, 147, 153B, 156, 157, 158B, 159, 161R, 162, 163, 171T, 174, 175, 182, 186, 187, 194, 195, 197, 202T, 202B, 203, 206T, 206B, 207, 213, 214, 215, 216, 217T, 219T, 219B, 220, 226T, 226B, 227T, 229B, 231, 238, 239.

Frances E. Schultz

Title page, 10, 67, 68, 87T, 110, 111T, 111B, 138, 146T, 151, 170, 171B, 177T, 183, 196.

Harper's Pictorial History of the Civil War, Half title page, 192. **Mary Evans Picture Library,** 221. **New Market Battle-field Park/Virginia Military Institute,** 233. **Steve Alley,** Back flap author photograph. (Hardback edition only). **David Playne,** Jacket photograph.